BASIC

ENGLISH GRAMMAR
Second Edition

TEACHER'S GUIDE

Betty Schrampfer Azar
Barbara F. Matthies
Shelley Hartle

PRENTICE HALL REGENTS

Publisher: *Mary Jane Peluso*
Editor: *Shelley Hartle*
Development Editor: *Janet Johnston*
Production/Composition: *Jan Sivertsen, Kelly Tavares*
Manufacturing Manager: *Ray Keating*
Art Director: *Wanda España*
Cover designer: *Joel Mitnick Design*
Interior designer: *Ros Herion Freese*

Published by PRENTICE HALL REGENTS

Printed in the United States of America

10 9 8

ISBN 0-13-368325-7

Contents

Preface

This *Teachers' Guide* is intended as a practical aid to teachers. You can turn to it for notes on the content of a unit and how to approach the exercises, for suggestions for classroom activities, and for answers to the exercises in the text.

General teaching information can be found in the introduction. It includes:
- the rationale and general aims of *Basic English Grammar*
- classroom techniques for presenting charts and using exercises
- comments on differences between American and British English
- a key to the pronunciation symbols used in this *Guide*

The rest of the *Guide* contains notes on charts and exercises.
The notes about the charts may include:
- suggestions for presenting the information to students
- points to emphasize
- common problems to anticipate
- assumptions underlying the contents
- additional background notes on grammar and usage

The notes that accompany the exercises may include:
- the focus of the exercise
- suggested techniques as outlined in the introduction
- possible specialized techniques for particular exercises
- points to emphasize
- assumptions
- answers
- expansion activities
- item notes on cultural content, vocabulary, and idiomatic usage
  (Some of these item notes are specifically intended to aid teachers who are
  non-native speakers of English.)

The authors of this *Teacher's Guide* would enjoy hearing comments and suggestions from other teachers who have ideas they would like to share. We can be contacted through the publisher:

Prentice Hall Regents
One Lake Street
Upper Saddle River, NJ 07458

Introduction

General Aims of *Basic English Grammar*

Basic English Grammar is a beginning level ESL/EFL developmental skills text. In the experience of many classroom teachers, adult language learners like to spend at least some time on grammar with a teacher to help them. The process of looking at and practicing grammar becomes a springboard for expanding the learners' abilities in speaking, writing, listening, and reading.

Most students find benefit and comfort in studying examples and explanations, for it allows them to make some sense out of the bewildering array of forms and usages of a language that is strange to them. These understandings provide the basis for practice in a relaxed, safe grammar classroom that encourages risk-taking as the students experiment with ways to communicate their ideas in a new language.

Teaching grammar does not mean lecturing on grammatical patterns and terminology. It does not mean bestowing knowledge and being an arbiter of correctness. Teaching grammar is the art of helping students make sense, little by little, of a huge, puzzling construct and engaging them in activities that enhance language acquisition in all skill areas.

The aims of this text are to acquaint the learners with fundamental structures of high frequency in English and to provide ample opportunities for practicing those structures. Perhaps the most important aim, however, is to supply a wealth and variety of material for teachers to adapt to their individual teaching situations. The text seeks to be interesting and easy to understand and to provide myriad learning opportunities, but in truth, grammar comes alive only with a teacher.

Students who study this text should be able to communicate on common everyday topics, such as their classes, hometowns, families, problems, and daily experiences. They should be able to understand the meaning of and produce the fundamental structures of English, such as questions, statements, and negatives. It is not expected that students who finish this text will be fluent. This text is a first step.

The grammar that is introduced in this text, *Basic English Grammar,* is revisited and expanded upon in the subsequent texts, so don't feel you need to add a lot of grammar information to that which is presented in the text. The students will cover more complex structures and revisit the same structures in more depth as they continue their English study. Learning a language takes repetition and practice. Don't expect your students to immediately gain mastery of all the grammar points you teach them. Be patient and encouraging. Learning a second language is a daunting undertaking.

The Azar Grammar Series

The Azar Grammar Series consists of three main texts: *Basic English Grammar* (red cover), a lower-level text; *Fundamentals of English Grammar* (black cover), designed for lower-intermediate and intermediate learners; and *Understanding and Using English Grammar* (blue cover), for intermediate through advanced students.

A supplementary text you might find useful is *Fun with Grammar*, by Suzanne Woodward (Prentice Hall Regents, 1997). It contains grammar games that are keyed to the Azar Grammar Series.

Classroom Techniques

Following are some techniques that have proven useful. *Suggestions for Presenting the Grammar Charts* are discussed first. Next are some notes on *Degrees of Teacher and Student Involvement.* Then *Techniques for Exercise Types* are outlined.

Suggestions for Presenting the Grammar Charts

A chart is a concise visual presentation of the structures to be learned in one section of a chapter. Some charts may require particular methods of presentation, but generally any of the following techniques are viable.

Technique #1: Use the examples in the chart, add your own examples to explain the grammar in your own words, and answer any questions about the chart. Elicit other examples of the target structure from the learners. Then go to the accompanying exercise immediately following the chart.

Technique #2: Elicit oral examples from the students before they look at the chart in the textbook. To elicit examples from the students, ask leading questions whose answers will include the target structure. (For example, for the present progressive, ask: "What are you doing right now?") You may want to write the elicited answers on the board and relate them to the examples in the chart. Then proceed to the exercises.

Technique #3: Assign the chart and accompanying exercise(s) for out-of-class study. In class the next day, ask for and answer any questions about the chart, and then immediately proceed to the exercises. (With advanced students, you might not need to deal with every chart and exercise thoroughly in class. With intermediate students, it is generally advisable to clarify charts and do most of the exercises.)

Technique #4: Lead the students through the accompanying exercise prior to discussing the chart. Use the material in the exercise to discuss the focus of the chart as you go along. At the end of the exercise, call attention to the examples in the chart and summarize what was discussed during the exercise.

Technique #5: Before presenting the chart in class, give the students a short written quiz on its content. Have the students correct their own papers as you review the answers. The quiz should not be given a score; it is a learning tool, not an examination. Use the items from the quiz as examples for discussing the grammar in the chart.

Presentation techniques often depend upon the content of the chart, the level of the class, and the students' learning styles. Not all students react to the charts in the same ways. Some students need the security of thoroughly understanding a chart before trying to use the structure. Others like to experiment more freely with using new structures; they refer to the charts only incidentally, if at all. Given these differing learning strategies, you should vary your presentation techniques and not expect students to "learn" or memorize the charts. The charts are just a starting point for class discussion and a point of reference.

Demonstration can be very helpful to explain the meaning of structures. You and the students can act out situations that demonstrate the target structure. For example, the present progressive can easily be demonstrated (e.g., "I *am writing* on the board right now.").

In discussing the target structure of a chart, use the chalkboard whenever possible. Not all students have adequate listening skills for "teacher talk," and not all students can visualize and understand the various relationships within, between, and among structures. Draw boxes and circles and arrows to illustrate connections between the elements of a structure.

The students need to understand the terminology, but don't require or expect detailed definitions of terms, either in class discussion or on tests. Terminology is just a tool, a useful label for the moment, so that you and the students can talk to each other about English grammar.

Most students benefit from knowing what is going to be covered in the following class session. The students should be assigned to read the charts at home so that they can become initially familiar with the target structure and, it is to be hoped, come to class with questions.

For every chart, try to relate the target structure to an immediate classroom or "real-life" context. Make up or elicit examples that use the students' names, activities, and interests. The here-and-now classroom context is, of course, one of the grammar teacher's best aids.

Degrees of Teacher and Student Involvement

Most of the exercises in the text are intended to be teacher-led, but other options are group work, pair work, and student-led work.

TEACHER-LED EXERCISES

In an eclectic text such as this, many approaches are possible, based on various sound theories of language learning and teaching. The teacher plays many roles and can employ a wide variety of techniques.

In essence, all exercises in the main text are "teacher-led." Even so, there is a wide range of possible teacher involvement: from explaining "rules" to eliciting deductive understandings, from supplying answers to eliciting responses, from being the focus of the students' attention to being solely an initiator and facilitator. Consider the students' goals and the time that is available, then decide whether to focus a lot of attention on every item in an exercise or to go through it quickly and spend time on related activities. It is beneficial for students to push hard and work intensively on English grammar, but it is also beneficial for the students to spend relaxed time in class exchanging ideas in structure-oriented conversations or similar pursuits.

GROUP WORK AND PAIR WORK

Many, but not all, exercises in the text are suitable for group or pair work. Suggestions for such alternatives are included in the comments on the exercises in the chapter notes.

Exercises done in groups or pairs may often take twice as much time as they would if teacher-led, but it is time well spent if you plan carefully and make sure that the students are speaking in English to each other. There are many advantages to student-student practice.

When the students are working in groups or pairs, their opportunities to use what they are learning are greatly increased. They will often explain things to each other during pair work, in which case both students benefit greatly. The students in group work are often much more active and involved than in teacher-led exercises.

Group and pair work also expands the students' opportunities to practice many communication skills at the same time that they are practicing target structures. In peer interaction in the classroom, the students have to agree, disagree, continue a conversation, make suggestions, promote cooperation, make requests, be sensitive to each other's needs and personalities, and the like—the kinds of exchanges that are characteristic of any group communication, whether in the classroom or elsewhere.

In addition, group and pair work helps to produce a comfortable learning environment. In teacher-centered activities, students may sometimes feel shy and inhibited or may experience stress. They may feel that they have to respond quickly and accurately and that *what* they say is not as important as *how* they say it—even though you strive to convince them to the contrary. If you set up groups that are non-competitive and cooperative, the students usually tend to help, encourage, and even joke with each other. This encourages them to experiment with the language and speak more.

Students should be encouraged to monitor each other to some extent in group work, especially when monitoring activities are specifically assigned. You shouldn't worry about "losing control" of the students' language production, and they shouldn't worry about learning each other's mistakes. (But perhaps you should remind them to give some *positive* as well as corrective comments to each other in order to maintain good feelings.) Not every mistake needs to be corrected, but you can take some time at the end of an exercise to call attention to mistakes that you heard frequently as you monitored the groups.

WAYS OF USING EXERCISES FOR GROUP OR PAIR WORK

1. Divide the class into groups of two to six, usually with one student as leader. You may appoint the students to the groups or sometimes let them divide themselves. You may appoint a leader or let the students choose one. Leadership can be rotated. Be sure that the leader understands what to do, and set a reasonable time limit for finishing the activity.

2. For ORAL (BOOKS CLOSED) exercises, only the leader has his/her text open. If these exercises are used for pair work, one student has an open text and the other doesn't. Halfway through an exercise, the pair may change roles.

3. For ORAL or some other types of exercises, the students can discuss completions, transformations, etc., among themselves prior to, or instead of, class discussion. You can move about the classroom, answering questions as necessary.

4. For exercises that require writing in the textbook, each group should produce one paper with answers that all (or at least a majority) of the members agree are correct. The leader can present the group's answers for class discussion or hand in a collaborative paper for your correction (and sometimes even for a grade). Similarly, pairs of students can compare their answers prior to class discussion and come to an agreement on their correctness.

STUDENT-LED EXERCISES

Once in a while you may wish to ask a student to assume the teacher role in some of the ORAL or ORAL (BOOKS CLOSED) exercises; the student conducts the exercise by giving the cues and determining the appropriateness of the response, while you retire to a corner of the room. It is helpful, but not essential, for you to work with the student leader outside of class in preparation for his/her role as teacher. Generally, a student-led oral exercise will take twice as much class time as it would if teacher-led, but if the time is available, it can be a valuable experience for the student-teacher and fun for the class as a whole.

Techniques for Exercise Types

Some of the exercises in the text have specific labels: ORAL (BOOKS CLOSED), ORAL, WRITTEN, ORAL/WRITTEN, ERROR ANALYSIS, PREPOSITIONS. It is important to note that the "oral" and "written" labels on particular exercises are only suggestions to the teacher. If you deem it appropriate, you can have the students write out an oral exercise or discuss a written exercise.

Exercise: ORAL (BOOKS CLOSED)

   a. For exercises of this type, which range from simple manipulation to open-ended communicative interaction, the students are to have their books closed. These exercises are not intended as drills to be completed rapidly without interruption. You are not "drilling" grammar into the students; rather, you are giving them the chance to practice speaking and to experiment with target structures. You are providing a good opportunity for the students to develop their listening and speaking skills while expanding their ability to use the structures. With their books closed, they can concentrate on what you and others are saying and can practice speaking without relying on written words.

   b. Be flexible in handling these exercises. You don't have to read the items aloud as though reading a script from which there should be no deviation. Modify the format to make it more workable for your particular class. Try to add more oral-aural items spontaneously as they occur to you. Change the items in any way you can to make them more relevant to your students. (For example, if you know that some students plan to watch the World Cup soccer match on TV soon, include a sentence about that.) Omit irrelevant items. Sometimes an item will start a spontaneous discussion of, for example, local restaurants or current movies or certain experiences the students have had. These spur-of-the-moment dialogues are very beneficial to the students. Encourage and facilitate the discussion, and then, within a reasonable length of time, bring attention back to the grammar at hand.

   c. To initiate an ORAL (BOOKS CLOSED) exercise, give the class an example or two of the format. Sometimes you will want to give explicit oral directions. Sometimes you will want to use the chalkboard to write down key words to help the students focus on the target structure or consider the options in their responses.

   d. Repeat a cue in ORAL (BOOKS CLOSED) exercises as often as necessary. Start out with normal spoken English, but then slow down and repeat as needed. You may want to write on the board, do a pantomime, demonstrate, draw a picture—whatever may help the students understand what you're saying. One of your goals is to convince students that they *can* understand spoken English. They shouldn't feel failure or embarrassment if they don't understand a spoken cue immediately. If an exercise is too difficult for your class as a whole or for particular students, let them do it with their books open.

   e. In general, ORAL (BOOKS CLOSED) exercises follow a chart or an open-book exercise. First, students should build up their understanding of the structure and practice using it. Then they will feel more confident during these oral exercises, which for most students are riskier and far more difficult than written work.

   Essentially, in the ORAL (BOOKS CLOSED) exercises, the teacher is saying to the students, "Okay, now you understand such-and-such [for example, word order in noun clauses], so let's play with it a bit. With any luck, you'll be happily surprised by how much you already know. Mistakes are no big problem. They're a natural part of learning a new language. So just give it a try and let's see what happens."

   f. Sometimes ORAL (BOOKS CLOSED) exercises precede a chart or open-book exercises. The purpose of this order is to elicit student-generated examples of the target structure as a springboard to the discussion of the grammar. If you prefer to introduce any particular structure to your students orally, you can always use an ORAL (BOOKS CLOSED) exercise prior to the presentation of a chart and written exercises, no matter what the given order is in the textbook.

Exercise: ORAL

   Exercises of this type are intended to be done with books open but require no writing and no preparation. In other words, the students can read what is in the text, but they don't have to write in their books. You don't have to assign these exercises ahead of time; they can be done directly in class. These exercises come in many forms and are often suitable for group or pair work.

Exercise: ORAL/WRITTEN

This label indicates that the material can be used for either speaking practice or writing practice. Sometimes it indicates that the two are combined: for example, a speaking activity may lead to a writing activity.

Exercise: WRITTEN

In this type of exercise, the intention is for the students to use their own paper and submit their writing to you. Some of the WRITTEN exercises require sentence completion, but most are designed to produce short, informal compositions. In general, the topics or tasks concern aspects of the students' lives in order to encourage free and relatively effortless communication as they practice their writing skills. While a course in English rhetoric is beyond the scope of this text, many of the basic elements are included and may be developed and emphasized according to your purposes.

For best results, whenever you make a writing assignment, let your students know what you expect: "This is what I suggest as content. This is how you might organize it. This is how long I expect it to be." If at all possible, give your students composition models, perhaps taken from good compositions written by previous classes, perhaps written by you, perhaps composed as a group activity by the class as a whole (e.g., you write on the board what the students tell you to write, and then you and the students revise it together).

In general, WRITTEN exercises should be done outside of class. All of us need time to consider and revise when we write. And if we get a little help here and there, that's not unusual. The topics in the exercises are structured so that plagiarism should not be a problem. Use in-class writing if you want to appraise the students' unaided, spontaneous writing skills. Tell your students that these written exercises are simply for practice and that—even though they should, of course, always try to do their best—mistakes will be considered only as tools for learning.

Encourage the students to use their dictionaries whenever they write. Point out that you yourself never write seriously without a dictionary at hand. Discuss the use of margins, indentation of paragraphs, and other aspects of the format of a well-written paper.

Ask your students to use lined paper and to write on every other line so that you and they have space to make corrections.

Exercise: ERROR ANALYSIS

ERROR ANALYSIS exercises focus on common mistakes made in typical student use of the target structures of a chapter. The main purpose of these exercises is to sharpen the students' self-monitoring skills. The exercises are challenging and fun, as well as a good way to summarize the grammar in a unit. If you wish, tell the students they are either newspaper editors or English teachers; their task is to locate all mistakes and write corrections.

The recommended technique is to assign an ERROR ANALYSIS for in-class discussion the next day. The students benefit most from having the opportunity to find the errors themselves prior to class discussion. These exercises can, of course, be handled in other ways: seatwork, written homework, group work, pair work.

You can make up your own error analysis exercises by presenting to the class student errors collected from their written completion exercises and compositions. It is usually best at this level to keep the focus on one or maybe two errors in one sentence. Adapt the mistakes in the students' writing to suit your purposes. The errors in such an exercise should be ones students can correct from their knowledge of English grammar. Awkward, convoluted sentences full of errors of many kinds are usually not suitable for class discussion; a wide-ranging discussion of numerous grammar points tends to confuse more than elucidate.

Some teachers may object to allowing students to see errors written in a textbook. There is little chance, however, that any harm is being done. Students look at errors all the time in their own writing and profit from finding and correcting them. The benefits of doing ERROR ANALYSIS exercises far outweigh any possible (and highly unlikely) negative results. Mistakes are a natural part of learning a new language, and indeed all language users make mistakes sometimes. Even native speakers or highly proficient non-native speakers—including you yourself—have to scrutinize, correct, and revise what they write. This is a normal part of the writing process.

Exercise: PREPOSITIONS

Exercises of this type focus on prepositions that are combined with verbs and adjectives. The intention is that the students simply make their "best guess" according to what "sounds right" to them when completing each item, then get the correct answers from class discussion and learn the ones they missed.

To reinforce the prepositions in an exercise, you can make up quick oral reviews (books closed) by rephrasing the items and having the students call out the prepositions. When you want the students to add onto a sentence you have begun, don't let your voice drop as it normally would at the end of speaking. Indicate with your voice that the sentence isn't complete yet. For example:

TEXT entry: Are you ready ___*for*___ the test?

Made-up oral reinforcement exercise:
TEACHER: "We're having a test tomorrow. Are you ready . . . ?"
STUDENTS call out: "for"
TEACHER: "Good. Ready **for**. Are you ready **for** the test?"

TEXT entry: Kathy was absent ___*from*___ class yesterday.

Made-up oral reinforcement exercise:
TEACHER: "Where was (Roberto) yesterday? He was absent . . . ."
STUDENTS call out: "from"
TEACHER: "Right. Absent **from**. (Roberto) was absent **from** class yesterday."

Additional Techniques

Most of the exercises in the textbook do not have specific labels. The following section outlines additional techniques, not only for labeled exercises but also for other activities.

The majority of the exercises in the text require some sort of completion, transformation, combination, sentence construction, or a combination of such activities. They range from those that are tightly controlled and manipulative to those that encourage free responses and require creative, independent language use. The techniques vary according to the exercise type.

FILL-IN-THE-BLANKS AND CONTROLLED COMPLETION EXERCISES

The label "fill-in-the-blanks" refers to those exercises in which the students complete the sentences by using words given in parentheses. The label "controlled completion" refers to those exercises in which the students complete cloze sentences according to directions. The possible ways of completing a sentence are limited. The directions may ask the students to use the words in a given list, to use the appropriate forms of a given structure, such as *be going to* or *used to*, or to select the completion from multiple choices. All of these types of exercises call for similar techniques.

Technique A: A student can be asked to read an item aloud. You can say whether the student's answer is correct or not, or you can open up discussion by asking the rest of the class if the answer is correct. For example:

TEACHER: "Mr. Wah, would you please read Number 2?"
STUDENTS: "Right now I'm in class. I *am sitting* at my desk I usually *sit* at the same desk in class every day."
TEACHER: (to the class): "Do the rest of you agree with Mr. Wah's answer?"

The slow-moving pace of this method is beneficial for discussion not only of grammar items but also of vocabulary and content. The students have time to digest information and ask questions. You have the opportunity to judge how well they understand the grammar.

However, this time-consuming technique doesn't always, or even usually, need to be used.

Technique B: You, the teacher, read the first part of the item, then pause for the students to call out the answer in unison. For example:

TEXT entry: Right now I'm in class. I (*sit*)_____ at my desk.
TEACHER: (with the students looking at their texts): "Right now I'm in class. I . . . . "
STUDENTS (in unison): "am sitting" (plus possibly a few incorrect responses scattered about)
TEACHER: "am sitting at my desk. *Am sitting.* Do you have any questions?"

This technique saves a lot of time in class, and is also slow-paced enough to allow for questions and discussion of grammar, vocabulary, and content. It is essential that the students have prepared the exercise by writing in their books, so it must be assigned ahead of time as homework or seatwork.

Technique C: If a particular exercise is little more than a quick review, you can simply give the answers so the students can correct their own previously prepared work in their textbooks. ("Number 2: Right now I'm in class. *I'm sitting* at my desk.") You can give the answers to the items one at a time, taking questions as they arise, or give the answers to the whole exercise before opening it up for questions. As an alternative, you can have one of the students read his/her answers for parts or all of an exercise and have the other students ask questions if they disagree.

Technique D: Divide the class into groups (or pairs) and, before the exercise is discussed in class, have each group prepare one set of answers that they all agree is correct. The leader of each group can present their answers.

Another option is to have the groups (or pairs) hand in their set of answers for correction and possibly a grade.

It's also possible to turn these exercises into games wherein the group with the best set of answers gets some sort of reward (perhaps applause from the rest of the class).

Of course, you can always mix Techniques A, B, C, and D—with the students reading some aloud, with you prompting unison response for some, with you simply giving the answers for others, or with the students collaborating on the answers for others. Much depends on the level of the class, their familiarity and skill with the grammar at hand, their oral-aural skills in general, and how flexible or limited your available class time is.

Technique E: When an exercise item has a dialogue between two speakers, A and B, ask one student to be A and another B and have them read the entry aloud. Then, occasionally, say to A and B: "Without looking at your text, what did you just say to each other?" (If necessary, let them glance briefly at their texts before they repeat what they've just said in the exercise item.) The students may be pleasantly surprised by their own fluency.

OPEN COMPLETION AND SEMI-CONTROLLED COMPLETION EXERCISES

The term "open completion" refers to those exercises in which the students use their own words to complete the sentences. "Semi-controlled completion" exercises allow for limited variations in the possible responses, permitting some independent input from the students.

Technique A: Exercises where the students must supply their own words to complete a sentence should usually be assigned for out-of-class preparation. Then in class, one, two, or several students can read their sentences aloud; the class can discuss the correctness and appropriateness of the completions. Perhaps you can suggest possible ways of rephrasing to make a sentence more idiomatic. Students who don't read their sentences aloud can revise their own completions based on what is being discussed in class. At the end of the exercise discussion, you can tell the students to hand in their sentences for you to look at, or simply ask if anybody has questions about the exercise and not have the students submit anything to you.

Technique B: If you wish to use an open or semi-controlled completion exercise in class without having previously assigned it, you can turn the exercise into a brainstorming session in which students try out several completions to see if they work. As another possibility, you may wish to divide the students into small groups and have each group come up with completions that they all agree are correct and appropriate. Then use only these completions for class discussion or as written work to be handed in.

Technique C: Some open or semi-controlled completion exercises are designated WRITTEN, which usually means the students need to use their own paper, as not enough space has been left in the textbook. It is often beneficial to use the following progression: (1) assign the exercise for out-of-class preparation; (2) discuss it in class the next day, having the students make corrections on their own papers based on what they are learning from discussing other students' completions; (3) then ask the students to submit their papers to you, either as a requirement or on a volunteer basis.

TRANSFORMATION AND COMBINATION EXERCISES

In transformation exercises, the students are asked to change form but not substance (e.g., to change the active to the passive). In combination exercises, the students are asked to combine two or more ideas or sentences into one sentence that contains a particular structure (e.g., an adjective clause).

In general, these exercises, which require manipulation of a form, are intended for class discussion of the form and meaning of a structure. The initial stages of such exercises are a good opportunity to use the chalkboard to draw circles and arrows to illustrate the characteristics and relationships of a structure. Students can read their answers aloud to initiate the class discussion, and you can write on the board as problems arise. Another possibility is to have the students write their sentences on the board. Also possible is to have them work in small groups to agree upon their answers prior to class discussion.

SENTENCE CONSTRUCTION AND DIALOGUE CONSTRUCTION EXERCISES

In sentence construction exercises, the students have to incorporate certain structures in sentences of their devising based on given information or situations. In dialogue construction, the students create situational conversations that include certain target structures. These exercises can be used for class discussion and/or written homework. In class discussion, students learn from what others have created. They can make corrections in their own work as the class discusses what other students have written. Often the dialogue construction can be done in pairs and then role-played before the class.

STRUCTURE IDENTIFICATION EXERCISES

Identifying structures does not play a large role in *Basic English Grammar*, but it is a useful technique in some instances, for example, in clarifying terminology. Having the students identify structures such as subjects and verbs also helps them focus on underlying sentence patterns: simple, compound, complex. In many respects, punctuation exercises on commas and periods are structure identification exercises; asking the students to punctuate sentences requires that they understand the sentence structure.

Almost any exercise can involve structure identification, if the teacher chooses, by asking the students to point out or name whatever the target structure may be: adjective clause, adverb clause, noun, verb tense, etc.

PRONUNCIATION EXERCISES

A few exercises focus on pronunciation of grammatical features, such as endings on nouns or verbs and contracted or reduced forms.

Some phonetic symbols are used in these exercises to point out sounds that should not be pronounced identically; for example, /s/, /əz/, and /z/ represent the three predictable pronunciations of the grammatical suffix that is spelled -s or -es. It is not necessary for students to learn a complete phonetic alphabet; they should merely associate each symbol in an exercise with a sound that is different from all others. The purpose is to help students become more aware of these final sounds in the English they hear to encourage proficiency of use in their own speaking and writing.

In the exercises on spoken contractions, the primary emphasis should be on the students' hearing and becoming familiar with spoken forms rather than on their production of these forms. The students need to understand that what they see in writing is not exactly what they should expect to hear in normal, rapid spoken English. The most important part of most of these exercises is for the students to listen to your oral production and become familiar with the reduced forms.

Language learners are naturally conscious that their pronunciation is not like that of native speakers of the language. Therefore, some of them are embarrassed or shy about speaking. In a pronunciation exercise, they may be more comfortable if you ask groups or the whole class to speak in unison. After that, individuals may volunteer to speak alone. The learners' production does not need to be "perfect," just understandable. You can encourage the students to be less inhibited by having them teach you how to pronounce words in their languages (unless, of course, you're a native speaker of the students' language in a monolingual class). It's fun—and instructive—for the students to teach the teacher.

SEATWORK

Many exercises can and should be assigned for out-of-class preparation, but sometimes it's necessary to cover an exercise in class that you haven't been able to assign previously. In "seatwork," you have the students do an unassigned exercise in class immediately before discussing it. Seatwork allows the students to try an exercise themselves before the answers are discussed so that they can discover what problems they may be having with a particular structure. Seatwork may be done individually, in pairs, or in groups.

HOMEWORK

The textbook assumes that the students will have the opportunity to prepare most of the exercises by writing in their books prior to class discussion. Students should be assigned this homework as a matter of course.

The use of the term "written" in this *Guide* suggests that the students write out an exercise on their own paper and hand it in to you. The amount generally depends upon such variables as class size, class level, available class time, your available paper-correcting time, not to mention your preferences in teaching techniques. Most of the exercises in the text can be handled through class discussion without the necessity of the students' handing in written homework. Most of the written homework that is suggested in the text and in the chapter notes in this *Guide* consists of activities that will produce original, independent writing.

Notes on American vs. British English

Students should be aware that the differences between American and British English are minor. Any students who have studied British English (BrE) should have no trouble adapting to American English (AmE) and vice-versa. In addition to American and British English, there are other varieties: Canadian English, Australian/New Zealand English, Scottish English, Irish English, West Indian English, West African English, Indian English, African-American English, etc. Although some differences exist among these various Englishes in grammar, spelling, vocabulary, and pronunciation, their speakers can communicate with each other with relatively little difficulty.

DIFFERENCES IN USAGE AND SPELLING

Differences in usage or spelling can be found in notes to the answers in this *Guide*. Differences in article and preposition usage in certain common expressions follow. These differences are not noted in the text; they are given here for the teacher's information.

AmE	**BrE**
be in **the** hospital	be in **Ø** hospital
be at **the** university	be at **Ø** university
go to **a** university/go to **Ø** college	go to **Ø** university
go to **Ø** class/be in **Ø** class	go to **a** class/be in **a** class
in **the** future	in **Ø** future (OR in **the** future)
did it **the next** day	did it **Ø** next day (OR **the** next day)
haven't done something **for/in** weeks	haven't done something **for weeks**
ten minutes **past/after** six o'clock	ten minutes **past** six o'clock
five minutes **to/of/til** seven o'clock	five minutes **to** seven o'clock

Differences in spelling of certain common words follow. British spellings should not be marked as incorrect in the students' writing. The students should simply be made aware of the variant spellings.

AmE	**BrE**
jewelry, traveler, woolen	jewellry, traveller, woollen
skillful, fulfill, installment	skilful, fulfil, instalment
color, honor, labor, odor	colour, honour, labour, odour
realize, analyze, apologize	realise, analyse, apologise
defense, offense, license	defence, offence, licence (n.)
theater, center, liter	theatre, centre, litre
check	cheque (bank note)
curb	kerb
forever	for ever/forever
jail	gaol
program	programme
specialty	speciality
story	storey (of a building)
tire	tyre

DIFFERENCES IN VOCABULARY

Differences in vocabulary usage usually do not significantly interfere with communication. Students should know that when American and British speakers read each other's literature, they encounter very few differences in vocabulary usage. A few differences follow:

AmE	BrE
attorney, lawyer	barrister, solicitor
bathrobe	dressing gown
can (of beans)	tin (of beans)
cookie, cracker	biscuit
corn	maize
diaper	nappy
driver's license	driving licence
drug store	chemist's
elevator	lift
eraser	rubber
flashlight	torch
gas, gasoline	petrol
hood of a car	bonnet of a car
living room	sitting room, drawing room
raise in salary	rise in salary
rest room	public toilet, WC (water closet)
schedule	timetable
sidewalk	pavement, footpath
sink	basin
soccer	football
stove	cooker
truck	lorry, van
trunk (of a car)	boot (of a car)
be on vacation	be on holiday

Key to Pronunciation Symbols

THE PHONETIC ALPHABET (Symbols for American English)

CONSONANTS

Most consonant symbols are used phonetically as they are in normal English spelling. However, a few additional symbols are needed, and some other letters are more restricted in their use as symbols. These special symbols are presented below. (Note that slanted lines indicate that phonetic symbols, not the spelling alphabet, are being used.)

/ θ / (Greek theta) = voiceless *th* as in ***th**in, **th**ank*
/ ð / (Greek delta) = voiced *th* as in ***th**en, **th**ose*
/ ŋ / = *ng* as in *si**ng**, thi**nk*** (but not in *danger*)
/ š / = *sh* as in ***sh**irt, mi**ss**ion, na**t**ion*
/ ž / = *s* or *z* in a few words like *plea**s**ure, a**z**ure*
/ č / = *ch* or *tch* as in *wa**tch**, **ch**urch*
/ ǰ / = *j* or *dge* as in ***j**ump, le**dge***

The following consonants are used as in conventional spelling:

/b, d, f, g, h, k, l, m, n, o, p, r, s, t, v, w, y, z/

Spelling consonants that are <u>not</u> used phonetically in English: c, q, x

VOWELS

The five vowels in the spelling alphabet are inadequate to represent the 12–15 vowel sounds of American speech. Therefore, new symbols and new sound associations for familiar letters must be adopted.

Front	**Central**	**Back** (lips rounded)
/i/ or /iy/ as in *b**ea**t*	/ɚ/ or /ər/ as in *w**or**d*	/u/, /u:/, or /uw/ as in *b**oo**t*
/ɪ/ as in *b**i**t*		/ʊ/ as in *b**oo**k*
/e/ or /ey/ as in *b**ai**t*		/o/ or /ow/ as in *b**oa**t*
		/ɔ/ as in *b**ough**t*
/ɛ/ as in *b**e**t*	/ə/ as in *b**u**t*	
/æ/ as in *b**a**t*	/a/ as in *b**o**ther*	

Glides: /ai/ or /ay/ as in *b**i**te*
/ɔi/ or /ɔy/ as in *b**oy***
/au/ or /aw/ as in *ab**ou**t*

British English has a somewhat different set of vowel sounds and symbols. You might want to consult a standard pronunciation text or BrE dictionary for that system.

COMMON FIRST NAMES USED IN THE TEXT

FEMALE

Alice	Jackie	Olga
Amanda	Jane	
Amy	Janet	Patricia
Anne	Jean	Peggy
Annie	Jennifer	
Anita	Jessica	Rachel
Anna	Jin-Won	Rita
	Joan	Rosa
Barbara	Joon-Kee	
Beth	Joy	Sally
	Judy	Sandy
	Julia	Sara
Carol	Jung-Po	Shelley
Carmen		Sonya
Chris		Stacy
Cindy	Karen	Stacy
	Kate	Sue
	Kathy	Susie
Diane	Kim	
Donna	Kristin	Tina
Elizabeth	Linda	Yoko
Ellen	Liz	Yolanda
Emily		Yuko
Erica	Marge	
	Maria	
Fatima	Marie	
Fumiko	Marika	
	Mary	
Gina	Masako	
Georgia	Meg	
Graciela	Michelle	
Heidi	Nadia	
Helen	Nancy	
	Natasha	
Ingrid	Nicole	

MALE

Abdul	Hamid	Pedro
Abdullah	Hiroki	Pierre
Ahmed		Peter
Akihiko	Igor	Po
Alex	Ivan	
Ali		Rick
Andy	Jack	Robert
	Jake	Roberto
Bakir	James	Ron
Ben	Jason	
Benito	Jerry	Sam
Bill	Jim	Samir
Bob	Jimmy	Spiro
Bobby	Joe	Spyros
Boris	Joel	Steve
	John	Steven
Carl	Johnny	
Carlos		Ted
Chris	Ken	Tom
	Kim	Tommy
David	Khalid	Tony
Dennis	Kunio	Toshi
Dick		
Don	Marco	
Doug	Mark	
	Matt	
Ed	Mehmet	
Eduardo	Mike	
Eric	Mustafa	
Ernesto		
	Luis	
Francisco		
Fred	Omar	
	Oscar	
Gary		
George	Pablo	
Greg	Paul	

Notes and Answers

Chapter 1: USING *BE* AND *HAVE*

ORDER OF CHAPTER	CHARTS	EXERCISES
Getting acquainted		Ex. 1
Be + noun	1-1 → 1-3	Ex. 2 → 10
Contractions with *be*	1-4	Ex. 11
Negative with *be*	1-5	Ex. 12
Be + adjective	1-6	Ex. 13 → 21
Be + a location	1-7	Ex. 22 → 24
Summary	1-8	Ex. 25 → 26
Yes/no questions with *be*	1-9	Ex. 27 → 29
Questions with *be:* using *where*	1-10	Ex. 30 → 32
Using *have* and *has*	1-11	Ex. 33
Using *my, your, his, her, our, their*	1-12	Ex. 34 → 37
Using *this, that, these, those*	1-13 → 1-14	Ex. 38 → 42
Asking questions with *what* and *who* + *be*	1-15	Ex. 43 → 48
Review		Ex. 49 → 57

General Notes on Chapter 1

This chapter presents very simple sentences for near-beginners. The assumption is that all students of this textbook can read words in English and that the teacher can both model and monitor good spoken and written English. The purpose of the lessons in Chapter 1 is to give learners basic phrases for exchanging information with other speakers of English. Thus, they begin by getting acquainted with each other. Then the text presents simple statements of definition and description and introduces a basic vocabulary of nouns and adjectives. Simple questions, negative verb phrases, and contractions are also presented early so that learners get plenty of practice with them throughout the course. A few prepositions of location are also illustrated and practiced.

You, the teacher, should judge whether your students need to complete every item in every exercise, or whether they can move along a bit faster. There is more than enough material for most learners. You must strike a balance between giving enough practice and not overdoing. It is unwise to expect perfect mastery of the structures in one chapter before moving to the next. Most of the structures will appear again in later exercises, so your students will have many opportunities to learn them during the course. In all chapters, the last exercises provide a review of all the structures presented in the chapter. Some of them, therefore, could be used as items on a test.

NOTE: It is not helpful to correct every mistake learners make. You may want to correct errors in their use of the target structure (for example, correcting *Where you from? or *I be from Japan.), but it is equally if not more important to help them use the language naturally and discover some of its peculiarities for themselves.

Also, if your students are true beginners and you know their native language, you might be tempted to translate the explanations for them. Try to avoid this. It encourages translation rather than understanding. The book's explanations are simple so that, with little repetition and rephrasing, most learners can catch the meaning. The exercises give a lot of practice for each point.

NOTE: The (★) is used two different ways throughout this *Teacher's Guide*. It appears <u>before</u> a group of words to indicate that they are incorrect. It appears <u>after</u> a group of words to indicate that there is more information contained in a footnote.

☐ EXERCISE 1, p. 1. *Getting acquainted.*

Oral and written.

This introductory exercise is designed as an ice-breaker for the first day of class. It shows learners how *be* is used in simple questions and answers while giving them an opportunity to get acquainted with classmates.

SUGGESTION: Allow the students to introduce each other to you and to the rest of the class. Put the students in pairs and ask them to find out the other person's name and country of origin. The students should write this information down. Then ask the students in turn to write their partner's name and country on the board as they orally introduce this person to the class.

First, model what you want the students to do by choosing one student as your partner. Ask the two questions in the illustration on page 1 of the text, then have the student ask you those two questions. Then introduce the student to the class, saying, "This is (. . .)" or "I would like you to meet (. . .)" or something similar. Write the student's name and country on the board. Then ask that student to do the same, introducing you to the class and writing your name and country on the board. Choose another student and model the pattern again if necessary until you are sure the class understands what they are supposed to do.

Encourage incidental communication and interaction; brief conversations may arise from the models in the drawings. Spell names aloud to review the spoken alphabet.

If you are teaching a multicultural class, mix nationalities in the pairs. If you are teaching a monolingual class, ask one student in each pair to find out the other student's hometown or address instead of country of origin.

SUGGESTION: Make up some items similar to the ones in Exercise 53 at the end of Chapter 1, pages 39–41. Hand them out and have the students complete them. Collect them, but don't correct them. After you have finished Chapter 1, return them and ask the students to correct their own work. There should be a noticeable improvement in their ability to complete simple dialogues such as the ones in Exercise 53 correctly and meaningfully.

CHART 1-1: NOUN + *IS* + NOUN: SINGULAR

- Chart 1-1 introduces some basic vocabulary for discussing grammar: *singular, noun, verb, article, consonant, vowel.* These terms are used frequently throughout the text, and the students will become familiar with them very quickly. Give these terms attention when you discuss the chart with your students. See the INTRODUCTION, pp. xii–xiii, for suggestions on different ways of presenting charts in class.

- To convey the concept of what a noun is, you may ask the students to name things and people in the classroom: *floor, door, desk, man, woman,* etc.

- In this lesson, names like *Canada* and *Mexico* are called singular nouns because they require singular verb forms. Perhaps point out in Exercises 2 and 3 that names of people, places, and languages (i.e., proper nouns) are capitalized.

- You may want to direct the students' attention to APPENDIX 1, which contains the alphabet and lists the vowels and consonants.

- Many languages do not use a verb where English requires a form of *be,* so a common error in spontaneous student usage of the grammar in the first ten charts of this chapter is omission of *be* (e.g., ★*I a student.* or ★*She not in class today.*).

☐ **EXERCISE 2, p. 2. *A or AN.* (Chart 1-1)**

Controlled completion.★

The students are practicing indefinite articles as a step along the way to producing the sentence pattern in Chart 1-1. The main focus of the first half of this chapter is sentence patterns with *be.*

After you discuss the chart with the class, give them a few minutes to complete the exercise by themselves. Then students can read their answers aloud; point out the sentence structure as you go through the exercise. Or, since the sentences are short, they could be written on the board by students. That would give you nine sentences on the board to use as additional examples of the pattern in Chart 1-1. You could go through each one, pointing out nouns and articles and the position of *is.*

Alternatively, students may be more comfortable if they all say an answer together rather than as individuals. You might proceed like this:

TEACHER: Look at the example. *(pause)* We use *a* with *horse,* not *an.* What letter does *horse* begin with?
CLASS: "H"
TEACHER: Is "h" a vowel or a consonant?
CLASS: A consonant.
TEACHER: Why do we use *a,* not *an,* in front of *horse?*
CLASS: "H" is a consonant.
TEACHER: Yes, we use *a* in front of *horse* because *a* is used in front of a consonant. Then we say ***an** animal.* Why?

★See INTRODUCTION: Classroom Techniques (pp. xii–xx) for descriptions of possible techniques to use in the various kinds of exercises: *controlled completion, oral (books closed), written,* etc., and ways of handling teacher and student involvement: *teacher-led, student-led, group work, pair work.*

CLASS: *Animal* begins with a vowel.

TEACHER: Right! Now, look at sentence number 2. *(pause)* Everybody, say this sentence now.

CLASS: English is a language.

TEACHER: Yes — *a language*. English is *a* language. Great!

Etc.

You may have to spend some time reviewing the alphabet and distinguishing between vowels and consonants.

Try to help the learners understand new vocabulary words without their using a dictionary. Some of the difficult vocabulary is illustrated *(bee, bear, ant)*. This vocabulary is recycled in subsequent exercises. You may have to explain some of the other vocabulary in this exercise (for example, by drawing a horse, or by using or drawing maps).

A large map of the world would be helpful for this and following exercises. The map of the world on page 407 of the text might be useful if a wall map isn't available. Also, there is a picture of a horse on page 85. Note that giving the students page numbers to look at is a way of reviewing and practicing numbers. There is also a map of the world at the back of this *Teacher's Guide,* on pp. 176–177, that you can photocopy.

EXPANSION: After you finish going through the exercise, have the students close their books. Then, using a few of the items in this exercise, write sentences on the board that contain errors and ask the class to correct them; e.g., write *English is language.* or *A bee is a insect.* or *Korea a country is.* Perhaps also include errors in capitalization.

ANSWERS: **2.** a   **3.** a   **4.** a   **5.** a   **6.** A . . . a   **7.** A . . . a   **8.** A . . . an **9.** A . . . an   **10.** An . . . an

☐ **EXERCISE 3, p. 3.   *Noun + BE + noun, singular.   (Chart 1-1)***

Controlled completion.

A map would be helpful.

First, pronounce the words in the box and have the class repeat. Everyone can read the first three sentences in chorus, then either the whole class or individuals can call out the rest. It's not necessary for the students to write every answer in their books; some students will put their pens aside and simply join in orally, but others will insist on writing every answer completely and correctly. Learning styles differ.

Ask questions about the vocabulary and encourage free responses from the class: *Who speaks Arabic? What countries use Arabic? What country is Rome in?* Etc. This exercise can be used as a springboard for listening and speaking practice. At least some of the students in the class will think this textbook and this class are too easy for them. It's important to identify and challenge those students by expanding the scope of this and other exercises to meet their needs while at the same time not overtaxing and scaring the less advanced students — the teacher's famous juggling act.

ANSWERS: **4.** Asia is a continent.   **5.** Tokyo is a city.   **6.** Spanish is a language. **7.** Mexico is a country.   **8.** London is a city.   **9.** A bee is an insect.   **10.** South America is a continent.   **11.** A dog is an animal.   **12.** China is a country. **13.** Russian is a language.   **14.** A cow is an animal.   **15.** A fly is an insect.

☐ **EXERCISE 4, p. 3.**   *Noun + BE + noun, singular.   (Chart 1-1)*

Oral; open completion.

This exercise gives students a chance to use their own knowledge to complete the sentences. Help them with pronunciation, and congratulate them on their answers.

Ask for different completions from a number of students. This is an exercise where the more advanced students can display their abilities and vocabularies. If a student uses a word that most of the rest of the class is unfamiliar with, ask that student to locate the place on a map or draw the animal or insect.

POSSIBLE RESPONSES: **2.** France/Canada/Thailand   **3.** London/Tokyo/Jakarta **4.** Asia/Africa/North America/South America/Antarctica/Europe/Australia   **5.** A bear/ A dog/A horse/An elephant   **6.** A bee/A fly/A mosquito

---

CHART 1-2:   NOUN + *ARE* + NOUN: PLURAL

• This chart introduces the grammatical term "plural." You could write sentence (c) from Chart 1-1 and sentence (a) from Chart 1-2 to show the differences. Allow students to discover all the differences between the two, then lead them through the rest of the points in Chart 1-2.

• Note the spelling variations of the plural *-s* ending. Model pronunciation of final *-s* and have the class repeat after you. (Focused work on pronunciation of final *-s/-es* follows in Chapter 2.)

☐ **EXERCISE 5, p. 4.**   *Noun + BE + noun, plural.   (Chart 1-2)*

Transformation.

These sentences are simple definitions and introduce vocabulary. Some of these words are illustrated in the drawing: *a rose, a rabbit, a carrot, a chicken.* If you wish and the class is interested, discuss other vocabulary in the illustration: *a bush, a beak, wings, a tail, orange* (color of a carrot), etc.

Model pronunciation of final *-s* and have the class repeat.

ANSWERS: **2.** Computers are machines.   **3.** Dictionaries are books.   **4.** Chickens are birds.   **5.** Roses are flowers.   **6.** Carrots are vegetables.   **7.** Rabbits are animals.

☐ **EXERCISE 6, p. 5.**   *Noun + BE + noun.   (Charts 1-1 and 1-2)*

Controlled completion.

You might find it useful to bring a world map or globe to class to help locate the countries mentioned in this exercise.

One suggestion for handling this exercise: Have the students write in their books before you discuss the correct answers. Perhaps have the students check each other's answers first, too. The completed sentences can be written on the board. That is a good way of your making sure the students understand the correct answers (as their listening skills may not be adequate at this point for simple oral discussion of correct answers). Also, at this level especially, copying sentences can be helpful in directing the students' attention to capitalization, spelling, final periods, and the like. An added benefit is that you have a whole board full of examples to use as a way of reviewing the grammar in Charts 1-1 and 1-2. Thorough discussion is a good way to familiarize the students with grammar terminology they will need throughout their English study, e.g., *singular, plural, noun.* (Be sure to keep the grammar terminology you use to the barest minimum.)

An alternate approach: Don't have the class write in their books at all. Use this as a quick oral review exercise if the text is too simple for your class.

ANSWERS: **3.** Spanish is a language. **4.** Spanish and Chinese are languages. **5.** Asia is a continent. **6.** Asia and Africa are continents. **7.** Thailand and Viet Nam are countries. **8.** Thailand is a country. **9.** Butterflies are insects. **10.** A butterfly is an insect. **11.** An automobile is a machine. **12.** Automobiles are machines. **13.** London is a city. **14.** London and Baghdad are cities.

☐ **EXERCISE 7, p. 5.** *Noun + BE + noun.* *(Charts 1-1 and 1-2)*

Oral; open completion.

It's probably too early to divide the students into groups, but if your class seems advanced and at ease with the grammar, working in small groups would be beneficial to them. Otherwise, use this as a teacher-led exercise and elicit as many responses as feasible. Engage your students in short spontaneous conversations based on their completions.

Note the new vocabulary: *peninsula* and *season*.

SAMPLE ANSWERS: **1.** Nepal is a country. **2.** Paraguay and Turkey are countries. **3.** Japanese and Korean are languages. **4.** Polish is a language. **5.** Hong Kong is a city. **6.** Jakarta and Singapore are cities. **7.** Dogs and cats are animals. **8.** A butterfly is an insect. **9.** Iberia is a peninsula. **10.** Maple and Main are streets in this city. **11.** Korea and Japan are countries in Asia. **12.** Florence is a city in Europe. **13.** A cactus is a plant. **14.** A carrot is a vegetable. **15.** Winter is a season.

☐ **EXERCISE 8, p. 6.** *Noun + BE + noun.* *(Charts 1-1 and 1-2)*

Oral (books closed).

To make the students comfortable, try choral response first. Students should close their books and listen to your cues, as follows:

TEACHER: What are cows?
  CLASS: Cows are animals.
TEACHER: Yes, good. Cows are animals. What is English?
  CLASS: English is a language.
TEACHER: Good. English is a language. What is England?
  Etc.

If any students look lost and panicked, tell them it is perfectly okay to keep their books open during this exercise.

Follow a round of choral responses with one of individual responses by repeating some of the given items or making up your own.

Emphasize pronunciation of final *-s/-es*.

Perhaps follow the oral practice with written practice. You give the cue, and the students write the response. If, on the other hand, time is short, it is not necessary to include every item (in this or any other exercise in the text).

ANSWERS: **1.** English is a language. **2.** England is a country. **3.** Butterflies are insects. **4.** Chickens are birds. **5.** Europe is a continent. **6.** Roses are flowers. **7.** A carrot is a vegetable. **8.** Russian and Arabic are languages. **9.** Spring is a season. **10.** Japan and Venezuela are countries. **11.** A computer is a machine. **12.** A bear is an animal. **13.** Bees are insects. **14.** An ant is an insect. **15.** Winter and summer are seasons. **16.** September and October are months. **17.** A dictionary is a book. **18.** Typewriters are machines. **19.** A Honda is an automobile/a car. **20.** *(free response)*

CHART 1-3: PRONOUN + *BE* + NOUN

- Languages of the world construct these simple sentences very differently. Some do not require *be*; others do not require articles; and others have the same pronoun for *he* and *she* (just as English has only the pronoun *they* for the plural). These differences may cause many mistakes as students try to learn the system of English. Encourage them to keep experimenting, and don't expect perfection.

- Some alert learners might ask about *my*, a possessive adjective in the bottom section. You might then point out that either an article or a possessive adjective — not both — may be used in front of a singular noun. (INCORRECT: ★*She is a my teacher.*) Possessive adjectives are introduced later in this chapter in Chart 1-12.

- Another possible problem is the pronoun *you*, which can be either singular or plural in meaning but always requires the plural form of *be*. This is an accident of English history.

- In discussing Chart 1-3 and Exercise 9, use yourself and students as props to demonstrate the meanings of the pronouns. For example, for *she*, point to a woman; for *we*, group yourself with another student or other students.

□ **EXERCISE 9, p. 6.** *Subject pronoun + BE + noun.* *(Chart 1-3)*

Controlled completion.
The focus of this exercise is on making sure the students understand the correct forms of simple present *be* and the correct singular or plural forms of the predicate nouns. This exercise has no other intention; it's just a way of ascertaining whether or not the students have understood the core grammar in the preceding chart.

Chapter 1 presents grammar and vocabulary slowly and deliberately, giving beginners no more than they can handle comfortably. If your class is more advanced, much of the material in this and the next chapter can be handled quickly and exercises can be shortened or deleted.

ANSWERS: **2.** I am a student.   **3.** She is a student.   **4.** They are students.
5. You are a student.   **6.** You are students.

□ **EXERCISE 10, p. 7.** *Subject + BE + noun.* *(Charts 1-1 → 1-3)*

Oral (books closed).
The symbol (. . .) throughout the text means that you are supposed to supply the name of a student.

Much of the emphasis in this exercise should be on the students' knowing one another; it's a follow-up, getting-to-know-each-other exercise, so include as many names as feasible in the course of the exercise to encourage the students' familiarity with one another's names and countries of origin. The grammar focus is basically secondary here.

Some beginners may have difficulty using all the correct singular and plural forms, but with your patient encouragement they will improve.

CHART 1-4:   CONTRACTIONS WITH *BE*

- Some learners — and even some teachers — are not comfortable with contractions. But these are the most natural forms in spoken English, so they are introduced early in this chapter. You should encourage students to use contractions when they speak answers to the lessons in this book, but don't insist.

- NOTE: Contractions are not used in formal written English, but you should encourage them in written answers to exercises in this book.

- Start familiarizing the students with the term "apostrophe." They will meet it again whenever you discuss contractions and in the unit on possessive nouns.

☐ **EXERCISE 11, p. 8.   *Contractions with BE.   (Chart 1-4)***

Controlled completion.
This exercise reviews pronouns while practicing contractions of *be*.

Some students may not know whether certain names are masculine or feminine, so you may need to supply that information. The names the students encounter here will be encountered again, as the text uses the same common names over and over. A list of all the first names used in the text can be found on page xxiv of this *Teacher's Guide*.

You might have students work in pairs for this exercise. One speaks while the other listens carefully and helps with correct answers and pronunciation. They can change roles after every item, after every four items, or halfway through.

ANSWERS: **2.** He's   **3.** He's   **4.** They're   **5.** It's   **6.** They're   **7.** They're
8. He's   **9.** She's   **10.** They're   **11.** They're   **12.** It's   **13.** We're
14. It's   **15.** I'm   **16.** You're

CHART 1-5:   NEGATIVE WITH *BE*

- The form and meaning of *be + not* are the focus of this chart. "Negative" is a grammar term the students will find useful.

- A common mistake of beginners from some language groups is the use of *no* instead of *not:* e.g., ★*Tom is no a teacher.* Another common mistake is the omission of *be:* e.g., ★*I not a teacher.*

- In example (c), you can point out that the only contracted form of *I am not* is *I'm not.*

☐ **EXERCISE 12, p. 9.   *Negative with BE.   (Chart 1-5)***

Controlled completion.
Give students time to complete this exercise prior to class discussion. Students could work alone or in pairs. The exercise looks easy, but it's a little tricky.

Vocabulary from earlier exercises is used again here, and the drawings should help learners understand the new vocabulary: *artist, professional photographer, gardener, bus driver,* and *police officer.* If your class is interested, discuss other vocabulary suggested by the illustrations: *steering wheel, paint brush, uniform, gloves, binoculars, stethoscope,* etc.

ANSWERS: **2.** Horses aren't insects. They're animals. **3.** Asia isn't a country. It's a continent. **4.** Bees and ants aren't animals. They're insects. **5.** Arabic isn't a country. It's a language. **6.** I'm not a professional photographer. I'm a student. **7.** Ann isn't a gardener. She's a photographer. **8.** Mike is a gardener. He isn't an artist. **9.** Jim isn't a bus driver. He's an artist. **10.** Sue isn't a photographer. She's a doctor/nurse. **11.** Mr. Rice is a police officer. He isn't a bus driver/an artist/a doctor/a gardener/a photographer. **12.** Ms. Black isn't an artist/a police officer/a gardener/a photographer/a doctor. She's a bus driver.

CHART 1-6: *BE* **+ ADJECTIVE**

• The term "adjective" might need more explanation, either from examples you make up or from the examples of adjective usage in the exercises that follow. The nine exercises that follow this chart are designed to help students understand what an adjective is and learn some common adjectives.

• Again, in this type of sentence many languages do not use a form of *be,* but *be* is required in English. You might want to point out that adjectives in English do NOT add *-s* when the noun is plural, as in example (b)— contrary to the use of adjectives in some other languages. INCORRECT: ★*Balls are rounds.*

• SUGGESTION: Use the illustration of the balls when discussing examples (a) and (b). The three balls are, from left to right, a basketball, a baseball or softball, and a soccer ball (AmE) or football (BrE). You could also bring several balls to class and perhaps a box to compare *round* and *square.*

☐ **EXERCISE 13, p. 10.** *BE* **+ adjective.** *(Chart 1-6)*

Oral.

This is a quick exercise that encourages effortless, spontaneous production of the target structure. First demonstrate what the students are supposed to do by drawing faces on the board. Mention that all three faces can show the same emotion if a student wishes.

EXPANSION: If you want to expand the exercise, you could add the adjectives *mean* or *evil.* Then demonstrate on the board the following: Draw "angry eyebrows" on a face and a downturned mouth to illustrate anger. Then draw "angry eyebrows" and a smiling mouth. The face suddenly becomes sinister-looking. Students might find this demonstration entertaining and/or curious.

☐ **EXERCISE 14, p. 11.** *BE + adjective.* *(Chart 1-6)*

Controlled completion.
Explain the word *opposite* in the directions. This exercise builds a vocabulary of basic adjectives by using opposites *(sad-happy, hot-cold,* etc.). Encourage learners to figure out the meanings of new words without using a dictionary. Help them with pronunciation, including the use of contractions in their answers.

ANSWERS: **2.** It's cold. **3.** He's poor. **4.** It's short. **5.** They're clean.
6. They're beautiful. **7.** They're expensive. **8.** They're fast. **9.** It's easy.
10. She's tall. **11.** They're old. **12.** It's noisy. **13.** It's open. **14.** They're dangerous. **15.** They're sour.

☐ **EXERCISE 15, p. 12.** *BE + adjective.* *(Chart 1-6)*

Oral (books closed).
Students close their books. Write the target adjectives on the board as you proceed. Begin with *round, square,* and *flat,* as in the example. Then write *full* and *empty,* and elicit sentences. Then *wet* and *dry,* etc. Prepare by bringing objects to class to use during this exercise and by planning which things in the classroom to use. You can make this exercise fun by your imaginative use of the adjectives and props.

   If you have time, repeat the exercise with students leading it. Assign individual students a pair (or trio) of adjectives to write on the board to elicit sentences. The leaders don't have to use the same props you used; encourage them to use their ingenuity. For example, for *round* they could use a fist, a head, or a wadded piece of paper.

☐ **EXERCISE 16, p. 12.** *BE + adjective.* *(Chart 1-6)*

Controlled completion.
You might begin by pronouncing the words in the box and making sure the students know their meanings. They could work in pairs, continuing to Exercises 17, 18, and 19. Give them a time limit, and tell them to take turns answering and listening. If students work in pairs, you should sample their answers after everyone is finished, or ask which items were hard to answer in order to give you a measure of their understanding.

ANSWERS: **2.** are cold **3.** is square **4.** are round **5.** is sweet
6. is large/big . . . is small/little **7.** is wet . . . is dry **8.** is sour **9.** is funny
10. is important **11.** are beautiful **12.** is . . . flat

☐ **EXERCISE 17, p. 13.** *BE + adjective.* *(Charts 1-5 and 1-6)*

Controlled completion.
ANSWERS: **3.** isn't **4.** are . . . are **5.** isn't . . . is **6.** isn't **7.** are
8. aren't **9.** isn't . . . is **10.** isn't . . . is **11.** is/isn't . . . isn't/is **12.** isn't/is . . . is/isn't **13.** is/isn't . . . isn't/is **14.** are/aren't **15.** is **16.** aren't . . . are
17. is/isn't . . . isn't/is **18.** is/isn't **19.** is/isn't **20.** aren't . . . are
21. are/aren't **22.** is/isn't **23.** aren't . . . are **24.** is . . . isn't

☐ **EXERCISE 18, p. 14.** *BE + adjective.* *(Charts 1-5 and 1-6)*

Oral.
Help with vocabulary as necessary.

☐ **EXERCISE 19, p. 15.** *BE + adjective.* *(Charts 1-5 and 1-6)*

> *Oral.*
> Use this exercise as an opportunity for general class discussion of your city. Encourage students to express their opinions and perhaps relate their experiences in this city.

☐ **EXERCISE 20, p. 15.** *BE + adjective.* *(Charts 1-5 and 1-6)*

> *Oral (books closed).*
> Students close their books. You give the cue and students make a complete sentence. If time is short, select only half of the items, some easy and others more challenging. If you have time to spare, use this exercise for group work in which the leader of each group has his/her book open and gives the cues.
>
> ANSWERS: **1.** is   **2.** isn't   **3.** isn't   **4.** is   **5.** aren't   **6.** are   **7.** are
> **8.** aren't   **9.** aren't   **10.** is   **11.** aren't   **12.** isn't   **13.** is   **14.** aren't
> **15.** is   **16.** isn't   **17.** is   **18.** aren't   **19.** are   **20.** is/isn't   **21.** isn't/is
> **22.** is/isn't   **23.** is/isn't   **24.** isn't/is   **25.** aren't   **26.** aren't   **27.** is   **28.** aren't
> **29.** is   **30.** is   **31.** are   **32.** are

☐ **EXERCISE 21, p. 15.** *BE + adjective.* *(Chart 1-6)*

> *Oral (books closed).*
> This exercise encourages the students to use their own knowledge and imaginations to answer your cue. Elicit several responses for each item if you have time.

CHART 1-7:   *BE + A LOCATION*

- Some students may ask about other prepositions with similar meanings, e.g., *above/over, under/below/beneath, behind/in back of.* You may not wish to discuss those now because some learners might be confused. If you decide to explain the differences, be prepared with clear examples, perhaps from a dictionary for ESL/EFL students.

- The preposition *at* is usually difficult to explain and understand. Uses of *at* and *in* are emphasized and differentiated in Chart 7-17.

- Note the new grammar terms "preposition" and "prepositional phrase." It is suggested that you not attempt to define a preposition but rather allow students' understanding to come from the examples. If students press you for a definition, you might say a preposition is a word that shows a particular relationship between nouns. For example, in the illustration *on* shows the relationship between the ball and the box. A humorous definition of prepositions is "little words that cause learners big problems." Some simple definitions of the term "phrase" are: "a group of related words that do not have a subject and a verb" (to contrast a phrase and a clause), or "a group of words that form a unit." These definitions are probably too confusing for students at this level. Perhaps easier is to define a phrase as "a short group of words." Easier still is not to attempt definitions at all at this point and to let the understandings emerge from the examples.

- Lead the students through an examination of the illustration. Use other objects in the classroom (e.g., an eraser and a book) to similarly demonstrate the meanings of the prepositions.

☐ **EXERCISE 22, p. 17.** *BE + a location. (Chart 1-7)*

Controlled completion.
This exercise is simply another series of illustrations of the meanings of the prepositions. Students can call out the answers.

ANSWERS: **2.** on **3.** above **4.** under **5.** between **6.** next to **7.** behind

☐ **EXERCISE 23, p. 19.** *BE + a location. (Chart 1-7)*

Structure identification.
Prepositional phrases are essential and extremely common structures in English sentences. The purpose of this exercise is to familiarize students with this structure.

ANSWERS: *(The prepositions are underlined.)* **2.** <u>at</u> the airport **3.** <u>from</u> Egypt **4.** <u>on</u> my desk **5.** <u>in</u> his pocket **6.** <u>on</u> First Street **7.** <u>next to</u> the bank **8.** <u>under</u> my desktop **9.** <u>between</u> my cheeks **10.** <u>on</u> the third floor . . . <u>above</u> Mr. Kwan's apartment.

☐ **EXERCISE 24, p. 19.** *BE + a location. (Chart 1-7)*

Oral (books closed).
Students' books are closed. They must listen carefully to your cues. You should expect them to follow your instructions and perform the actions.

CHART 1-8: SUMMARY: SENTENCE PATTERNS WITH *BE*

- This chart (1) summarizes the three completions for sentences with main verb *be*, and (2) introduces the two very important grammar terms "subject" and "verb."

- For review, ask the students to make the example sentences negative. You could also preview the next chart by asking them to change the example sentences to questions (even though you would end up with the somewhat unnatural question "Am I student?").

- In example (a), the noun phrase *a student* is called a "noun complement" later in the text (Chart 8-12).

- If structure recognition and identification are not important to your goals and purposes, skip class discussion of Chart 1-8 and omit Exercise 25.

☐ **EXERCISE 25, p. 20.** *Sentence patterns with BE. (Chart 1-8)*

Controlled completion and structure identification.
ANSWERS: **4.** are + N **5.** is + LOC **6.** is + ADJ **7.** are + N **8.** am + LOC **9.** is + LOC **10.** are + ADJ

☐ **EXERCISE 26, p. 21.** *Sentence patterns with BE. (Chart 1-8)*

Oral.
Say the sentences in normal spoken English. The students can repeat after you in unison just to familiarize themselves with the phenomenon of normal contracted speech. It's what they will hear — and will themselves produce naturally later as they gain experience with English. Don't insist on the students' using contracted speech now. More important at this stage is clear, understandable production, even if it is necessary for the learner to speak more slowly and carefully than native speakers.

ANSWERS: *(The contractions in this exercise are usually spoken but not written.)* **2.** Rita's a student. **3.** My book's on the table. **4.** My books're on the table. **5.** The weather's cold today. **6.** My brother's twenty-one years old. **7.** The window's open. **8.** The windows're open. **9.** My money's in my wallet. **10.** Mr. Smith's a teacher. **11.** Tom's at home now. **12.** The sun's bright today. **13.** My roommate's from Chicago. **14.** My roommates're from Chicago. **15.** My sister's a student in high school.

CHART 1-9:   YES/NO QUESTIONS WITH *BE*

● Two important structures are presented here: (1) word order in questions with *be,* and (2) verb use in short answers. Point out that contractions are not used in affirmative short answers.

☐ **EXERCISE 27, p. 22.** *Yes/no questions with BE.* **(Chart 1-9)**

Transformation.
Students can work in pairs. Try to make it clear that the words in parentheses are long answers and that the students are to supply only short answers.

ANSWERS: **3.** A: Are you homesick? B: No, I'm not. **4.** A: Is Bob homesick? B: Yes, he is. **5.** A: Is Sue here today? B: No, she isn't. OR No, she's not. **6.** A: Are the students in this class intelligent? B: Yes, they are. **7.** A: Are the chairs in this room comfortable? B: No, they aren't. OR No, they're not. **8.** A: Are you married? B: No, I'm not. **9.** A: Are you and Tom roommates? B: Yes, we are. **10.** A: Is a butterfly a bird? B: No, it isn't. OR No, it's not.

☐ **EXERCISE 28, p. 23.** *Yes/no questions with BE.* **(Chart 1-9)**

Oral (books closed).
Students work in pairs. One student's book is closed. The other one asks questions for items 1 through 14 and waits for a response. Then they change roles for items 15 through 27. They should use their own words for the phrases in parentheses.

☐ **EXERCISE 29, p. 23.** *Yes/no questions with BE.* **(Chart 1-9)**

Oral (books closed).
Students can change to other partners, then continue as in Exercise 28. Tell them to help each other with or ask you for word meanings, but not to use a dictionary. (Not using a dictionary keeps the focus on oral interaction in this kind of exercise.)

QUESTIONS: **1.** Is a mouse big? **2.** Is sugar sweet? **3.** Are lemons sweet? **4.** Are ice cream and candy sour? **5.** Is the world flat? **6.** Is the world round? **7.** Is your desk comfortable? **8.** Are your shoes comfortable? **9.** Are your eyes brown? **10.** Is the sun bright today? **11.** Is the weather cold today? **12.** Is your pen heavy? **13.** Are apples expensive? **14.** Are diamonds cheap? **15.** Is English grammar easy? **16.** Is the floor in this room clean? **17.** Are butterflies beautiful? **18.** Are turtles intelligent? **19.** Is your dictionary under your desk? **20.** Are your books on your desk? **21.** Is your desk in the middle of the room? **22.** Is your pen in your pocket?

CHART 1-10: QUESTIONS WITH *BE*: USING *WHERE*

• The forms of two types of questions are compared: (1) a yes/no question (i.e., a question that is answered by *yes* or *no*) and (2) an information question (a question that begins with a question word, also called a Q-word or WH-word, such as *where, when, why, who).*

• You might write the examples on the chalkboard, aligning them as they are in the chart to show the positions of the sentence parts. The similarity in form between yes/no and information questions is emphasized throughout the text — whether the question uses *am/is/are, do/does, did, was/were, have/has,* or modal auxiliaries.

☐ **EXERCISE 30, p. 24.** *Questions with BE: using WHERE.* *(Chart 1-10)*

Transformation.
Students must decide which type of question is necessary in each short conversation. The words in parentheses are not part of the conversation, just part of the meaning; they give the full meaning of the short answer.

ANSWERS: **3.** Is Cairo in Egypt? **4.** Where is Cairo? **5.** Are the students in class today? **6.** Where are the students? **7.** Where is the post office? **8.** Is the train station on Grand Avenue? **9.** Where is/does the bus stop? **10.** Where are Sue and Ken today?

☐ **EXERCISE 31, p. 25.** *Questions with BE: using WHERE.* *(Chart 1-10)*

Oral (books closed).
After you give the cue, Student A directs his/her question to any classmate.
  Where-questions are the target structure here, but the response part of this exercise is just as important and far more challenging. Create cues for item 12 that will test the students' knowledge of the city and their ability to state locations.
  Item 12 is a good way to again give the students information about the city they're living in and to promote communicative language use by having the students provide real information.

QUESTIONS: **1.** Where is your grammar book? **2.** Where is your dictionary? **3.** Where is your money? **4.** Where are your books? **5.** Where is *(name of a student)?* **6.** Where are *(names of two students)?* **7.** Where are your sunglasses? **8.** Where is your pen? **9.** Where is your apartment? **10.** Where are your parents? **11.** Where is the post office? **12.** Where is *(name of a store, landmark, or restaurant in this city)?*

☐ **EXERCISE 32, p. 25.** *Questions with BE: using WHERE.* *(Chart 1-10)*

Oral.
This is another good exercise for exchanging real information. You might begin by pronouncing all of the names. Perhaps point out that some of the locations are indicated by dots on the map, but let them discover that others have different symbols. Students can work in pairs, then you can ask the whole class whether any items remain unknown and lead the discussion about their location.
  Items 7 and 8 use *are:* *Where are the Great Lakes?* and *Where are the Rocky Mountains?* All of the other questions are singular and use *is.*

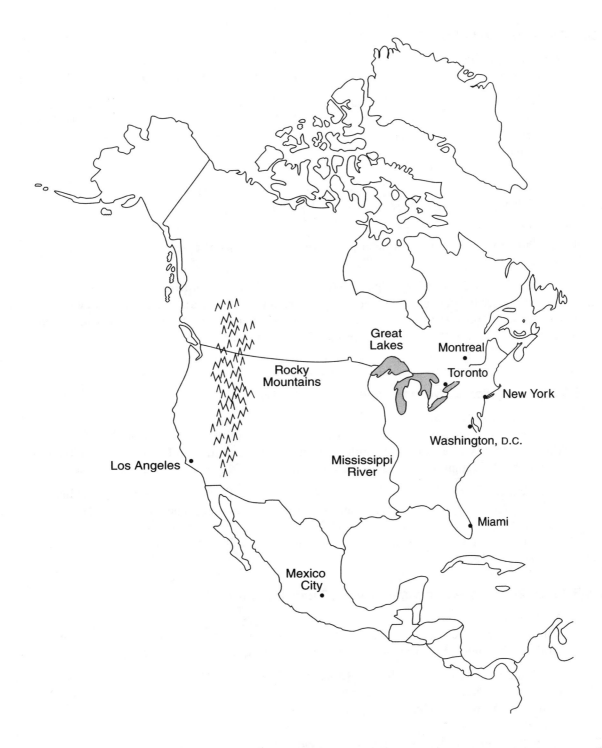

CHART 1-11: USING *HAVE* AND *HAS*

● The students are now moving from the use of main verb *be* to the use of main verb *have*. The main difficulty students have with this grammar is using *has* with third person singular subjects (the pronouns *she/he/it* or singular noun subjects). A common mistake would be: ★*My teacher have a blue pen.* You might point out that the final *-s* is consistent in the forms *is* and *has*.

☐ **EXERCISE 33, p. 26.** *HAVE and HAS.* *(Chart 1-11)*

   Controlled completion.
   Learners must decide whether each item requires the basic form of *have* or the *-s* form, *has*.

   ANSWERS: **2.** have   **3.** has . . . has   **4.** have   **5.** has   **6.** have . . . have
   7. has   **8.** have . . . has   **9.** have   **10.** has . . . has   **11.** has [To *have* the flu is an
   idiomatic use of *have*. In English, one *has* an illness. This use of *have* might seem odd to some students.]
   12. have

CHART 1-12:   USING *MY, YOUR, HIS, HER, OUR, THEIR*
• This chart builds upon the known (subject pronouns) to introduce the new forms (possessive adjectives).   • The terms "possessive adjective" and "possessive pronoun" can be confusing. *My, your, her*, etc., are pronouns in that they are noun substitutes, but they can also function as adjectives (i.e., they modify nouns); hence the term "possessive adjectives," to distinguish them from "possessive pronouns" *(mine, yours, hers,* etc.). See Charts 8-9 and 8-15 for possessive pronouns.

☐ **EXERCISE 34, p. 27.** *Possessive adjectives.* *(Chart 1-12)*

   Controlled completion.
   This is a very mechanical exercise; it does not represent real conversation, but it gives learners
   the opportunity to ensure their understanding of the grammar. They have to think about the
   concepts of singular and plural and about antecedents for possessive adjective usage.

   ANSWERS: **2.** Your   **3.** Her   **4.** His   **5.** Our   **6.** Your   **7.** Their
   8. My [Note: You might call students' attention to the hyphen in the number *twenty-one*. Numbers are spelled
   out in APPENDIX 2 at the back of the textbook.]   **9.** Her   **10.** Your   **11.** Your [*Mustache* can be
   defined as the hair between a man's nose and mouth.]   **12.** Their   **13.** Our   **14.** Her
   15. His   **16.** Our

☐ **EXERCISE 35, p. 28.** *Possessive adjectives.* *(Charts 1-11 and 1-12)*

   Controlled completion.
   This combines the lessons from Charts 1-11 and 1-12. If that grammar is review for your
   students, not new, this exercise can be finished very quickly or skipped.

   ANSWERS: **2.** has . . . His   **3.** have . . . Your   **4.** has . . . Her   **5.** have . . . Their
   6. have . . . Their   **7.** have . . . Our   **8.** have . . . My   **9.** have . . . Our   **10.** have . . .
   Your   **11.** has . . . Her   **12.** has . . . His

☐ **EXERCISE 36, p. 28.** *Possessive adjectives.* *(Chart 1-12)*

   Controlled completion.
   One purpose of this exercise is to familiarize the students with the vocabulary for clothing and
   colors. Another is to provide a context for a passive understanding of the present progressive
   (e.g., *is wearing*). The first sentence in each item uses the present progressive, which is not
   explained until Chapter 3. The meaning of the verb form is "at this moment in time, right now"
   if students ask about it. It is not necessary to explain more about this until Chapter 3.

   ANSWERS: **1.** Her   **2.** His   **3.** My   **4.** Their   **5.** Your   **6.** Our
   7. Your   **8.** Her   **9.** His   **10.** Their   **11.** His   **12.** My

VOCABULARY CHECKLIST, p. 29.

Have the students ask you questions about words they don't understand or would like you to pronounce. Use items and colors in the classroom to explain the vocabulary.

☐ **EXERCISE 37, p. 29.** *Summary.* *(Charts 1-1 → 1-12)*

Oral (books closed).
This exercise gives learners an opportunity to use the grammar they have been studying while practicing vocabulary. Encourage the use of complete sentences.

Using the formats suggested in the examples, lead the students through all or most of the colors and clothing types represented in the classroom. The method is for you to have a series of short conversations with individual students using the true and present classroom context; the goal is for the students to engage in effortless and clear communication using familiar structures and vocabulary — a real coup for a beginning student.

CHARTS 1-13 AND 1-14:   USING *THIS, THAT, THESE, THOSE*

• Some languages have very different systems for indicating near and far objects. Demonstrate the English system by putting a book near you *(this book)* and one away from you *(that book)*. Use other objects in the classroom for additional contextualized examples.

• This chart gives the singular English forms *this* and *that*; Chart 1-14 gives the plural forms *these* and *those*. These words are often called "demonstratives."

• Learners often have difficulty differentiating the pronunciation of *this* and *these*. It may help to tell them that the vowel in *these* is spoken a bit longer, and the *-s* in *these* is pronounced /z/. The *-ese* in *these* should sound exactly like the *-ease* in *please*. The *-is* in *this* should sound exactly like the *-iss* in *kiss*.

• You might wish to emphasize good pronunciation of the *th*-sound /ð/. For some learners it's too difficult to think about correct forms and good pronunciation at the same time, and pronunciation quickly slips into old habits when a student is concentrating on form and meaning. It will all come together eventually as the student gains experience.

• You could point out that *this, that, these,* and *those* can be used both as adjectives and as pronouns. In Chart 1-13, (a) and (b) illustrate their use as adjectives; (c) and (d) illustrate their use as pronouns. This information is not crucial and can easily be omitted.

☐ **EXERCISE 38, p. 30.** *THIS and THAT.* *(Chart 1-13)*

Oral (books closed).
You give the cue and the responding student touches or points to things in the classroom. The students must think about *this* vs. *that* as well as the possessive adjectives in their answers. Give them time to think of a good answer.

Some students might naturally slip into use of possessive pronouns *(mine, hers, etc.)*. For example, they might say *This book is mine. That book is yours.* If they already know how to use possessive pronouns, that's great. Don't discourage them simply because they didn't follow the exact pattern of the exercise. Keep the focus on *this* and *that*.

Add or substitute items from your classroom to the list of cues. Keep all the items singular at this point.

☐ **EXERCISE 39, p. 30.** *THIS and THAT.* *(Chart 1-13)*

> *Oral (books closed).*
> This is a review of colors while the target structure is being practiced. Continually model the pronunciation of *th*.

☐ **EXERCISE 40, p. 31.** *THIS, THAT, THESE, and THOSE.* *(Charts 1-13 and 1-14)*

> *Controlled completion.*
> Errors in singular-plural usage of *this, that, these,* and *those* are common. This exercise encourages students to pay careful attention to singular and plural.
>   Emphasize the pronunciation differences between *this* and *these*, with *this* ending in an /s/ sound and *these* ending in a /z/ sound. The vowel sounds are also different.
>
> *ANSWERS:*   **2.** This . . . Those   **3.** These . . . Those   **4.** This . . . That
> **5.** These . . . Those   **6.** This . . . Those   **7.** these . . . those   **8.** This . . . Those

☐ **EXERCISE 41, p. 31.** *THAT and THOSE.* *(Chart 1-14)*

> *Oral (books closed).*
> This exercise practices plural forms only. Add or substitute items from your classroom to the list of cues.

☐ **EXERCISE 42, p. 32.** *THIS, THAT, THESE, and THOSE.* *(Charts 1-13 and 1-14)*

> *Oral (books closed).*
> This exercise mixes singular and plural forms. Add or substitute items from your classroom.

CHART 1-15:   ASKING QUESTIONS WITH *WHAT* AND *WHO* + *BE*

• The words in parentheses are usually omitted in conversations because both speaker and listener can see the same thing or person.

• NOTE: In singular questions with *who*, the demonstrative pronoun *that* (or possibly *this)* is used to ask about a person, but in the plural *these* and *those* are not used as pronouns. (INCORRECT: ★*Who are those?* CORRECT: *Who are they?* ALSO CORRECT: *Who are those people?*) The students don't need this information, but an unusually alert student might have a query about it.

☐ **EXERCISE 43, p. 32.** *Questions with WHO and WHAT + BE.* *(Chart 1-15)*

> *Controlled completion.*
> Students can work in pairs, but they should exchange roles so that everyone has a chance to supply answers. They have to think about the differences between singular and plural as well as between people and things.
>
> *ANSWERS:*   **2.** What are   **3.** Who is/Who's   **4.** What is/What's   **5.** Who are
> **6.** What is/What's   **7.** Who is/Who's   **8.** Who are   **9.** What is/What's
> **10.** What are

☐ **EXERCISE 44, p. 33.** *Questions with WHAT and WHO + BE.* *(Chart 1-15)*

Oral.
Students can work in pairs. This is intended as a very short exercise that gives the students a little practice with these very common questions.

☐ **EXERCISE 45, p. 34** *Parts of the body.*

Vocabulary.
This exercise is designed to familiarize the students with the vocabulary they will need to use in the following exercise. Freely add more vocabulary related to the body, whatever your students want and can handle: *neck, shoulder, chest, ribs, belly button*, etc.

☐ **EXERCISE 46, p. 34.** *THIS, THAT, THESE, THOSE, and questions with BE.* *(Charts 1-13 → 1-15)*

Oral (books closed.)
After the students have learned the vocabulary in Exercise 45, they close their books and use that vocabulary while they are practicing with *this, that, these,* and *those.* Include any extra vocabulary you taught the students in Exercise 45.

☐ **EXERCISE 47, p. 35.** *THIS, THAT, THESE, THOSE, and questions with BE.* *(Charts 1-13 → 1-15)*

Oral.
This is a very natural way to exchange information. Students should work in pairs, helping each other learn the vocabulary that is illustrated in the drawing. Supply vocabulary meanings only if asked.

It's very tempting to use this illustration as a preview of the present progressive (after the class is done with the exercise as pair work). If you think your class is ready and will enjoy the challenge rather than feel frustrated, ask them leading questions using the present progressive (e.g., *What is the cow doing?*), but be prepared to supply the answer yourself as well as spend some time explaining new vocabulary. Some examples: *The cow is eating grass. The clouds are drifting above the trees. The bat is hanging from a branch in the tree. The bat is sleeping. The turtle is climbing out of the water onto the river bank. The bird is flapping its wings. The dog is running. The horses are facing each other.*

☐ **EXERCISE 48, p. 36.** *THIS, THAT, THESE, THOSE, and questions with BE.* *(Charts 1-13 → 1-15)*

Pair work.
Students can be creative, perhaps making their drawings at home if time is short. Simple stick-figure drawings are fine. You should do a drawing on the board first to illustrate the simple kind of drawing you want them to do. If you don't draw very well, that's good. Show the students that any kind of simple drawing is fine.

☐ **EXERCISE 49, p. 36.** *Review.* *(Chapter 1)*

Structure identification.
The end-of-the-chapter review section begins here. This exercise reviews basic structures and their labels. The students will encounter these structures and this terminology over and over again in the course of the textbook.

In PART II, have the students identify the antecedents. For example, in item 6 *Bats* is the antecedent for *they* as well as *their.*

ANSWERS:

PART I: **2.** Flowers = *noun* . . . beautiful = *adj.*   **3.** Birds = *noun* . . . wings = *noun*
4. Bats = *noun* . . . birds = *noun*   **5.** Bats = *noun* . . . blind = *adj.*
PART II: **7.** I = *pronoun* . . . It = *pronoun* . . . My = *poss. adj.*   **8.** My = *poss. adj.* . . . . your =
poss. adj.   **9.** It = *pronoun*   **10.** She = *pronoun* . . . They = *pronoun* . . . Her = *poss. adj.*
PART III: **12.** from Beijing   **13.** on my desk   **14.** at school   **15.** between my index
finger and my ring finger

☐ EXERCISE 50, p. 37.   *Review.*   *(Chapter 1)*

Error analysis.
These sentences contain typical errors. This kind of exercise encourages the students to pay attention to important details as they develop self-monitoring skills. See the INTRODUCTION to the *Teacher's Guide,* pp. xvi–xvii, for more information about error analysis exercises.

    At this point, the learners should be able to correct each error and understand the underlying grammar. If they can do this exercise easily and well, you and they have done a really good job in Chapter 1! Congratulate them lavishly and don't forget to congratulate yourself too.

ANSWERS: **2.** I <u>am not</u> hungry.   **3.** I am <u>a</u> student. He is <u>a</u> teacher.   **4.** Yoko <u>is</u> not here. She <u>is</u> at school.   **5.** I'm from Mexico. Where <u>are you</u> from?   **6.** <u>Is Roberto</u> a student in your class? OR <u>Roberto is</u> a student in your class, isn't he?   **7.** Those pictures are <u>beautiful</u>.   **8.** This is <u>your</u> dictionary. It <u>is not</u> my dictionary.   **9.** Mr. Lee <u>has</u> a brown coat.   **10.** They <u>aren't</u> here today.   **11.** <u>This book is</u> expensive. OR <u>These</u> books are expensive.   **12.** Cuba is <u>an</u> island.   **13.** Florida and Korea <u>are</u> <u>peninsulas</u>.

☐ EXERCISE 51, p. 38.   *Review.*   *(Chapter 1)*

Controlled completion; multiple choice.
This is a multiple-choice exercise, similar to parts of international English tests. Some students may not be familiar with this type of test.

    You may ask the students to do this exercise individually in class as though they were actually taking a test. The usual amount of time allotted per item in a multiple-choice test is 30 seconds, so you would give the students 6 minutes to complete this exercise. Since this is a beginning class, however, be flexible. If some students don't finish in 6 minutes, give them some more time.

    This is not a tricky or difficult exercise. The expectation is that students will easily mark the correct answers and gain self-confidence.

ANSWERS: **1.** C   **2.** C   **3.** B   **4.** B   **5.** B   **6.** C   **7.** C   **8.** C
9. A   **10.** A   **11.** C   **12.** B

☐ EXERCISE 52, p. 39.   *Review.*   *(Chapter 1)*

Controlled completion.
Again, this is a simple exercise. Students have to supply truthful answers using correct grammar. They should be able to do this confidently and effortlessly.

ANSWERS: **1.** aren't   **2.** is   **3.** am/am not   **4.** are   **5.** are   **6.** are . . . aren't
7. isn't . . . is   **8.** is   **9.** are   **10.** isn't . . . is

☐ **EXERCISE 53, p. 39.** *Review.* *(Chapter 1)*

Open completion.
This exercise is more complicated than it may look. The students must have control of a number of basic structures to complete these dialogues. If the learners find this exercise easy, they should be pleased by their progress and proud of themselves.

ANSWERS: **1.** B: I am   A: are   B: am from   **2.** A: is   B: has   A: are B: have   **3.** A: What is   B: is a   A: Who is   B: my   A: Who are

POSSIBLE COMPLETIONS: **4.** A: artist/doctor/actor/etc.   B: I'm . . . student **5.** A: these/those   B: they are   A: this/that   B: it isn't/it's not   **6.** A: an orchid . . . an orchid   B: a flower   **7.** A: Is a bear . . . are wolves . . . Is a bat   **8.** A: Are Thailand and Vietnam . . . Is Argentina . . . Is Italy   B: Europe   **9.** A: is your brother   B: at home A: are Tina and Bill   B: in class   **10.** A: What is . . . What is   B: It's/It is   A: Are B: They're/They are

☐ **EXERCISE 54, p. 42.** *Review.* *(Chapter 1)*

Oral; pair work.
This is lots of fun for most learners. They have to listen carefully to their partners, and the speakers have to speak clearly.

☐ **EXERCISE 55, p. 42.** *Review.* *(Chapter 1)*

Oral; pair work.
This is a review of the prepositions of location in Chapter 1. One of its main purposes is for the students to have fun interacting with each other by making up funny directions such as "Put your foot on your desk." or "Put your pen in Ali's pocket." The students will take their cue from you. Give them funny examples and set a jovial mood. In some classes, students will vie with each other to give the funniest or most outrageous directions.

☐ **EXERCISE 56, p. 42.** *Review.* *(Chapter 1)*

Open completion.
This exercise is most effective when students copy the whole thing so that it looks like an essay. Tell them to indent the beginning of each paragraph, as in lines 1, 3, 6, 12, and 16. This exercise is preparation for Exercise 57, which follows.

ANSWERS: **2.** I am/I'm . . . I am/I'm   **3.** My . . . is   **4.** He is/He's . . . My **5.** is . . . She is/She's   **6.** have   **7.** are . . . is   **8.** She is/She's . . . is   **9.** She is/She's . . . my   **10.** is . . . He is/He's   **11.** has   **12.** It is/It's . . . It is/It's   **13.** is **14.** His . . . He is/He's   **15.** He is/He's   **16.** They are/They're . . . my **17.** They are/They're

☐ **EXERCISE 57, p. 43.** *Review.* *(Chapter 1)*

Open completion.
As in Exercise 56, students should copy the whole thing. The blanks in the book are purposefully not long enough for the necessary information. What the students should end up with is an essay about themselves using the structures they practiced in Chapter 1.

Chapter 2: EXPRESSING PRESENT TIME (Part 1)

ORDER OF CHAPTER	CHARTS	EXERCISES
Simple present	2-1	Ex. 1
Frequency adverbs with *be*	2-2 → 2-3	Ex. 2 → 5
Spelling and pronunciation of final *-s/-es*	2-4 → 2-5	Ex. 6 → 8
Final *-s/-es* with words ending in *-y*	2-6	Ex. 9
Has, does, goes	2-7	Ex. 10
Summary: final *-s/-es*	2-8	Ex. 11 → 13
Simple present: negative	2-9	Ex. 14 → 18
Yes/no questions	2-10	Ex. 19 → 21
Information questions	2-11 → 2-12	Ex. 22 → 25
Summary: information questions, *be* and *do*	2-13	Ex. 26 → 29
Using *it* to talk about time	2-14	Ex. 30
Prepositions of time	2-15	Ex. 31 → 32
Using *it* to talk about weather	2-16	Ex. 33 → 35
Review		Ex. 36 → 43

General Notes on Chapter 2

This chapter focuses on the simple present tense. Many languages do not have the variety of verb tenses that English employs, so learners must adjust their assumptions about the relationships between real time and the meanings of verb tenses. The simple present tense, the subject of Chapter 2, is used in talking or writing about repeated, habitual activities. Its main complication is the addition of *-s* to a verb whose subject is a singular noun or *she/he/it*. Final *-s* has variations in spelling and pronunciation which are presented in this chapter. Negative and question forms of the simple present tense are also introduced.

**CHART 2-1:   FORM AND BASIC MEANING OF THE
SIMPLE PRESENT TENSE**

- This chapter and this chart focus on the most common use of the simple present tense: expressing habits, routine activities, customary situations. Of course, there are other uses for this tense, but this is a good place to start.

- Help students recall the use of *-s* on a verb with a singular third-person subject *(she/he/it* or a singular noun). In Chapter 1 they learned to use *is* and *has*; now they see *-s* added to many verbs.

☐ **EXERCISE 1, p. 45.**   *Simple present tense.   (Chart 2-1)*

Sentence construction.
The purpose of this exercise is to provide vocabulary and phrases students can use to express their own habitual activities in the morning. First answer any questions about vocabulary in the left column. Then have the students complete the sentences in the right column. Students choose the order of their morning activities and then just add the pronoun "I" and end the sentence with a period.

EXPANSION: When the students have finished writing, ask them to describe their mornings orally, books closed (or open if they wish). This oral work can be teacher-led, or the students can be divided into pairs. Follow the oral part by having the students describe their mornings in a written paragraph.

Note that item (m) is checked because it was used for item 2. Checking off an item helps students keep track of which ones they have used in their lists. When an item contains a slash (/), the student can choose between the words before and after the slash.

Notice that the exercise introduces some common phrasal verbs. *Put on, pick up, turn off* are separable phrasal verbs. In other words, they can be separated by a noun phrase, e.g., in (c): *put on my clothes* OR *put my clothes on. On, up,* and *off* can function as prepositions, but here they function as particles. ("Particles" are connected to the verbs they follow; "prepositions" are linked with the nouns that follow them. The students don't need to know the distinction between prepositions and particles at this stage in their language study.)

Brush, stretch, yawn, and rub may need to be demonstrated.

CHART 2-2:   USING FREQUENCY ADVERBS: *ALWAYS,
USUALLY, OFTEN, SOMETIMES, SELDOM,
RARELY, NEVER*

- Two points to learn here are the meaning of each adverb and its location in a sentence. Point out also that the word *frequency* is used when talking about habits; therefore, frequency adverbs are frequently used with the simple present tense. (Frequency adverbs are also used with other tenses.)

- Pronunciation note: *often* may be pronounced with the /t/ sound, but usually without it.

- The illustration with cups of tea shows that the percentages of frequency are not precise; learners should see them as generalizations, not as absolute quantities.

□ **EXERCISE 2, p. 46.** *Frequency adverbs.* *(Chart 2-2)*

Oral; structure identification and controlled completion.
This is an exercise in word order and in recognition of subjects and verbs. Lead the students quickly through it, simply making sure they understand the information in Chart 2-2 (including the meanings of the adverbs).

ANSWERS: (Frequency adverbs are in italics.)   **2.** I = subject; <u>get up</u> = verb → I *usually* get up at 7:00.   **3.** I = subject; <u>drink</u> = verb → I *often* drink two cups of coffee in the morning.   **4.** I = subject; <u>eat</u> = verb → I *never* eat carrots for breakfast.   **5.** I = subject; <u>watch</u> = verb → I *seldom* watch TV in the morning.   **6.** I = subject; have = verb → I *sometimes* have tea with dinner. [*have tea* = drink tea]   **7.** <u>Bob</u> = subject; <u>eats</u> = verb → Bob *usually* eats lunch at the cafeteria.   **8.** <u>Ann</u> = subject; <u>drinks</u> = verb → Ann *rarely* drinks tea.   **9.** I = subject; <u>do</u> = verb → I *always* do my homework.   **10.** <u>We</u> = subject; <u>listen</u> = verb → We *often* listen to music after dinner.   **11.** <u>John and Sue</u> = subject; <u>watch</u> = verb → John and Sue *never* watch TV in the afternoon. [*TV* = television]   **12.** <u>students</u> = subject; <u>speak</u> = verb → The students *always* speak English in the classroom.

□ **EXERCISE 3, p. 47.** *Frequency adverbs.* *(Chart 2-2)*

Oral.
Students can work in pairs or small groups, taking turns with the answers. They should be encouraged to tell the truth and to monitor the correct word order in each other's answers.

If you use it as a teacher-led exercise, go through it somewhat quickly, slowing occasionally to get multiple responses to certain items. Change it to a books-closed exercise if your class can handle it.

In item 10, *spend time* = use a period of time for some purpose.

In item 20, *a snack* = a small thing to eat that is not part of a main meal.

Items 21–25: In the phrase *go to bed,* note the absence of an article before *bed.* A fairly common error students make is to say ★"*I usually go to <u>the</u> bed at eleven.*"

CHART 2-3:   USING FREQUENCY ADVERBS WITH *BE*

• Ask students to locate the verb in each example in this chart. Then ask them where the frequency adverb is located in relation to the verb. They should see the difference between sentences with *be* and with other verbs. You might use the chalkboard to show this.

□ **EXERCISE 4, p. 48.** *Frequency adverbs.* *(Charts 2-2 → 2-3)*

Structure identification and controlled completion.
This is a type of editing exercise. Students add a caret (^) where the frequency adverb should be added to the sentence, then write the adverb above the caret. This exercise is written instead of oral so students have a visual representation of the word order differences presented in Charts 2-2 and 2-3.

Items 1–4: *on time* is the opposite of *late;* note the use of the preposition *for* after *on time* and *late.*

ANSWERS: **3.** Sue is *often* late for class.   **4.** Sue *often* comes to class late.   **5.** Ron is *never* happy.   **6.** Ron *never* smiles.   **7.** Bob is *usually* at home in the evening.   **8.** Bob *usually* stays at home in the evening.   **9.** Tom *seldom* studies at the library in the evening.   **10.** Tom is *seldom* at the library in the evening.   **11.** I *rarely* eat breakfast.   **12.** I *often* take the bus to school.   **13.** The weather is *usually* hot in July.   **14.** Sue *never* drinks coffee.   **15.** She *sometimes* drinks tea.

☐ **EXERCISE 5, p. 48.** *Frequency adverbs.* *(Charts 2-2 → 2-3)*

Written.

Most learners can write a simple paragraph in a chronological (time) sequence. Perhaps assign this as homework. When you mark it, focus on the correct use of final *-s* and the location of frequency adverbs. Don't penalize students for other errors; praise their successes.

The use of *after that* to show a sequence of events can be problematical. *(After that* means "and then.") A common error is for students to write *After I eat lunch* as a complete sentence instead of *After that I eat lunch.* Another common problem is to confuse uses of *after* as a preposition and a subordinating conjunction. Note the difference:

Preposition (followed by pronoun object *that*): *I go to the cafeteria for breakfast.* ***After that*** *I go back to my room.*

Preposition: *I got back to my room* ***after*** *breakfast.*

Subordinating conjunction: *I go back to my room* ***after*** *I eat breakfast.*

Students aren't introduced to adverb clauses of time until Chart 5-18. These difficulties with the use of *after* will probably occur in the students' writing, but it is probably too soon to try to explain the grammar.

CHART 2-4: **PRONUNCIATION OF FINAL -*S***

- Learners usually have difficulty hearing and saying these forms. You should not expect perfection now, but you should continually help students when they use these forms. Problems with correct use of final *-s/-es* continue well into the advanced stages of most learners' study of English, well beyond the point at which they understand the grammar. Use of final *-s/-es* needs constant teacher attention and student self-monitoring.

- In this chart and the following exercises, have the students exaggerate the pronunciation of final *-s*. In actuality, final /s/ and /z/ are tiny, unstressed sounds; students have difficulty hearing them and, subsequently, often omit them in their speaking and writing.

- The vocabulary used to explain the information in this chart is difficult for learners. Take some time to make sure students understand the terms "voiced" and "voiceless." Perhaps start out with the vocabulary item "voice." Then explain that *voiced* means "with the voice" and *voiceless* means "without the voice." (Explain perhaps that the suffix *-less* means "without.") *Voiced* means we use our voice boxes; model sounds for them to repeat and have the students feel their voice boxes. For *voiceless* sounds, we're simply pushing air out our mouths with our lips, teeth, and/or tongue in particular formations. For example, for /f/ we put our upper front teeth on top of the bottom lip and blow air out.

- In example (d), point out that the *-gh* in *laugh* is pronounced /f/, a voiceless sound.

☐ **EXERCISE 6, p. 49.** *Pronunciation of final -S.* *(Chart 2-4)*

Pronunciation.

You should model the pronunciation of each verb and then have the students pronounce it before one or more of them read the whole sentence. Exaggerate final *-s,* but also demonstrate what a small sound it is in normal spoken English.

In item 1, the pronunciation of *Cindy* is /sɪndi/.
In item 6, the pronunciation of *Tina* is /tinə/.
In item 7, the pronunciation of *Seattle* is /siyǽtəl/.

ANSWERS: **1.–7.** *(pronunciation given)* **8.** stands = stand/z/ **9.** lives = live/z/ **10.** smiles = smile/z/ **11.** comes = come/z/ **12.** rains = rain/z/ **13.** remembers = remember/z/ **14.** snows = snow/z/

☐ **EXERCISE 7, p. 50.** *Pronunciation of final -S.* *(Chart 2-4)*

> *Pronunciation.*
> You should model the pronunciation of each verb, and then have the students pronounce it before one or more of them read the whole sentence.
>
> *ANSWERS:* **1.–6.** *(pronunciation given)* [In item 4, the pronunciation of *Sara* is /sɛrə/.]
> **7.** claps = clap/s/ **8.** bites = bite/s/ **9.** gets up = get/s/ up **10.** asks = ask/s/
> **11.** talks = talk/s/ **12.** coughs = cough/s/ [The pronunciation of *coughs* is /kɔfs/.]

CHART 2-5:	SPELLING AND PRONUNCIATION OF FINAL -ES	

- There are three different pronunciations of final -*s*. This is the third pronunciation of the -*s* ending.

☐ **EXERCISE 8, p. 51.** *Spelling: final -ES.* *(Charts 2-4 and 2-5)*

> *Fill-in-the-blanks.*
> All three pronunciations of the -*s* ending are used here, with an emphasis on the /əz/ pronunciation.
>
> *ANSWERS:* **2.** teaches = teach/əz/ **3.** fixes = fix/əz/ [*Fixes* is pronounced /fɪksəz/.]
> **4.** drinks = drink/s/ **5.** watches = watch/əz/ **6.** kisses = kiss/əz/ **7.** wears = wear/z/
> **8.** washes = wash/əz/ [In items 8 and 9, the letter "c" in *Eric* and *Jessica* is pronounced /k/.]
> **9.** walks = walk/s/ **10.** stretches = stretch/əz/ . . . yawns = yawn/z/

CHART 2-6:	ADDING FINAL -S/-ES TO WORDS THAT END IN -Y	

- The focus here is on the spelling. All of these endings use the /z/ pronunciation.

☐ **EXERCISE 9, p. 52.** *Spelling: final -ES.* *(Chart 2-6)*

> *Fill-in-the-blanks.*
>
> *ANSWERS:* **2.** seldom cries **3.** studies **4.** usually stays **5.** flies **6.** always carries **7.** prays **8.** seldom buys **9.** worries **10.** enjoys

---

CHART 2-7:	IRREGULAR SINGULAR VERBS: *HAS, DOES, GOES*	

- Irregular verbs in English have unusual pronunciations and spellings. Students must simply learn them.

- It is also true in English that some words that look like they ought to rhyme simply do not. *Do* and *go* do not rhyme. Similarly, *meat* and *great* do not rhyme. There are many other examples: *rough* and *cough*, *know* and *now*, *says* and *pays*, *heard* and *beard*. This feature of English can be quite frustrating for students.

☐ **EXERCISE 10, p. 53.** *Irregular singular verbs.* **(Chart 2-7)**

Fill-in-the-blanks.
This exercise is a quick check on the learners' understanding of the information in Chart 2-7.

ANSWERS: **3.** have   **4.** has   **5.** goes   **6.** go [*Go to the beach* means "go to the sandy shore of a lake or ocean."]   **7.** does   **8.** do   **9.** goes . . . go   **10.** has

---

CHART 2-8:	SUMMARY: SPELLING AND
	PRONUNCIATION OF -*S* AND -*ES*

• This summarizes the pronunciation and spelling rules given in Charts 2-4 through 2-7.

☐ **EXERCISE 11, p. 54.** *Summary.* **(Charts 2-4 → 2-8)**

Oral (books closed.)
Students' books are closed. This exercise gives practice in using singular and plural verbs. The learners not only must think about those correct forms and the correct pronunciation of forms with final -*s*, but must also produce complete sentences from their own experience.

In item 13, *put on* is a separable two-word verb, so both *put on my clothes* and *put my clothes on* are correct. The verb phrases in items 7 and 11 cannot be separated in this way.

☐ **EXERCISE 12, p. 55.** *Summary.* **(Charts 2-4 → 2-8)**

Oral (books closed); written.
This exercise uses listening, speaking, writing, and grammatical knowledge. When you mark the papers, praise the students' successes. You may wish to mark only their use of verbs and frequency adverbs, since that is the focus here. If you mark all the errors, ask the students to rewrite the paragraph completely, incorporating all of your corrections.

☐ **EXERCISE 13, p. 55.** *Simple present review.* **(Charts 2-1 → 2-8)**

Fill-in-the-blanks.
See the INTRODUCTION, pp. xvii–xviii, for suggestions for handling fill-in-the-blanks exercises. Students may work in pairs and help each other complete the sentences correctly. You may want to use item 12 as a test or ask the students to write out the whole paragraph.

ANSWERS: **2.** usually studies   **3.** bites   **4.** cashes   **5.** worry . . . never worries . . . studies   **6.** teach . . . teaches [*Ms.* is pronounced /mɪz/. Note: *Ms.* is used as a common title for a woman instead of *Miss* (unmarried) or *Mrs.* (married). *Ms.* makes no reference to marital status.]   **7.** fly . . . have   **8.** flies . . . has   **9.** always does . . . never goes [*Jason* is pronounced /jeysən/.   **10.** always says   **11.** always pays . . . answers . . . listens . . . asks   **12.** enjoys . . . often tries . . . likes . . . invites . . . go . . . watch . . . usually has . . . watches . . . makes . . . always washes . . . cleans . . . never cook . . . is . . . loves

CHART 2-9: THE SIMPLE PRESENT: NEGATIVE

• Allow the students time to look carefully at the examples. The word "negative" as a grammar term was introduced in Chart 1-5. They should notice that two words are necessary in a negative sentence: a helping verb (or auxiliary) and *not*. They should also notice that the -*s* ending is added only to the helping verb, not to the main verb. This will be difficult to learn and remember; you must expect it to be a recurring problem.

• The students learned the formation of the negative with main verb *be* in Chart 1-5. Remind them of this when you discuss this chart and point out that when the main verb is *be*, you cannot add the helping verb *do* to form the negative. Only *not* is used with a form of *be*.

☐ **EXERCISE 14, p. 57.** *Simple present: negative.* *(Chart 2-9)*

Fill-in-the-blanks.
Allow students time to figure out all the answers before you ask them to respond. When they respond, be sure they pay attention to the word order and the -*s* endings, and encourage them to use contractions when they speak. Note that the verb is *be* in items 7, 10, 11, and 14, so the helping verb *do* cannot be added.

ANSWERS: **3.** doesn't know   **4.** don't need [BrE: needn't]   **5.** doesn't snow
6. don't speak   **7.** am not   **8.** don't live   **9.** doesn't have   **10.** isn't   **11.** aren't
12. don't have   **13.** doesn't have   **14.** isn't   **15.** doesn't rain

☐ **EXERCISE 15, p. 58.** **Simple present: affirmative and negative.** **(Charts 2-1 and 2-9)**

Fill-in-the-blanks.
This exercise includes both affirmative and negative.
  Historical note: If you have read works by Shakespeare, you have seen phrases like "she knows not" or "he wants not," but modern English no longer uses those forms. All speakers of English say "she doesn't know," "he doesn't want," etc.

ANSWERS: **2.** knows . . . doesn't know   **3.** want . . . don't want   **4.** isn't . . . doesn't want   **5.** doesn't drink . . . drinks   **6.** am not . . . don't have   **7.** doesn't belong . . . belongs [*Pierre* (a French name) is pronounced /pyɛr/ in English.]   **8.** don't live . . . have
9. is . . . isn't . . . don't need   **10.** is . . . don't have

☐ **EXERCISE 16, p. 59.** *Simple present: negative.* *(Chart 2-9)*

Semi-controlled completion.
Students are asked to use the words in the list, but accept and discuss any correct completion.

ANSWERS: **2.** don't speak   **3.** doesn't shave [*Beard* is pronounced /bɪrd/ (like *feared*).]
4. doesn't carry [Note: a briefcase is a leather case for carrying papers and books. A bookbag is a cloth bag for carrying books, sometimes worn over the shoulder.]   **5.** don't go   **6.** doesn't smoke
7. don't eat   **8.** don't do   **9.** doesn't make   **10.** doesn't drink   **11.** don't do
12. doesn't put on [*To walk barefoot* means "to walk with no shoes on" (as in the picture).]

☐ **EXERCISE 17, p. 60.** *Simple present: negative.* *(Chart 2-9)*

Oral (books closed).
This is a quick review of the use of *don't* and *doesn't*.

□ **EXERCISE 18, p. 60.** *Simple present review.* *(Chapters 1 and 2)*

Oral.

Students can work in pairs. This exercise is usually fun because they have to tell the truth, which sometimes depends on their own opinions. Some of the vocabulary may be difficult, but the students can help each other understand it.

SUGGESTION: Use some of the items for a books-closed review exercise the next class period or the next several class periods.

ANSWERS: **5.** A restaurant doesn't sell shoes. **6.** A restaurant serves food. **7.** People wear clothes. **8.** Animals don't wear clothes. **9.** A child needs love, food, care, and toys. **10.** A child doesn't need a driver's license. **11.** Refrigerators aren't hot inside. **12.** Refrigerators are cold inside. **13.** Electricity isn't visible./ Electricity is invisible. [*Visible* means "can be seen."] **14.** Light is visible. **15.** Fresh vegetables are good for you. **16.** Junk food isn't good for you. **17.** Cats have whiskers. **18.** Birds don't have whiskers. **19.** An architect designs buildings. [*Architect* is pronounced /ˈɑrkɪtɛkt/.] **20.** Doctors don't design buildings. **21.** Doctors take care of sick people. **22.** A bus carries people from one place to another. **23.** The weather is/isn't very hot today. **24.** It is/isn't very cold today. **25.** Glass breaks. **26.** Rubber is flexible. [*Flexible* means "can easily bend or change shape."] **27.** Rubber doesn't break. **28.** English is/isn't an easy language to learn. **29.** People in this city are/aren't friendly. **30.** It rains/doesn't rain a lot in this city. **31.** Apples have seeds. **32.** Scientists don't have all the answers to the mysteries of the universe. [*Mysteries* are unknown or poorly understood events.]

CHART 2-10:   THE SIMPLE PRESENT: YES/NO QUESTIONS

• These are called yes/no questions because they produce simple answers beginning with *Yes* or *No*. English has two categories, depending on the main verb in a sentence. Examples (a) and (b) introduce the helping verb *do/does* in questions. Students should recall the similarity with the use of *do/does* in negative sentences (Chart 2-9). Example (c) shows the other category of yes/no questions: with *be* as the main verb. The verb *be* is the first word in these questions.

• It is not easy for learners to remember to use *do/does* in some questions and to put the words in correct order. You will have to help them with these structures throughout the course.

□ **EXERCISE 19, p. 61.** *Simple present: yes/no questions.* *(Chart 2-10)*

Transformation.

The words in parentheses don't need to be spoken. They just give information for the response.

ANSWERS: **3.** A: Do you speak Japanese? B: No, I don't. **4.** A: Does Ann speak French? B: Yes, she does. **5.** A: Do Ann and Tom speak Arabic? B: No, they don't. **6.** A: Do you do exercises every morning? B: Yes, I do. **7.** A: Do you have a Spanish–English dictionary? [*A Spanish–English dictionary* is a bilingual dictionary to help with translation from one language to the other.] B: No, I don't. **8.** A: Does Sue have a cold? B: Yes, she does. **9.** A: Does the teacher come to class every day? B: Yes, she/he does. **10.** A: Do Jim and Sue do their homework every day? B: No, they don't. **11.** A: Does it rain a lot in April? B: Yes, it does. **12.** A: Do your parents live in Baghdad? B: Yes, they do.

□ **EXERCISE 20, p. 62.** *Simple present: yes/no questions.* *(Chart 2-10)*

Oral (books closed).
The students must listen carefully to you and to each other in order to give accurate responses. Use familiar names instead of the words in parentheses. This can be a lively, fast-paced exercise with students talking to each other after you give the cue. Encourage spontaneous oral interaction rather than treating the exercise as a drill.

□ **EXERCISE 21, p. 62.** *Simple present: yes/no questions.* *(Charts 1-9 and 2-10)*

Transformation.
Lead the students through the examples carefully so that they understand they are supposed to use their classmates' names. In the examples, substitute their names for those in parentheses.

ANSWERS: **4.** A: Does (. . .) come to class every day? B: Yes, he does. **5.** A: Are (. . .) and (. . .) in class today? B: Yes, they are. **6.** A: Does (. . .) sit in the same seat every day? B: Yes, she does. **7.** A: Does (. . .) have a mustache? [*Mustache* is pronounced /<u>mæ</u>stæš/. BrE: *Has he a mustache?* is infrequent and is not taught in this text.] B: Yes, he does.
8. A: Does (. . .) have a bicycle? B: No, she doesn't. **9.** A: Is (. . .) wearing blue jeans today? B: Yes, he is. **10.** A: Does (. . .) wear blue jeans every day? B: Yes, he does.
11. A: Are (. . .) and (. . .) from Indonesia? B: No, they aren't. OR No, they're not.
12. A: Do (. . .) and (. . .) have dictionaries on their desks? B: No, they don't.
13. A: Is (. . .) writing in her book right now? B: Yes, she is. **14.** A: Does (. . .) study hard? B: Yes, she does. **15.** A: Do (. . .) and (. . .) speak English? B: Yes, they do.

**CHART 2-11: THE SIMPLE PRESENT: ASKING
INFORMATION QUESTIONS WITH *WHERE***

• This chart contrasts two types of questions: yes/no questions and information questions. You might want to write (a) and (b) on the chalkboard, then ask students to point out all the similarities and differences between them. The key points are the use of the same word order and the use of final -*s* on the helping verb with a singular subject.

□ **EXERCISE 22, p. 64.** *Information questions with WHERE.* *(Chart 2-11)*

Transformation.
Point out the similarity in sentence structure in the pairs of sentences in items 1 and 2, 3 and 4, and 5 and 6. Perhaps draw a grid on the board showing the placement of *do/does,* the subject, and the main verb.

ANSWERS: **3.** Where does Peter work? **4.** Does Peter work at the post office?
5. Do you live in an apartment? **6.** Where do you live? **7.** Where does Bill eat dinner every day? **8.** Where do you sit during class? **9.** Where does Jessica go to school? [*Wisconsin* is pronounced /wɪs<u>kæn</u>sən/.] **10.** Where is your book? **11.** Where do you go every morning? **12.** Where are the students right now? **13.** Where do kangaroos live?

□ **EXERCISE 23, p. 65.** *Information questions with WHERE.* *(Chart 2-11)*

Oral (books closed).
Books are closed. You give the cue verb, then one student asks a question and another gives a response. Encourage students to use each other's names. They can refer to the list of names they

made in the first exercise in Chapter 1 if necessary. This exercise could also be done in pairs and small groups, with one student keeping his/her book open.

Items 11–16 require a question with the verb *be* in its correct form as well as the information in parentheses. For example, in item 13:

STUDENT A: Where is London?
STUDENT B: It's in England.

CHART 2-12:	THE SIMPLE PRESENT: ASKING INFORMATION QUESTIONS WITH *WHEN* AND *WHAT TIME*

- Questions with *when* and *what time* follow the same pattern as questions with *where* (see Chart 2-11). Ask students why examples (a) and (b) use the helping verb *do*, while (c) and (d) use *does*. They should see that *Anna* is a singular noun that requires *does*.

- A question with *what time* usually asks about time on a clock:
  A: *What time do you have class?*
  B: *At eight-thirty.*

 A question with *when* can be answered by any time expression:
  A: *When do you have class?*
  B: *At eight-thirty. | Every day. | Monday morning. | In the afternoon. | Etc.*

This information is presented in Chart 5-13, p. 203, but you may wish to mention it at this point.

☐ **EXERCISE 24, p. 66.**   *WHEN and WHAT TIME.*   *(Chart 2-12)*

Transformation.
Two students can read one item as a short dialogue. If everyone is satisfied with the response, two more students can read the next item. As you listen to the students, encourage them to speak so everyone can hear, but it's not necessary to correct every pronunciation mistake. Be sure that they say *do* or *does* clearly in every question.

Review ways of saying the time as you go through the exercise in class. For example, *6:45* can be said "six forty-five," "a quarter to seven," "fifteen (minutes) before seven," etc.

ANSWERS: **3.** When/What time do you get up?   **4.** When/What time does Maria usually get up?   **5.** When/What time does the movie start?   **6.** When/What time do you usually go to bed?   **7.** When/What time do you usually eat lunch?   **8.** When/What time does the restaurant open?   **9.** When/What time does the train leave?   **10.** When/What time do you usually eat dinner?   **11.** When/What time does the library close on Saturday? **12.** When/What time do your classes begin?

☐ **EXERCISE 25, p. 67.**   *WHEN and WHAT TIME.*   *(Chart 2-12)*

Oral (books closed).
Students' books are closed. After demonstrating the example, you choose two students for item 1. You say the cue to one student, who includes it in a question. Then the other student answers, preferably with a short answer. If this is too difficult, everyone can look again at Chart 2-12 and at the cues in the exercise.

Spontaneous discussion should be encouraged.

```
┌─────────────────────────────────────────────────────────────────────┐
│  CHART 2-13:   SUMMARY: INFORMATION QUESTIONS        │
│                WITH BE AND DO                        │
└─────────────────────────────────────────────────────────────────────┘
```

• Learners benefit greatly from a contrastive summary like this. You might write the grammatical categories (Q-WORD + *be* + SUBJECT) on the chalkboard and point to each as you say one of the examples. Discuss singular and plural verb use. Proceed in a similar way with the examples that use the helping verb *do/does*. Exercises 26–29 give plenty of practice with these questions.

☐ **EXERCISE 26, p. 68.** *BE and DO in questions.* *(Charts 1-9, 1-10, and 2-10 → 2-13)*

Controlled completion.
SUGGESTION: Give everyone time to read a whole dialogue and write in a form of the verb *be* or the helping verb *do/does*. Then ask partners to practice the dialogue and to discuss any differences in their answers. After that, ask a pair to speak the dialogue for the rest of the class to hear so that everyone can make sure of the correct completions.

ANSWERS: **(1)** does **(2)** Do **(3)** is **(4)** Are **(5)** are **(6)** do **(7)** Do **(8)** Are **(9)** Does **(10)** Do **(11)** Does **(12)** Is **(13)** does **(14)** Does **(15)** Are **(16)** Do

☐ **EXERCISE 27, p. 69.** *BE and DO in questions.* *(Charts 1-9, 1-10, and 2-10 → 2-13)*

Transformation.
This is a summary review of simple present questions; it also introduces new vocabulary.

ANSWERS: **3.** When does the weather start to get hot? **4.** Do you dream in color? **5.** Does Igor come from Russia? [*Igor* and *Ivan* are male names; *Olga* is a female name.] **6.** Where does Olga come from? **7.** Is Ivan from Russia? **8.** Where is Red Square? **9.** Do birds sleep? . . . Where do they sleep? **10.** What is the biggest animal on earth? **11.** Are whales fish? . . . Are they mammals? . . . Do they breathe air? **12.** Is a seahorse a mammal? **13.** What is a seahorse? **14.** Does a starfish have a mouth? . . . Where is it? . . What does a starfish eat? [Note: Clams and oysters are soft sea animals that have two hard shells; many people like to eat them fresh or boiled. Shrimp are small sea animals that have thin shells; many people eat them boiled or fried in oil. Shrimp turn pink outside when cooked, but the meat is white.]

☐ **EXERCISE 28, p. 71.** *BE and DO in questions.* *(Charts 1-9, 1-10, and 2-10 → 2-13)*

Open completion.
Exercises 28 and 29 could be assigned as homework, since students will need time to think of good questions and answers. Then in class discussion you could elicit completions from several students for each item. Another possibility would be to ask the students to use their own paper and hand in the dialogues. You can decide how to mark their papers. To save time with a large class, you could choose to mark only the same three items from Exercise 28 on everyone's paper, probably one each with *be*, *do*, and *does*.

☐ **EXERCISE 29, p. 71.** *BE and DO in yes/no questions.* *(Chart 2-13)*

Oral/written.
Tell students to write their information like a report, using the form of one or more paragraphs (like Exercise 5, p. 48).

CHART 2-14: USING *IT* TO TALK ABOUT TIME

• Speakers of the English language have developed the custom of using *it* + *be* to refer to time and to the weather (Chart 2-16). Your students' home languages might not use this pattern. It is a very common pattern in everyday conversations, so it is helpful for learners to get used to it as soon as possible.

• These sentences use the pronoun *it* with no real meaning. Some grammar books call this "dummy *it*" or "filler *it*" because it merely fills the empty subject position in the sentence. If some students are puzzled about this required but meaningless pronoun, just assure them that languages are not always logical in their structures. Many phrases are a matter of history or custom, not pure logic.

☐ **EXERCISE 30, p. 72.** *WHAT + IT in questions about time.* **(Chart 2-14)**

Open completion.
Obviously, B's responses are not truthful for your students' situation. So, you might want to add a few more items about the current day, date, and time where you are.

ANSWERS: **2.** What day/date is it? OR What's the date today? **3.** What time is it?
4. What month is it? **5.** What time is it? **6.** What day/date is it? OR What's the date today? **7.** What day is it? **8.** What day/date is it? OR What's the date today?
9. What time is it? [The answer can be said "six-oh-five," "five past six," or "five after six."]
10. What time is it? [The answer can be said "ten fifty-five," "five minutes to eleven," or "five of eleven."]

CHART 2-15: PREPOSITIONS OF TIME

• Few prepositions in English have exact meanings, so they are difficult to learn. The prepositions of time in the chart are important and fairly easy to understand. Some people find it helpful to see them on a pyramid:

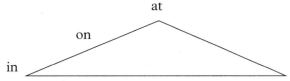

On this pyramid, *at* is at the point, a very short, specific point in time. *In* is at the broadest, most general base of the pyramid. *On* is restricted to the middle, which represents a 24-hour period of time or a 2-day weekend. (Americans say "on the weekend" while the British say "at the weekend.")

• The phrases "*at* night" and "*in* the evening/morning/afternoon" have no logical explanation. Students must simply memorize those phrases. Sometimes when the students ask "Why?" a grammar teacher simply has to say, "That's just the way it is."

☐ **EXERCISE 31, p. 73.** *Prepositions of time.* **(Chart 2-15)**

Controlled completion.
Exercises 31 and 32: After you lead them through about half of Exercise 31, students can work in small groups to complete this and Exercise 32 in a short time. Encourage them to discuss difficult items and arrive at the correct answers together.

☐ **EXERCISE 32, p. 74.** *Prepositions of time.* *(Chart 2-15)*

Controlled completion.

CHART 2-16: USING *IT* TO TALK ABOUT WEATHER	

- Remind students of the use of *it* when talking about time (Chart 2-14).

☐ **EXERCISE 33, p. 74.** *IT + the weather.* *(Chart 2-16)*

Oral.

This is principally a vocabulary development exercise. The list of terms comes from weather reports, and learners might not need or want to know all of them. You might choose only the most common ones rather than taking time to discuss the fine points of meaning, especially in the last six items; however, your more advanced students may appreciate the information and challenge.

☐ **EXERCISE 34, p. 75.** *IT + the weather.* *(Chart 2-16)*

Oral.

In the United States, the Fahrenheit scale is used much more than Celsius (which is sometimes called Centigrade). This exercise allows learners to associate both scales with descriptive terms.

NOTE: In the box, *0°C* is spoken "zero degrees Celsius"; *-18°C* is spoken "minus 18 degrees Celsius" or "18 degrees below zero Celsius."

ANSWERS: **2.** 0° C, cold, freezing **3.** 38° C, hot **4.** 24° C, warm **5.** − 18° C, very cold, below freezing

☐ **EXERCISE 35, p. 75.** *IT + the weather.* *(Chart 2-16)*

Transformation.

These formulas are handy ways of converting Fahrenheit and Celsius temperatures. Your students may not be interested in these calculations, so you could omit this exercise. On the other hand, if you divide the students in groups, the exercise can lead to task-based interactive problem-solving that encourages creative language use.

Note how a mathematical statement is spoken:

$$12°C \times 2 = 24 + 30 = 54°F$$

"Twelve degrees Celsius times two equals twenty-four plus thirty equals (approximately) fifty-four degrees Fahrenheit."

$$60°F - 30 = 30 \div 2 = 15°C$$

"Sixty degrees Fahrenheit minus thirty equals thirty divided by two equals (approximately) fifteen degrees Celsius."

ANSWERS: The **approximate** conversion numbers are as follows:

2. 34° F   **3.** 90° F   **4.** 50° F   **5.** 62° F   **6.** 7.5° C   **7.** 20° C   **8.** 14° C
9. 35° C

*The **exact** conversion numbers are as follows:**

1. 22°C = 71.6°F   **2.** 2°C = 35.6°F   **3.** 30°C = 86°F   **4.** 10°C = 50°F   **5.** 16°C =
60.8°F   **6.** 45°F = 7.2°C   **7.** 70°F = 21.1°C   **8.** 58°F = 14.4°C   **9.** 100°F = 37.8°C

☐ EXERCISE 36, p. 76.   *Review.   (Chapter 2)*

Error analysis and pronunciation.
Exercises 36–43: These review exercises give learners more complete contexts for using the
structures in this chapter. You might save one part of each exercise to use in a test but assign the
rest as either seatwork or homework.

Exercises 38, 41, 42, and 43 require the students to use their own words and ideas, so you
should check their accuracy on these tasks before testing them. You could either mark written
homework or circulate around the classroom as they are working in small groups and answer
their questions or comment on their responses. It's advisable to praise their successes more than
criticize every mistake.

ANSWERS: **(2)** walks = walk + /s/   **(3)** catches = catch + /əz/   **(4)** shares = share + /z/
(5) comes = come + /z/   **(6)** *(no change)*   **(7)** *(no change)*   **(8)** speaks . . . speaks =
speak + /s/   **(9)** *(no change)*   **(10)** tries = try + /z/ . . . gives = give + /z/ [Note: Do not add -s to an
infinitive *(to teach, to speak).*]   **(11)** *(no change)*   **(12)** enjoys = enjoy + /z/ . . . misses = miss + /əz/
(13) *(no change)*   **(14)** *(no change)*   **(15)** eats = eat + /s/ . . . curls = curl + /z/   **(16)** doesn't =
d/əz/n't   **(17)** opens = open + /z/ . . . moves = move + /z/   **(18)** squeezes = squeeze + /əz/
(19) breaks = break + /s/ . . . goes = go + /z/   **(20)** spits = spit + /s/   **(21)** *(no change)*

☐ EXERCISE 37, p. 76.   *Review.   (Chapter 2)*

Fill-in-the-blanks.

ANSWERS: **2.** Do monkeys eat   **3.** A: don't remember . . . Do you remember
B: write . . . like . . . try   **4.** don't understand . . . doesn't have . . . sleeps . . . doesn't take . . .
worry   **5.** are . . . moves . . . doesn't move . . . is . . . run . . . doesn't move . . . moves . . .
reaches . . . carries . . . hits   **6.** A: Do you study   B: study . . . studies . . . Do you spend
A: spend . . . don't like   B: are you   A: want . . . don't want   B: think [*Drop out of school* means stop
attending school for a long time.]   **7.** have . . . washes . . . Do you know . . . is . . . doesn't change . . .
keeps. . . never washes . . . wears . . . is always . . . is always . . . always says . . . takes [*Neat* means
"tidy, orderly," the opposite of *messy* or *a mess.* "It takes all kinds of people to make a world" is a folk saying.]

☐ EXERCISE 38, p. 79.   *Review.   (Chapter 2)*

Open completion.
In item 9, *south of the United States* means outside of its borders. *In the southern part of the United
States* or *in the South* means a region inside its borders.

---

* To get exact numbers, use these formulas: °C = 5/9(°F − 32) OR: F = 9/5(°C) + 32

□ **EXERCISE 39, p. 80.** *Review.* *(Chapter 2)*

Error analysis.
See the INTRODUCTION, pp. xvi–xvii for suggestions on handling error review exercises.

ANSWERS: **2.** Ann <u>usually comes</u> to class on time. **3.** Peter <u>watches</u> TV every evening. **4.** Anita <u>carries</u> a briefcase to work every day. **5.** She <u>enjoys</u> her job. **6.** I <u>don't</u> know Joe. **7.** Mike <u>doesn't</u> like milk. He never <u>drinks</u> it. **8.** Tina doesn't <u>speak</u> Chinese. She <u>speaks</u> Spanish. **9.** <u>Are</u> you a student? **10.** Does your roommate <u>sleep</u> with the window open? **11.** A: *(no change)* B: Yes, I <u>do</u>. **12.** Where <u>do</u> your parents live? **13.** What time <u>does</u> your English class <u>begin</u>? OR What time <u>is</u> your English class? **14.** Olga <u>doesn't</u> need a car. She <u>has</u> a bicycle. **15.** <u>Does</u> Pablo <u>do</u> his homework every day?

□ **EXERCISE 40, p. 80.** *Review.* *(Chapter 2)*

Controlled completion; multiple choice.
It is expected that the students will have no difficulty with this exercise. Scores of 100% or 90% should help boost their self-confidence.

ANSWERS: **1.** B **2.** B **3.** A **4.** C **5.** C **6.** C **7.** A **8.** B **9.** B **10.** C

□ **EXERCISE 41, p. 81.** *Review.* *(Chapter 2)*

Open completion.

□ **EXERCISE 42, p. 82.** *Review.* *(Chapter 2)*

Oral/written.
This exercise encourages authentic language use of the target structures in this chapter.

□ **EXERCISE 43, p. 83.** *Review.* *(Chapter 2)*

Oral/written.
If you are teaching in an English-speaking country, your students could go outside the classroom and interview some people to practice these structures. They could take notes on a chart like the one in the book, then write a brief report on their findings.

Chapter 3: EXPRESSING PRESENT TIME (Part 2)

ORDER OF CHAPTER	CHARTS	EXERCISES
Present progressive	3-1	Ex. 1 → 4
Spelling of -ing	3-2	Ex. 5 → 8
Present progressive: questions	3-3	Ex. 9 → 11
Simple present vs. present progressive	3-4	Ex. 12
Nonaction verbs	3-5	Ex. 13
See, look at, watch, hear, listen to	3-6	Ex. 14
Need and *want* + noun or infinitive	3-7	Ex. 15 → 16
Would like vs. *like*	3-8 → 3-9	Ex. 17 → 20
Think about and *think that*	3-10	Ex. 21 → 23
Review		Ex. 24
There + be	3-11	Ex. 25 → 28
There + be: yes/no questions	3-12	Ex. 29 → 32
There + be: questions with *how many*	3-13	Ex. 33 → 36
Prepositions of location	3-14	Ex. 37 → 39
Review		Ex. 40 → 45

General Notes on Chapter 3

Chapter 3 introduces the present progressive (or present continuous). This verb form is used mainly to describe temporary situations at the moment of speaking. Because it adds *-ing* to the verb, some attention is given to spelling. Questions and negative forms are introduced, and the difference between the meanings and uses of simple and progressive present verbs is pointed out and practiced. Next, students are introduced to common uses of the simple present to express needs, wants, likes, and thoughts; included in this section is also an introduction to infinitive complements, modal auxiliary patterns, and noun clauses marked by *that*. Also in this chapter is a section on indicating locations, including *there is/are* and some common prepositions. The review section introduces many vocabulary items in useful contexts.

CHART 3-1: BE + -ING: THE PRESENT PROGRESSIVE TENSE

- The progressive tense (or aspect) expresses an activity that is in progress at the moment of speaking. This activity is usually of short duration: it began in the recent past, is continuing at present, and will probably end at some point in the near future.

COMPARE: *Mr. Jones usually wears a jacket, but today he's wearing a sweater.*

The best way to make this meaning clear to learners is through a lot of practice that makes use of meaningful contexts. Use yourself to demonstrate the meaning by performing actions and describing them at the same time: *I am standing, I am sitting, I am walking, I am talking, I am writing on the board, I am opening the door, I am looking at the ceiling,* etc. Perhaps have students perform the same actions and say the same sentences. You stand and say, "I am standing." Then the class mimics you by standing and saying, "I am standing."

- Suggest to the students that they describe their own actions silently to themselves as they go through their days: *I'm walking to class. I'm opening the door. I'm sitting down. I'm eating lunch. I'm listening to music.* Etc.

☐ **EXERCISE 1, p. 84.** *Present progressive.* *(Chart 3-1)*

Oral (books closed).
This exercise uses the verb "wear" and familiar vocabulary to practice the basic form and meaning of the present progressive. Lead the students to answer your questions. Keep the pace lively, but be patient as the learners struggle to understand your questions and formulate their own answers.

NOTE: The word *else* in *What else is Jin Won wearing?* means "additional." *What else* is a common phrase to invite more information.

In item 9, *running shoes* are also called "sneakers," "gym shoes," "jogging shoes," or "tennis shoes."

☐ **EXERCISE 2, p. 85.** *Present progressive.* *(Chart 3-1)*

Oral.
One use of the present progressive is to describe activities in progress in pictures. This exercise shows some typical activities. Some of the vocabulary may be unfamiliar. Write new words on the board.

EXPANSION: Write the activities shown in this exercise on 3" x 5" cards or slips of paper: *eat a carrot, paint a picture, read a newspaper,* etc. Pass out the cards. Then ask the students, in turn, to pantomime the activities on their cards so that other students can describe the activity in progress.

ANSWERS: (from left to right) The rabbit is eating a carrot. The monkey is painting a picture (of a clown). The elephant is reading a newspaper/wearing glasses. The tiger is talking on the telephone/making a telephone call. The horse is sleeping/snoring. The cat is drinking a cup of coffee/tea. The dog is playing the piano. The mouse is singing. The bird is taking a bath. The giraffe is driving a car.

☐ EXERCISE 3, p. 86.   *Present progressive.   (Chart 3-1)*

Oral (books closed).

Lead the students through the example, using their names. Then continue with other actions in the list. The example shows sentences beginning with *I, we, they,* and *he/she.* It's not necessary to include all of those subjects for each item. It is also not necessary to include all 20 items if time is short or if your students have few problems with their answers. Adapt the material to your class.

Anticipate that some of the vocabulary in this exercise is new for at least some students: *ceiling, shake hands, turn around in a circle, clap.* Unfamiliar vocabulary, of course, makes following the cues in a books-closed exercise impossible for the students, so take time to write new words on the board and discuss them. The definitions of the new words can come from actions you demonstrate.

If any students are visibly uncomfortable or distressed, tell them they may open their books (but not their dictionaries — they can more profitably get the meanings of the new words by paying attention to what's going on in the classroom).

☐ EXERCISE 4, p. 86.   *Present progressive.   (Chart 3-1)*

Oral (books closed).

A pantomime is an action performed without speaking. Lead this exercise like Exercise 3.

New vocabulary: *wave, push, pull, kick, count.*

EXPANSION: After you've gone through the cues in the text, ask students (preferably volunteers) to perform any pantomime of their choosing. They can do some of the same ones given in the cues or make up their own (e.g., *brush one's teeth, open an umbrella, shave, wash one's hands).*

CHART 3-2:   SPELLING OF *-ING*

• The spelling of *-ing* forms has clear rules. Understanding these rules right from the beginning of their study of English can help students avoid lots of writing errors down the road. (If correctness of written English is not important to your students' needs, this and similar charts can be handled briefly or omitted.)

• SUGGESTION: Demonstrate the points made in the chart by writing the wrong spelling (e.g., **writting, siting, rainning*) on the board and explaining the underlying rules for correct spelling. Clearly label the wrong spellings on the board by also writing something like WRONG or NO. Perhaps draw a circle around the misspelled word and then draw a slash through the circle.

• The unstated part of Rule 1 is that the consonant is NOT doubled. Emphasize that when we drop final *-e,* we do NOT double the consonant.

• Explain the meaning of the verb *double.*

☐ EXERCISE 5, p. 87   *Spelling of -ING.   (Chart 3-2)*

Transformation.

The *-ing* forms of many of the words in this and the following exercise are common sources of spelling errors for many learners.

Give the students time in class to complete the exercise prior to class discussion. If you wish, students can work in pairs.

The correct spellings should be written on the board, and the students should check their answers carefully. It would be helpful for the students to check each other's answers. Sometimes some students cannot see their own spelling errors, especially beginning students whose native languages do not use the same alphabet as English.

ANSWERS: **2.** smiling   **3.** running   **4.** raining   **5.** sleeping   **6.** stopping   **7.** writing   **8.** eating   **9.** counting   **10.** wearing   **11.** riding   **12.** cutting   **13.** dancing   **14.** putting   **15.** sneezing   **16.** planning   **17.** snowing   **18.** fixing   **19.** saying   **20.** crying

☐ **EXERCISE 6, p. 88.**   *Spelling of -ING.*   *(Chart 3-2)*

Transformation.

ANSWERS: **1.** dreaming   **2.** coming   **3.** looking   **4.** taking   **5.** biting   **6.** hitting   **7.** hurting   **8.** clapping   **9.** keeping   **10.** camping   **11.** shining   **12.** winning   **13.** joining   **14.** signing   **15.** flying   **16.** paying   **17.** studying   **18.** getting   **19.** waiting   **20.** writing

☐ **EXERCISE 7, p. 88.**   *Present progressive.*   *(Chart 3-1)*

Oral.
This exercise is meant to be fun. It is books-open because some of the vocabulary is unfamiliar.
NOTE: The description must be given while the action is continuing so that the present progressive is appropriate. The short actions in items 12, 14, and 15 might have to be repeated until the answer is spoken.

☐ **EXERCISE 8, p. 89.**   *Spelling of -ING.*   *(Chart 3-2)*

Written (books closed).
Call out the item's number, then pantomime the action and ask, "What am I doing?" Students write only one word for each item. To check their answers, they can exchange papers and mark any mistakes they see. You might sample a few items by having students spell their answers out loud as you write them on the board.

ANSWERS: **1.** smiling   **2.** crying   **3.** laughing   **4.** sitting   **5.** standing   **6.** sleeping   **7.** clapping   **8.** writing   **9.** eating   **10.** running   **11.** singing   **12.** reading   **13.** drinking   **14.** sneezing   **15.** flying   **16.** cutting

---

CHART 3-3:   THE PRESENT PROGRESSIVE: QUESTIONS

• Short answers are quite natural, even preferred, in conversation. So are contractions, which some learners try to avoid. Note that when *be* is the main verb in an affirmative short answer (e.g., *Yes, she is; Yes, I am),* no contraction is possible, as noted in Chart 1-9.

• Long answers normally do not occur in conversational English. The inclusion of the long answer here is for teaching-learning reasons, so that students can understand what underlies the short answer.

• Point out again that subject-verb word order is the same in yes/no and information questions:
    BE (HELPING VERB) + SUBJECT + MAIN VERB

• You might model the spoken contractions of *is* and *are* with *where* and *why* in examples (c) and (d): "Where's" and "Why're."

☐ **EXERCISE 9, p. 89.** *Present progressive: questions.* *(Chart 3-3)*

Transformation.

ANSWERS: **3.** A: Is Anna eating lunch? B: Yes, she is. [incorrect: Yes, she's.] **4.** Where is she eating lunch? [spoken and written: "Where's"] **5.** A: Is Mike drinking a cup of coffee? B: No, he isn't. **6.** What is he drinking? **7.** A: Are the girls playing in the street? B: No, they aren't. OR No, they're not. **8.** Where are they playing? [spoken: "Where're"] **9.** Why are they playing in the park? [spoken: "Why're"] **10.** [*Hi* = an informal greeting; *kids* = young children] A: Are you drawing pictures with your crayons? [*crayons* = sticks of colored wax for drawing] B: No, we aren't. OR No, we're not. A: Oh? Then what are you drawing? . . . Why are you drawing maps? [spoken: "what're" and "why're"]

☐ **EXERCISE 10, p. 91.** *Present progressive: questions.* *(Chart 3-3)*

Oral (books closed)
Write the verbs listed in Exercise 4 on page 86 of the textbook, one per piece of paper or 3" x 5" card. Give one to each student, then explain the directions. This becomes a sort of game, giving learners a chance to recall vocabulary while practicing the present progressive.

☐ **EXERCISE 11, p. 91.** *Present progressive: questions.* *(Chart 3-3)*

Transformation.
This exercise includes *what* in addition to *where* and *why* in questions with the present progressive. Students were introduced to questions with *what* with main verb *be* in Chart 1-15. This exercise extends that use of *what* to its use with the present progressive.

ANSWERS: **2.** Why are you smiling? [spoken: "Why're"] **3.** What are you reading? [spoken: "What're"] **4.** Why are you reading your grammar book? [spoken: "Why're"] **5.** Where is Roberto sitting? [spoken and written: "Where's"] **6.** Where are you going? [spoken: "Where're"] **7.** Why are you going downtown? [spoken: "Why're"] **8.** What is Akihiko wearing today? [spoken and written: "What's"]

CHART 3-4:   THE SIMPLE PRESENT vs. THE PRESENT PROGRESSIVE

- Another way to explain the difference in meanings between the simple present and the present progressive is to point out (using terms beginners can understand) that the simple present expresses more permanent or unchanging situations while the present progressive expresses more temporary or unique situations.

- In examples (e) through (h), point out that the subject-verb word order in the questions is the same:
  BE/DO (HELPING VERB) + SUBJECT + MAIN VERB

☐ **EXERCISE 12, p. 93.** *Simple present vs. present progressive.* *(Chart 3-4)*

Fill-in-the-blanks.
If possible, assign this exercise as homework to be discussed in class the next day. The students need time to think this one through. It is a summary exercise that includes the affirmative, negative, and question forms of both the simple present and the present progressive. If you can't give the students time to prepare out of class, go slowly as the learners decide which form is required. The later items have more information and vocabulary to think about, so allow time for students to read and understand each item before the answer is announced.

ANSWERS: **2.** read . . . don't read   **3.** A: are you reading   B: am/'m reading
4. cooks   **5.** is/'s cooking   **6.** doesn't eat [*Vegetarian* is pronounced /vɛjət̲ɛ̲riən/.]   **7.** Do
you cook   **8.** A: Do you want [*Want* is not used with a present progressive form (See Chart 3-5).] . . .
Is this   B: is hanging   **9.** A: Does Tom have . . . does he wear . . . Is he wearing   B: don't
know [*Know* is not used with a present progressive form (See Chart 3-5).]   A: think   **10.** talks . . .
is talking   **11.** sit . . . help . . . is helping   **12.** rains . . . isn't raining . . . is shining
[Ask a student to spell *shining* out loud; be sure everyone remembers not to double the letter "n" here.] . . .
Does it rain   **13.** is eating [*Bye* is a short, informal form of *goodbye*.]   **14.** eats [*Family* can be a
grammatically confusing noun for learners. It is a collective noun that usually takes a singular verb but may also
take a plural verb in some circumstances. As for pronoun agreement, *family* is usually referred to with the plural
pronouns: My family *is* wonderful. I love *them* very much. *They* are wonderful people.] . . . doesn't let [*let* =
permit, allow]   **15.** A: Are you working   B: I'm not studying . . . I'm writing   A: Do you
write   B: don't write   A: Does she write   B: get [*get* = receive] . . . Do you write   A: like
16. flies . . . is flying   **17.** A: does the teacher usually stand   B: stands   A: is she standing
B: is standing   **18.** [*Excuse me* is a polite way to begin a conversation with a stranger.]   A: Are you
waiting   B: am [incorrect: I'm]   A: does the bus stop   **19.** A: Do animals dream? [*I suppose so* =
This is my opinion, but it isn't strong.]   B: aren't [*lots of* = a lot of, many]   A: is/'s sleeping . . .
are . . . is yipping [*yip* = make a small, high vocal sound] and moving . . . am/'m . . . is/'s dreaming . . .
dream [Check on students' spelling of *sleeping*, *yipping*, and *dreaming*.]

**CHART 3-5:   NONACTION VERBS NOT USED IN THE
                PRESENT PROGRESSIVE**

- "Nonaction" verbs are stative verbs: they describes "states" rather than actions.
- In example (a), the verb *be* in *I'm hungry* is also an example of this rule.
   INCORRECT: *I am being hungry.*

☐ **EXERCISE 13, p. 96.   *Simple present vs. present progressive.   (Chart 3-5)***

Fill-in-the-blanks.

ANSWERS: **2.** is snowing . . . like   **3.** know   **4.** is talking . . . understand   **5.** is
eating . . . likes . . . tastes   **6.** ["*Sniff-sniff*" should not be spoken; it tells the reader to inhale quickly a
couple of times.] smell . . . Do you smell   **7.** is telling . . . believe . . . think   **8.** [*Ugh!* = an
expression of strong disapproval or dislike] smells   **9.** is sitting [Check the students' spelling of this
verb.] . . . is sitting . . . hates   **10.** is holding . . . loves . . . is licking

---

**CHART 3-6:   *SEE, LOOK AT, WATCH, HEAR, AND
                LISTEN TO***

- As stative or nonaction verbs, *see* and *hear* are not used in the progressive. The other verbs in this
chart have more active meanings, so they can have progressive forms. This is sometimes difficult for
learners to understand. The text uses these five verbs to try to convey the concept of nonaction vs.
action verbs, as well as simply to give the students usage information about these very common words.

☐ **EXERCISE 14, p. 97.** *SEE, LOOK AT, WATCH, etc.* *(Chart 3-7)*

Oral.
You should read an item aloud and then call on one student to answer your question. Ask him/her to respond with complete sentences, not short answers. Change some items to use things that are in your students' everyday experience.

CHART 3-7: ***NEED* AND *WANT* + A NOUN OR AN INFINITIVE**

- The purpose of this chart is to introduce common, simple statements made with infinitives. Their use following these two extremely frequent verbs, *need* and *want,* is only the starting point. The students will encounter infinitives in other structures as the text progresses.

- For pedagogical purposes, this text defines an infinitive as *to* + *the simple form of a verb,* which is the most common form of infinitive by far. Strictly speaking, an infinitive is the uninflected form of a verb, either with or without *to* in front of it. In this text and the others in the series, the uninflected form of a verb is called the "simple form of a verb."

- A common error in infinitive usage after a main verb is the omission of *to:* ★*I want go to a movie tonight.*

- Be sure students understand that *need* and *want* must add *-s* with a singular noun or pronoun subject, e.g., *He needs food; She wants to eat.* The text might be misleading since it gives no example of third person singular with *need* or *want.*

☐ **EXERCISE 15, p. 98.** *NEED and WANT + infinitive.* *(Chart 3-7)*

Controlled and/or open completion.
The students don't have to limit their completions to the words in the box; they can make up their own completions.
    In the two verb phrases "listen to" and "talk to," *to* is a preposition. Note for the students that the word *to* has more than one grammatical use: it can be used as a preposition or as part of an infinitive.

EXPECTED ANSWERS: **2.** to go . . . to buy/to get   **3.** to watch   **4.** to play [*Soccer* is usually called "football" in BrE, which is not the same as the American game of football, played with an oblong, not round, ball.]   **5.** to call/to talk to   **6.** to go/to walk . . . to cash   **7.** to do/to finish   **8.** to wash   **9.** to marry   **10.** to pay   **11.** to take . . . to walk   **12.** to play/ to listen to   **13.** to take [incorrect: to study an English course]   **14.** to go

---

☐ **EXERCISE 16, p. 99.** *NEED and WANT + infinitive.* *(Chart 3-7)*

Fill-in-the-blanks.
Give students time to figure out the word order, the addition of *do,* and the full meaning before they answer. Assigning this exercise as homework would be helpful.
    During class discussion, ask two students to read a dialogue aloud with the correct completion. Then ask them to repeat the short conversation without looking at their text (or maybe just peeking a little).

ANSWERS: **2.** do you want to go   **3.** do you need to be   **4.** Jean doesn't want to go . . . she needs to study   **5.** I want to take   **6.** Peter wants to go back . . . he wants to change   **7.** We don't need to come   **8.** A: do you want to go   B: I want to visit   **9.** I need to look up   **10.** A: Do you want to come   B: I need to get

CHART 3-8: *WOULD LIKE*

- Charts 3-7 through 3-10 deal with four essential verbs: *want, need, like,* and *think*. They are common, apparently simple words that the students need to know how to use in order to express their wants, needs, likes, and thoughts in everyday discourse. While learning how to use these words, the students are being introduced to (1) infinitive complements, (2) modal auxiliaries, and (3) noun clauses marked by *that*.

- *Would like* is a useful phrase that allows learners to communicate politely. It also introduces them to patterns of modal auxiliaries: i.e., both the helping and main verbs are uninflected, and the modal precedes the subject in a question. The next modal students will encounter is *will* in Chapter 6, followed closely by *may* and *might*. Chapter 7 deals with *can* and *could*, and Chapter 10 introduces *should* and *must*. The periphrastic modals "be going to," "be able to," and "have to" are also included as appropriate. *Would* is just the beginning.

□ **EXERCISE 17, p. 100.** *WOULD LIKE.* *(Chart 3-8)*

Oral.

The purpose of this exercise is to practice using polite expressions. Another important point is the pronunciation footnote at the bottom of page 100. Learners often omit final contracted sounds in their own production, both oral and written, because they don't hear them. Final contracted /s/ and /d/ are unstressed and difficult for students to hear. One of the benefits of studying grammar is that students can understand the underlying structures of what they hear; they learn what they are "supposed to hear." Say aloud to yourself, "Bob'd like some tea" and "My friend's not coming." Notice how the /d/ is practically swallowed and the /s/ is just a very tiny sound. It's easy to understand that learners are reproducing what they think they hear when they say or write ★"Bob like some tea" or ★"My friend not coming." Making students aware of unstressed contracted sounds of basic grammatical structures is an important part of grammar instruction.

ANSWERS: **1.** (spoken: "Tony'd /toniəd/ like a cup of coffee.")   **2.** He would like/He'd like some sugar in his coffee.   **3.** Ahmed and Anita would like some sugar in their coffee, too. (spoken: "Ahmed and Anita'd /ənitəd/ like some sugar in their coffee, too.")   **4.** They would like/They'd like some sugar in their coffee, too.   **5.** A: Would you like a cup of coffee? B: Yes, I would. Thank you.   **6.** I would/I'd like to thank you for your kindness and hospitality.   **7.** My friends would like to thank you, too. (spoken: "My friends'd /frɛnzəd/ like to thank you, too.")   **8.** A: Would Robert like to ride with us?   B: Yes, he would. (incorrect: Yes, he'd.)

□ **EXERCISE 18, p. 101.** *WOULD LIKE.* *(Chart 3-8)*

Oral.

You should ask these questions as naturally as possible, using your students' names. Keep the pace lively, and add an occasional comment (e.g., "Really? Me too!") to a student's answer so that it becomes a real exchange of information. Occasionally ask another student to follow up the first student's answer with a comment.

CHART 3-9: *WOULD LIKE* vs. *LIKE*

• Confusion between the uses of *like* and *would like* is a common problem for new learners. The purpose of this chart is to clarify these uses. Include the information in the footnote at the bottom of page 100 in the textbook in your discussion of this chart. (See the above comments on Exercise 17.)

☐ **EXERCISE 19, p. 101.   *WOULD LIKE* vs. *LIKE*.   (Chart 3-9)**

Oral.
This exercise should clarify the difference in meaning between *would like* and *like*.

☐ **EXERCISE 20, p. 101.   *Review*.   (Charts 3-7 → 3-9)**

Open completion.
This exercise encourages students to express their own ideas in the target structures. See pp. xviii–xix in the INTRODUCTION to this *Teacher's Guide* for ways of handling open completion exercises.

Items 9 and 10 are a little tricky. Item 9 encourages the use of parallel infinitives: e.g., *I need to go to the library and (to) look up some information.* Students have not yet been introduced to the concept of parallelism. You may need to explain it briefly, and possibly explain that *to* is usually omitted in the second parallel infinitive. Other parallel structures are possible in item 9: e.g., *I need to talk to **Maria and Toshi** today.* Item 10 is looking for a question word: *Where would you like to go this evening? What would you like to do this evening? What time would you like to leave this evening?*

CHART 3-10:   *THINK ABOUT* AND *THINK THAT*

• *Think about* [examples (a) and (b)] has both simple present and present progressive forms. In *think about, think* is a sort of "action verb" with thoughts actively going through one's mind. In *think that, think* is a "nonaction verb," as introduced in Chart 3-5. Exercises 21–23 focus on these two different uses of the verb *think.*

• A common mistake is the use of *think that* in the present progressive: ★*I'm thinking that this is a nice city.* The chart seeks to clarify when *think* can be used in the progressive and when not.

☐ **EXERCISE 21, p. 102.   *THINK ABOUT* and *THINK THAT*.   (Chart 3-10)**

Open completion.
Students should first read the item and decide on their opinions about it. Then they should make a statement like examples (c) through (g) in Chart 3-10. You might want to expand the number of items, seeking opinions about movies, other sports, other school subjects, etc. To avoid controversy, you might wish to stay away from matters of religion or politics.

The illustration on page 103 shows the positions on a baseball team. The batter is on the opposing team, and the umpire is the judge. The illustration is intended to engender incidental, spontaneous conversation about a topic at least some of the students find interesting. Grammar classes should routinely contain short periods of time devoted to spontaneous oral interaction. It's important for the teacher to give the students opportunities to speak freely.

☐ **EXERCISE 22, p. 103.** *THINK ABOUT and THINK THAT.* *(Chart 3-10)*

Open completion.
Give students a few minutes to use their imaginations and come up with good answers, or assign the exercise as homework. The sentences can be either written or spoken, depending on your preference. During class discussion, elicit responses from several students for each item and encourage incidental conversation in which the students state (and perhaps defend) their opinions.

☐ **EXERCISE 23, p. 104.** *THINK ABOUT and THINK THAT.* *(Chart 3-10)*

Oral.
Students can work in pairs or small groups, comparing their opinions. This is less threatening than having to state them in front of the whole class. Encourage students to help each other with corrections.

The purpose of this exercise is to encourage spontaneous conversation as the students gain experience expressing their opinions in English.

☐ **EXERCISE 24, p. 104.** *Review.* *(Charts 3-1 → 3-10)*

Fill-in-the-blanks.
Because this is a contextualized story, students should take time to read and understand it. Assign it as homework, if possible. During class discussion of the answers, pay attention to spelling as well as verb forms.

EXPANSION: Following class discussion of the correct answers or the next class day, give the students copies of the illustration (including the names of the people and animals) and ask them to write about it. If they can remember the content of the exercise in the text, they should write that. If they can't, they can make up their own story about the picture.

ANSWERS: **(1)** is sitting **(2)** is reading **(3)** is sitting . . . is studying
(4) is listening to **(5)** hears . . . isn't listening to **(6)** is concentrating
(7) + **(8)** is thinking about **(9)** is studying **(10)** likes . . . thinks **(11)** is thinking about **(12)** understands . . . likes **(13)** doesn't like **(14)** is cooking
(15) is cutting **(16)** is rising **(17)** doesn't like . . . knows **(18)** is making
(19) is thinking about **(20)** gets **(21)** loves . . . wants **(22)** doesn't know
(23) is standing **(24)** is taking off **(24)** + **(25)** is wearing **(26)** is thinking about
(27) wants to watch **(28)** needs to go **(30)** is eating **(31)** tastes **(32)** doesn't see
(33) doesn't smell . . . is sleeping **(34)** is dreaming about **(35)** is playing
(36) doesn't see **(37)** is looking at **(38)** is singing **(38)** + **(39)** isn't listening to
(40) likes **(41)** to listen to

CHART 3-11: *THERE + BE*

- *There + be* is a way of introducing a topic or calling attention to something. The word *there* is another "dummy" subject (similar to *it* in Charts 2-14 and 2-16), also called an "expletive." *There* does not receive much stress when spoken in this phrase. This is not the same as the adverb *there*. Notice the difference:

  1. There's a book on the shelf. (little stress on *There's*)
  2. There's my book! I'm glad I found it. (heavy stress on the adverb *There*)

- Emphasize that expressing a location is integral to this structure. For example, *There's a bird* is an incomplete thought. A location needs to be stated: *There's a bird in the tree.*

☐ **EXERCISE 25, p. 106.** *THERE + BE.* *(Chart 3-11)*

Controlled completion.
This exercise helps learners think about singular and plural subject-verb agreement. Agreement is a common problem in students' use of this structure.

In items 6 and 7, you could substitute other locations to suit your class.

ANSWERS: **3.** are **4.** is **5.** are **6.** is **7.** are **8.** are **9.** is **10.** are

☐ **EXERCISE 26, p. 107.** *THERE + BE.* *(Chart 3-11)*

Oral.
Follow this books-open exercise with students' books closed and make up cues from your classroom: *in this room / (four) windows; a clock / on the wall;* etc. — whatever exists in your room.

Using this kind of exercise with books closed puts a great load on students' short-term memory (remembering cues, checking word order, and using the singular or plural form of *be),* but they should be able to handle it when they are talking about actual things that exist right in front of their eyes.

ANSWERS: **3.** There is (There's) a map on the wall. **4.** There are (There're) some pictures on the wall. **5.** There are (There're) three windows in this room. **6.** There are (There're) fifteen students in this room. **7.** There is (There's) some milk in the refrigerator. **8.** There is (There's) a bus stop at the corner of Main Street and 2nd Avenue. **9.** There are (There're) ten provinces in Canada. **10.** There is (There's) a good program on television tonight.

☐ **EXERCISE 27, p. 107.** *THERE + BE.* *(Chart 3-11)*

Oral.
This exercise can be done in small groups to make sure everyone can see the items. It will go more quickly too. You could then ask everyone to visualize another place (e.g., some other part of the building or a nearby street) and tell what things they recall seeing in that place.

EXPANSION: Tell one student to turn his/her back to the table. Put four or five items on the table. Tell the student to turn around and study the table for a certain length of time (5 or 10 seconds), then turn away from the table again and report what he/she remembers seeing. This is a game. It's supposed to be fun, not really a test of memory.

☐ **EXERCISE 28, p. 107.** *THERE + BE.* *(Chart 3-11)*

Oral/written.
You could make a memory game of this. Have one student begin with two statements, then move to the next student, who must repeat the first student's information and add one more statement. The third student must repeat what the first two said, then add another statement. Keep moving on until no one can add new information about the classroom.

EXPANSION: Have the students describe another place using *there + be:* their room, a place in this city, their parents' home, etc.

CHART 3-12: *THERE + BE*: YES/NO QUESTIONS

• This chart explains the question form of *there + be*, with *there* in the subject position.

• This chart also passively introduces *any*. Students will have to use *any* in the following exercises. The determiner "any" is similar in meaning to "some"—an inexact quantity. *Any* is used with plural count nouns or noncount nouns in questions and in negative statements. (See Chart 4-12.) Exercise 29 contains only plural count nouns and noncount nouns, so the students don't have to make choices at this point in their use of *any*.

• Learners may have difficulty with noncount nouns, such as *milk,* which require singular verb forms. (See Chart 4-9.)

☐ **EXERCISE 29, p. 108.** *THERE + BE: yes/no questions.* (Chart 3-12)

Oral.
Students should work in pairs.

ANSWERS: **1.** A: Is there any milk in the refrigerator?   B: Yes, there is.   **2.** A: Are there any onions in the refrigerator?   B: No, there aren't.   **3.** A: Is there any cheese in the refrigerator?   B: Yes, there is.   **4.** A: Is there any butter in the refrigerator?   B: Yes, there is.
5. A: Are there any eggs in the refrigerator?   B: Yes, there are.   **6.** A: Is there any bread in the refrigerator?   B: No, there isn't.   **7.** A: Are there any apples in the refrigerator?   B: Yes, there are.   **8.** A: Are there any potatoes in the refrigerator?   B: No, there aren't.   **9.** A: Is there any orange juice in the refrigerator?   B: Yes, there is.   **10.** A: Are there any strawberries in the refrigerator?   B: Yes, there are.   **11.** A: Are there any oranges in the refrigerator?   B: No, there aren't.   **12.** A: Is there any fruit in the refrigerator?   B: Yes, there is.   **13.** A: Is there any meat in the refrigerator?   B: Yes, there is.   **14.** A: Are there any roses in the refrigerator?   B: No, there aren't.   **15.** A: Is there any flour in the refrigerator?   [*flour* = powder made from grinding grain, such as wheat; pronunciation is the same as *flower.*] B: No, there isn't.

☐ **EXERCISE 30, p. 108.** *THERE + BE: yes/no questions.* (Chart 3-12)

Oral.
This can be done in pairs. After half of the exercise, students should exchange roles so that everyone practices both asking and answering. Encourage free conversation.

☐ **EXERCISE 31, p. 108.** *THERE + BE: yes/no questions.* (Chart 3-12)

Oral.
You could have several students give answers to each item. Note the progression in these items from the building to the whole universe.

☐ **EXERCISE 32, p. 109.** *THERE + BE: yes/no questions.* (Chart 3-12)

Oral.
Students could work in pairs. Encourage free conversation.
  In item 7, a *landmark* is something one can see that helps identify a particular location, such as a unique building or a rock formation.
  In item 10, *elevator* (pronounced /ɛləveytɚ/) is a *lift* in British English.

<table>
<tr><td>

CHART 3-13:

</td><td>

THERE + BE: **ASKING QUESTIONS WITH**
HOW MANY

</td></tr>
</table>

- This chart introduces the useful question phrase *how many* by putting it into one of its usual grammatical contexts: questions with *there + be*.

- Word order is difficult in these questions. Many other languages form this question with very different sequences. The following exercises give plenty of practice.

- *How many* is used only with plural count nouns. Students will be introduced to this grammar in Chapter 4. For the time being, they do not need this information as the exercises contain only plural count nouns; students can focus on word order and meaning.

☐ **EXERCISE 33, p. 109.** ***THERE + BE with HOW MANY.*** **(Chart 3-13)**

Oral (books closed).
The intention is for the teacher to give the cue to Student A. Alternatively, students could work in pairs, with Student A's book open. In either case, Student B must listen carefully with book closed.

    Because the word order is difficult, you might wish to lead the whole class in asking and answering the first two or three items in chorus. Since all verbs with *how many* are plural, students can focus on the word order.

ANSWERS: **1.** A: How many pages are there in this book? B: *(free response)* [Students can simply look at the last page number or can include the front matter as well as the appendices and index in their page total.]   **2.** A: How many chapters are there in this book? B: *(free response)*
3. A: How many letters are there in the English alphabet? B: Twenty-six.   **4.** A: How many states are there in the United States? B: Fifty.   **5.** A: How many provinces are there in Canada? B: Ten.   **6.** A: How many countries are there in North America? B: Three.
7. A: How many continents are there in the world? B: Seven [By some recent definitions, there are six continents, with Europe and Asia considered one continent named "Eurasia."]   **8.** A: How many windows are there in this room? B: *(free response)*   **9.** A: How many floors are there in this building? B: *(free response)*   **10.** A: How many people are there in this room? B: *(free response)*

☐ **EXERCISE 34, p. 109.** ***THERE + BE with HOW MANY.*** **(Chart 3-13)**

Oral.
Students in pairs should have short conversations following the model. They should exchange roles after a few items so everyone has a chance to ask and to answer.

☐ **EXERCISE 35, p. 110.** ***THERE + BE.*** **(Charts 3-11 → 3-13)**

Oral.
Students can have fun with this exercise, asking about things that are not in the picture and helping each other with vocabulary as well as grammar.

    For a test, you might find a similar picture, perhaps in a book for children.

☐ **EXERCISE 36, p. 110.** *Review.* **(Charts 3-5 → 3-13)**

Open completion.
Students can speak their answers to partners, or you may collect them as written work.

CHART 3-14: PREPOSITIONS OF LOCATION

• To help learners remember the general meanings of these prepositions, you could draw a triangle like the one below. This is the same as the one given in this *Teacher's Guide* for Chart 2-15. It illustrates that *at* is for a specific point, *in* is for large areas, and *on* is between them.

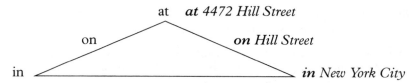

This relationship does not hold for other meanings of these prepositions, however.

• Lead students through a discussion of the illustrations. Compare A and C, D and F, H and I (note the use of *the* in I), J and K. In E, one could also say, "The cup is beneath (or below) the book." In G, one could also say, "The cup is in the hand."

• Pay special attention to the difference in meaning between *in back of* vs. *in the back of* as well as *in front of* vs. *in the front of*. It's good for students to know that the inclusion or omission of *the* can change the meaning of a phrase.

• A note on the historical development of the English language: Early English used noun endings and cases to show relationships like the location of one thing relative to another. Modern English has lost those endings and cases, so it uses prepositions to show location and other relationships. This feature of English is very different from many other languages and takes a long time to learn.

☐ **EXERCISE 37, p. 112.** *Prepositions of location.* *(Chart 3-14)*

Controlled completion.
Lead students through the items slowly so they have time to understand. Ask for alternative answers when they are possible.

ANSWERS: **2.** under **3.** above [Note: The apple is not touching the plate.]
4. beside/near/next to **5.** far (away) from **6.** in/inside **7.** between **8.** around
9. outside/next to **10.** front [no *the*] **11.** back [no *the*] **12.** the front **13.** the back

☐ **EXERCISE 38, p. 114.** *Prepositions of location.* *(Chart 3-14)*

Oral.
Students work in pairs. They don't have to use exactly the sentences in the example for every item, but they should use prepositions in complete sentences. Both partners should give a response for each item.

☐ **EXERCISE 39, p. 114.** *Prepositions of location.* *(Chart 3-14)*

Controlled completion.

ANSWERS: **1.** in **2.** in **3.** on **4.** at . . . in **5.–6.** *(free response with "in")*
7. *(free response with "on")* **8.** *(free response with "at")*

☐ **EXERCISE 40, p. 115.** *Review.* *(Chapter 3)*

Oral and open completion.
Exercise 40 is a long exercise. It builds vocabulary and gives the students plenty of practice. Students can work in pairs. The students don't need to do the entire exercise. Devote whatever

time your class has available. Do part of the exercise one day and part another. Perhaps assign it for pair work outside of class.

Before the pair work begins, students should look at the vocabulary checklists and ask about words that are unfamiliar. You or their classmates can explain the meanings.

EXPANSION: After the students have had time to do the exercise in pairs, hand out photocopies of the illustrations for oral or written work. Students should be able to describe a picture confidently, effortlessly, clearly, and completely.

ANSWERS:

PART B:

1. Mary is eating at/in a restaurant. [The preposition *at* gives her location; *in* can also be used because she is inside the restaurant. (See Chart 7-17 for more information about *at* vs. *in*.)]   **2.** I see a cup of coffee, a vase of flowers, a candle, a bowl of salad, a glass of water, a plate, and a piece of meat.
3. Mary is holding a knife in her right hand. She is holding a fork in her left hand.
4. There's some salad in the bowl.   **5.** There's a steak/a piece of meat on the plate.
6. There's coffee in the cup.   **7.** A candle is burning.   **8.** No, Mary isn't eating breakfast.
9. No, Mary isn't at home. She's at/in a restaurant.   **10.** She's cutting a steak/a piece of meat.

PART C:

11. at   **12.** on   **13.** in   **14.** is . . . in   **15.** at/in   **16.** isn't   **17.** isn't

PART B, p. 116:

1. John is studying.   **2.** I see a clock, a sign, some books, some bookshelves, a librarian, a desk, a plant, a table, two chairs, and two students.   **3.** No, John isn't at home. He's at the library. [The preposition *at* shows his location; *in* is also possible.]   **4.** No, John isn't reading a newspaper.   **5.** The librarian is standing behind the circulation desk.   **6.** John is right-handed.

PART C:

7. at/in   **8.** at   **9.** in/on [Often *in a chair* may indicate that the chair is soft and comfortable; *on a chair* may indicate that the chair is hard and has no arms.]   **10.** under   **11.** on   **12.** on
13. on   **14.** isn't   **15.** is . . . behind   **16.** beside/near/next to

PART B, p. 117:

1. Mary is signing/writing a check. [She is actually signing it with her name.]   **2.** Mary's address is 3471 Tree Street, Chicago, Illinois 60565.   **3.** Mary's full name is "Mary S. Jones."
4. Mary's middle initial is "S."   **5.** Mary's last name is "Jones."   **6.** Mary wants twenty-five dollars.   **7.** Mary's name and address are in the upper left corner of the check.
8. The bank's name and address are in the the lower left corner of the check. OR Mary's bank account number is in the lower left corner of the check.   **9.** The name of the bank is "First National Bank."

PART C:

10. check   **11.** her   **12.** of [See item 9; *of the bank* means possession, the same as *the bank's name*.]
13. at   **14.** in   **15.** in . . . of

PART A, p. 118:

Note the pronunciation: *woman* /wʊmən/, *women* /wɪmən/, *people* /pipəl/

PART B:

1. Mary is cashing a check.   **2.** No, Mary isn't at a store. She's at a bank. [also possible: *in a bank*]   **3.** I see a bank teller, a clock, a sign, a line [BrE: queue] of people, a check [BrE: cheque], a purse/handbag/ pocketbook, a briefcase, a hat, a tie/necktie, eyeglasses, a suit, a T-shirt, a beard and mustache, slacks, jeans, and a dress.   **4.** A woman is standing behind Mary.
5. A man is standing at the end of the line. [*At* is used because *the end* is a very specific location.]
6. There are three men in the picture.   **7.** There are two women in the picture.

8. There are five people in the picture.   **9.** Four people are standing in line. OR There are four people standing in line. [BrE and sometimes AmE: on line]

PART C:
10. at/in   **11.** are   **12.** at/in front of   **13.** behind/in back of   **14.** is . . . behind/in back of   **15.** isn't . . . at . . . of   **16.** is . . . at . . . of   **17.** is . . . between

PART A, p. 119:
Pronunciation: *grocery* /grosri/ or /grŏsri/

PART B:
1. John/He is cooking/making dinner.   **2.** I see a kitchen, a stove [BrE: a cooker], a pot, a salt shaker, a pepper shaker, a clock, a refrigerator, a sign, a shopping/grocery list, and a spoon.
3. John is in the kitchen./John is at the stove.   **4.** Yes, John/he is tasting his dinner.
5. No, John isn't a good cook. (because he doesn't like the taste of the food)   **6.** The refrigerator is beside/near/next to the stove. (behind John)   **7.** There's a shopping/grocery list on the refrigerator.   **8.** The food on the stove is hot.   **9.** The food in the refrigerator is cold.

PART C:
10. in   **11.** on   **12.** beside/near/next to   **13.** on   **14.** on   **15.** on . . . of   **16.** in

PART A, p. 120:
The phrase *living room* is sometimes hyphenated in BrE: *living-room*.

PART B:
1. John and Mary are sitting on a sofa. They're watching TV.   **2.** I see a TV set, an antenna, a table, a fishbowl, a fish, a rug, a dog, a cat, a lamp, a clock, and a sofa.   **3.** No, John and Mary aren't in a kitchen. They're in the living room.   **4.** The lamp is on the floor. The lamp is beside/near/next to/the sofa.   **5.** The rug is on the floor in front of the sofa.   **6.** The dog is on the rug.   **7.** The cat is on the sofa. OR The cat is beside/next to Mary.   **8.** No, the cat isn't walking. The cat's sleeping.   **9.** The dog is sleeping (too).   **10.** A fishbowl is on top of the TV. OR There's a fishbowl on top of the TV.   **11.** No, the fish isn't watching TV.
12. There's a singer on the TV screen. John and Mary are watching a singer on TV.

PART C:
13. are   **14.** are . . . on   **15.** aren't   **16.** on   **17.** is . . . on   **18.** is . . . on

PART B, p. 121:
1. John and Mary are talking to each other on the phone.   **2.** I see a clock, a refrigerator, a calendar, two phones, a table, a pen, a chair, a piece of paper, a telephone book, and a picture on the wall.   **3.** Yes, John/he is happy. Yes, Mary/she is happy. Yes, John and Mary/they are smiling.   **4.** No, they aren't sad./No, they're not sad.   **5.** John is standing. Mary is sitting.
6. No, John isn't in his bedroom. He's in his kitchen.   **7.** Mary is drawing a heart.
8. There's a telephone book on Mary's table. OR There's a piece of paper. OR There's/are a telephone book and a piece of paper on Mary's table. [strictly grammatically correct: *there are* followed by a compound subject, but commonly the singular verb "is" is used in this structure when the first noun in the compound subject is singular.]   **9.** There's a clock on the wall next to the refrigerator. OR There's a calendar on the wall next to the refrigerator. OR A clock and a calendar are on the wall next to the refrigerator.   **10.** The clock is on the wall next to the refrigerator.   **11.** It's eight-thirty/half past eight.   **12.** There's a picture of a mountain on the wall above the table.

PART C:
14. are . . . on   **15.** is . . . to . . . is . . . to . . . are . . . each   **16.** in . . . in front of/near/next to/beside   **17.** on   **18.** is . . . at . . . drawing   **19.** on   **20.** of . . . above

PART B, p. 122:
1. Mary is sleeping. She's dreaming about John.   **2.** John is sleeping. He's dreaming about Mary.   **3.** Mary and John are sleeping and dreaming about each other.   **4.** I see an alarm clock, two pillows, two heads, two beds.   **5.** Yes, she is. Mary is in her bedroom.

6. No, John isn't in class. He's in his bedroom.   **7.** John is/He's lying down.   **8.** Yes, Mary is/she's dreaming.   **9.** Yes, Mary and John/they are dreaming about each other. **10.** Yes, Mary and John/they are in love.

PART C:
11. are . . . in   **12.** is . . . about . . . is . . . about . . . are . . . about   **13.** on   **14.** aren't **15.** are . . . aren't   **16.** in [*In love* is an idiom.]

☐ EXERCISE 41, p. 123.   *Review.   (Chapter 3)*

Fill-in-the-blanks.
As students answer, check their spelling of words with doubled consonants.

ANSWERS: **2.** speaks . . . is speaking   **3.** are doing . . . do   **4.** am looking . . . is writing . . . is looking . . . is biting . . . is smiling . . . is sleeping . . . is chewing   **5.** works . . . has . . . often eats . . . usually brings . . . usually sits . . . sits . . . watches . . . watches . . . relaxes **6.** am looking . . . isn't . . . is . . . is sitting . . . is eating . . . are running . . . is sitting . . . is eating . . . is watching . . . always watches . . . are swimming . . . are flying . . . is riding . . . rides . . . is having . . . go

☐ EXERCISE 42, p. 124.   *Review.   (Chapter 3)*

Oral.
Alternatively, you could supply the picture(s). Students could work in small groups and check each other's correctness.

☐ EXERCISE 43, p. 124.   *Review.   (Chapter 3)*

Written.
Students could check each other's papers for correctness. Alternatively, you could use this exercise as homework or a test. Check for verb tenses, spelling, and prepositions.

☐ EXERCISE 44, p. 124.   *Review.   (Chapter 3)*

Controlled completion; multiple choice.
This is not a difficult or tricky multiple-choice test. Students should score 100% with little effort. Errors probably result from inattention, not lack of understanding.

ANSWERS: **1.** A   **2.** C   **3.** B   **4.** C   **5.** C   **6.** C   **7.** B   **8.** A **9.** C   **10.** C   **11.** B   **12.** C

☐ EXERCISE 45, p. 125.   *Review.   (Chapter 3)*

Error analysis.
Errors in this exercise include spelling, verb forms, singular-plural, prepositions, and words added or omitted. Finding the errors is a good way to review the grammar in this chapter, and it forces learners to pay close attention to details as they develop their self-monitoring skills.

ANSWERS: **1.** It's <u>raining</u> today. I <u>need</u> my umbrella.   **2.** Do you want <u>to</u> go downtown with me?   **3.** There <u>are</u> many problems in big cities today.   **4.** I like New York City. I <u>think</u> that it is a wonderful city.   **5.** <u>Is</u> Abdul <u>sleeping</u> right now?   **6.** Why <u>are you</u> going downtown today?   **7.** I'm listening <u>to</u> you.   **8.** <u>Do</u> you <u>hear</u> a noise outside the window? **9.** I'd like <u>to</u> see a movie tonight.   **10.** Kunio <u>is</u> at a restaurant right now. He usually <u>eats</u> at home, but today <u>he is eating</u> dinner at a restaurant.   **11.** I <u>like</u> flowers. They <u>smell</u> good. **12.** Mr. Rice <u>would like</u> to have a cup of tea.   **13.** How many students <u>are there</u> in your class?   **14.** Alex is <u>sitting</u> at his desk. He <u>is writing</u> a letter.   **15.** Yoko and Ivan are <u>studying</u> grammar right now. They want <u>to</u> learn English.   **16.** Where <u>are they</u> sitting today?

Chapter 4: NOUNS AND PRONOUNS

ORDER OF CHAPTER	CHARTS	EXERCISES
Introduction to nouns		Ex. 1
Subjects and objects	4-1	Ex. 2
Adjective + noun	4-2	Ex. 3 → 5
Subject and object pronouns	4-3	Ex. 6 → 7
Singular and plural nouns	4-4	Ex. 8 → 10
Irregular plural nouns	4-5	Ex. 11 → 12
Count and noncount nouns	4-6	Ex. 13 → 14
An vs. *A*	4-7	Ex. 15 → 16
A/an vs. *some*	4-8	Ex. 17 → 23
Measurements with noncount nouns	4-9	Ex. 24 → 32
The	4-10	Ex. 33 → 35
Making generalizations with no article	4-11	Ex. 36
Some and *any*	4-12	Ex. 37 → 39
Something, someone, anything, anyone	4-13	Ex. 40
Nothing and *no one*	4-14	Ex. 41
Review		Ex. 42 → 48

General Notes on Chapter 4

This chapter contains much more information than the title "Nouns and Pronouns" may indicate. It begins with the basic parts of a simple sentence, leading students to identify the parts with the traditional grammatical terms "subject," "verb," "object," "preposition," and "object of preposition." These terms are used in the charts and exercises in the rest of the textbook. The basic notions of countability and plurality are introduced as well as some commonly used irregular forms. Several elements of noun phrases are also introduced, including adjectives, articles, and phrases of measurement. Questions and negatives are practiced throughout the chapter.

□ EXERCISE 1, p. 127. *Nouns.*

Oral.

Your students will be able to supply ample examples of nouns from their vocabularies for each category. You might want to give them the traditional definition of a noun: "a word that names a person, place, or thing." They might find it helpful.

SAMPLE RESPONSES: **1.** pants, jeans, blouse, skirt, T-shirt, shoes, socks, hose, sweater, hat, coat, gloves, dress, etc. **2.** pear, peach, banana, orange, lemon, grapes, grapefruit, strawberry, melon, date, etc. **3.** tea, water, soda/pop, beer, milk, juice, wine, etc. **4.** ears, nose, mouth, cheek, neck, arm, hand, finger, chest, stomach, leg, knee, ankle, foot, toe, etc. **5.** dog, cat, goat, donkey, horse, llama, tiger, lion, giraffe, deer, antelope, monkey, etc. **6.** Chicago, Boston, Philadelphia, Toronto, Quebec, Vancouver, Seattle, San Francisco, Los Angeles, Miami, Denver, etc. **7.** Spanish, Portuguese, Vietnamese, Thai, Italian, French, Arabic, Japanese, Chinese, Polish, Russian, etc. **8.** geography, biology, English, mathematics, chemistry, physics, art history, dramatic arts, physical education, political science, etc. [Note: School subjects are capitalized when they are used in the title of a course. Compare: *I like to study history.* vs. *I'm taking History 101 this semester.*]

CHART 4-1:   NOUNS: SUBJECTS AND OBJECTS

• The purpose of this section of the chapter is to introduce basic terms that will be used throughout the rest of the book. Most grammar books use these same terms. There are two types of terms: categories and functions. *Noun* is a grammatical category; *subject* is one of the functions (or uses) of a noun in a sentence. *Verb* is both a category and a function; verbs are further divided into types such as *transitive* and *intransitive,* which are usually identified in dictionaries. *Prepositions* and *prepositional phrases* are categories which have a variety of functions, but those functions are not important in this lesson.

• The important point for your learners is that these grammatical units work together to communicate meanings from one person to another. They follow a certain predictable order in English that students benefit from learning and understanding.

□ EXERCISE 2, p. 128.   *Subjects and objects.*   *(Chart 4-1)*

Structure identification.

Some learners may be confused by this exercise initially because it may present them with a completely different way of looking at a sentence. They might like to work it out in small groups and talk over their solutions. This is an excellent way to deepen everyone's understanding. A thorough understanding of the grammar in this exercise will greatly benefit the learners as they work their way through the rest of the text—and the mysteries of English.

This exercise sneaks in the concept of parallel structure (in items 8, 9, 10, and 12). Point out that two nouns connected by *and* can function as a subject or object. The text calls this parallel structure "connected nouns." (See Chart 8-13, p. 357.)

EXPANSION: For further practice, make up your own simple sentences, using only simple present and present progressive verbs.

ANSWERS:

3. Children	like	candy	(none)	(none)
subj.	verb	obj.	prep.	obj. of prep.

4. The teacher	is erasing	the board	with	her hand
subj.	verb	obj.	prep.	obj. of prep.

	subj.	verb	obj.	prep.	obj. of prep.
5.	Mike	lives	(none)	in	Africa
6.	The sun	is shining	(none)	(none)	(none)
7.	Robert	is reading	a book	about	butterflies
8.	Tom and Ann	live	(none)	with	their parents
9.	Monkeys	eat	fruit and insects	(none)	(none)
10.	Mary and Bob	help	Sue	with	her homework
11.	Ships	sail	(none)	across	the ocean
12.	Water	contains	hydrogen and oxygen	(none)	(none)

CHART 4-2: ADJECTIVE + NOUN

- *Adjective* is another grammatical category; its function is the modification of nouns. Most adjectives in English come before a noun, which may be different from the word order in your students' languages. The other normal location for an adjective is after the main verb *be;* in this case, *be* is a "linking verb" which links the subject noun with its adjective modifier; *be* is like the equals sign (=) in an equation: *The weather = cold.*

- Students were introduced to the term "adjective" in Chapter 1. This chart expands upon that information a bit. It includes many of the adjectives used in Chapter 1 and also introduces some new vocabulary. Students will encounter adjectives again in chapters 7, 8, and 9.

- Note that the first two columns of "common adjectives" in Chart 4-2 are pairs with opposite meanings. Take time to discuss any unfamiliar words in this list. Demonstrate them or use them in sentences for the students. Ask the students leading questions using adjectives, such as "What is your favorite food?" or "What color is a ripe banana?"

- See if the class can come up with a few other adjectives to add to the list.

☐ **EXERCISE 3, p. 130.** *Adjective + noun.* *(Chart 4-2)*

Structure identification.
Some students may recall that *my* (item 2) and *her* (item 4) are possessive adjectives (Chart 1-12, p. 27). This category is not included in this exercise, but you might want to remind students of it.

ANSWERS: **2.** sister = *noun;* beautiful = *adjective;* house = *noun* **3.** Italian = *adjective* [Note the capital letter.]; restaurant = *noun* **4.** Maria = *noun;* favorite = *adjective;* songs = *noun;* shower = *noun* **5.** Olga = *noun;* American = *adjective;* hamburgers = *noun* **6.** sour = *adjective;* apples = *noun;* sweet = *adjective;* fruit = *noun* **7.** Political = *adjective;* leaders = *noun;* important = *adjective;* decisions = *noun* **8.** Heavy = *adjective;* traffic = *noun;* noisy = *adjective;* streets = *noun* **9.** Poverty = *noun;* serious = *adjective;* problems = *noun;* world = *noun* **10.** Young = *adjective;* people = *noun;* interesting = *adjective;* ideas = *noun;* modern = *adjective;* music = *noun*

□ **EXERCISE 4, p. 130.** *Adjective + noun.* *(Chart 4-2)*

Open completion.
Give students a few minutes to think of some opinions before you ask for their responses. If giving an opinion seems embarrassing to them, give them permission to say what "some people" think or to not tell the truth.

In items 5 and 6 there is a choice between *a* and *an*. This was explained in Chart 1-1 on page 2, but the students may need to be reminded of the difference.

SAMPLE COMPLETIONS: **2.** hot, spicy, cold, frozen, fried, broiled, Italian, Thai, etc. **3.** honest, strong, generous, intelligent, courageous, trustworthy, truthful, etc.   **4.** Rude, impolite, unkind, cruel, dishonest, selfish, etc.   **5.** large, big, serious, common, widespread, significant, undeniable, etc.   **6.** good, bad, terrible, funny, wonderful, odd, strange, terrific, unforgettable, interesting, etc.

□ **EXERCISE 5, p. 130.** *Uses of nouns.* *(Chart 4-2)*

Structure identification.
The "use" of a noun is its "grammatical function" in a sentence.

ANSWERS: **2.** Jack = *a noun used as the subject;* radio = *a noun used as the object of the verb "have";* car = *a noun used as the object of the preposition "in"*   **3.** Monkeys, apes = *nouns used as the subject;* thumbs = *a noun used as the object of the verb "have"*   **4.** Scientists = *a noun used as the subject;* origin = *a noun used as the object of the preposition "on";* earth = *a noun used as the object of the preposition "of"*   **5.** Janet = *a noun used as the subject;* office = *a noun used as the object of the preposition "in"*   **6.** Egypt = *a noun used as the subject;* summers, winters = *nouns used as objects of the verb "has"*   **7.** farmers = *a noun used as the subject;* villages = *a noun used as the object of the preposition "in";* fields = *a noun used as the object of the preposition "near"*   **8.** cities = *a noun used as the subject;* problems = *a noun used as the object of the verb "face"*   **9.** problems = *a noun used as the subject;* poverty, pollution, crime = *nouns used as objects of the verb "include"*   **10.** hour = *a noun used as the subject;* minutes = *a noun used as the object of the preposition "of";* day = *a noun used as the subject;* minutes = *a noun used as the object of the preposition "of"* [Yes, there are 1440 minutes in a day. 60 x 24 = 1440.]

┌───┐

CHART 4-3:   SUBJECT PRONOUNS AND OBJECT PRONOUNS

• The pronouns are listed in the traditional order: (a) and (b) first person singular; (c) and (d) second person singular; (e) through (j) third person singular; (k) and (l) first person plural; (m) and (n) second person plural; (o) and (p) third person plural. The term "first person" indicates the speaker/writer; the "second person" is someone who is spoken/written to; the "third person" is someone spoken/written about.

• Speakers of some languages may find it odd that English uses *he* for male and *she* for female but only *they* for the plural form with no distinction between the genders.

└───┘

□ **EXERCISE 6, p. 132.** *Subject and object pronouns.* *(Chart 4-3)*

Controlled completion.
In this and the following exercise, you may need to tell the students if a name is for a male or a female. The text uses a core of common English names that the students encounter over and over, but at this point the students may be unfamiliar with some of the names.

Ask the students to identify the antecedents. You could introduce the term "antecedent" if you wish, or simply use the verb *refer* to ask leading questions: e.g., "In sentence one, what noun does *she* refer to?"

ANSWERS: **2.** them   **3.** it   **4.** He   **5.** him   **6.** her . . . She . . . I   **7.** them . . . They   **8.** us   **9.** It   **10.** We . . . it

☐ **EXERCISE 7, p. 132.** *Subject and object pronouns.*   *(Chart 4-3)*

Controlled completion.

ANSWERS: **2.** it . . . It   **3.** we . . . I . . . you   **4.** they . . . They . . . them   **5.** it . . . It   **6.** he . . . him   **7.** A: us   B: I . . . We [*Chris* is used as both a man or a woman's name.]   **8.** B: I . . . We   A: It   B: me [*Great!* is an exclamation of happy approval meaning "Excellent!" *See you then* is a short form meaning "I'll meet you at that time."]   **9.** they . . . them . . . He . . . him [*beat someone in a game* = win the game]   **10.** B: It . . . her . . . She   A: her . . . her [*get along with someone* = be comfortable, compatible]   B: we . . . us . . . you

---

CHART 4-4:   NOUNS: SINGULAR AND PLURAL

- In Chapter 2, the students learned the spelling and pronunciation of verbs that end in -*s*/-*es*. This chart presents the spelling of nouns that end in -*s*/-*es*. Examples (d) and (f) present new information. The other examples represent spelling rules the students were introduced to in Chapter 2.

- The pronunciation of final -*s*/-*es* follows the same rules presented in Chapter 2 in Charts 2-4, 2-5, 2-6, and 2-8. In (a), point out the two pronunciations of final -*s*: /z/ and /s/ (pen/z/, apple/z/, cup/s/, elephant/s/). Example (e) gives the third possible pronunciation of final -*s*/-*es*: /əz/.

☐ **EXERCISE 8, p. 135.** *Singular and plural nouns.*   *(Chart 4-4)*

Controlled completion.
Discuss the meaning, spelling, and pronunciation of each answer as you go through the exercise.

ANSWERS:

LIST A:
2. countries   **3.** babies   **4.** keys   **5.** cities   **6.** parties   **7.** trays
8. dictionaries   **9.** ladies [Note: This is the formal greeting from a speaker to an audience.]
10. Cowboys

LIST B:
11. knives   **12.** wives   **13.** lives [pronounced /laivz/; note the difference from the verb "lives" /lɪvz/.]   **14.** thieves   **15.** leaves [*fall* (noun) = autumn, the season between summer and winter]

LIST C:
16. glasses   **17.** sexes [pronounced /sɛksəz/]   **18.** dishes [*silverware* = knives, forks, and spoons]
19. taxes   **20.** bushes   **21.** matches   **22.** tomatoes   **23.** potatoes   **24.** zoos
25. classes   **26.** sandwiches [The drawing shows a very large sandwich.]

□ **EXERCISE 9, p. 137.** *Singular and plural nouns.* *(Chart 4-4)*

Pronunciation.
Review for the students voiced vs. voiceless sounds. You could model one or two examples in each list, then have one or all students continue. Or you could have the class simply repeat after you. Have the students say the final -s/-es sounds loudly and clearly.

□ **EXERCISE 10, p. 138.** *Singular and plural nouns.* *(Chart 4-4)*

Pronunciation and structure identification.
This exercise has two parts: (1) identifying plural nouns, and (2) pronouncing them correctly.
In class, students can work in pairs, but you should review the plural nouns with the whole group so that everyone can check the pronunciation.
If you have a language lab, you could record these sentences on tape for students to practice.

ANSWERS: **1.** desks /s/ **2.** Oranges /əz/ **3.** Roses /əz/ . . . flowers /z/ . . . bushes /əz/ **4.** cats /s/ . . . dogs /z/ [This sentence contains a common idiom that describes a heavy rainfall, not a real situation of falling animals!] **5.** sentences /əz/ **6.** places /əz/ **7.** exercises /əz/ **8.** pieces /əz/ **9.** sandwiches /əz/ **10.** tigers /z/, monkeys /z/, birds /z/, elephants /s/, bears /z/ . . . snakes /s/ **11.** stores /z/ . . . sizes /əz/ . . . clothes /z/ **12.** students /s/ . . . books /s/ . . . bookbags /z/ **13.** teachers /z/ . . . offices /əz/ **14.** Engineers /z/ . . . bridges /əz/ **15.** ears /z/ . . . eyes /z/ . . . arms /z/ . . . hands /z/ . . . legs /z/ **16.** tables /z/ . . . tables /z/ . . . edges /əz/ [An edge is a sharp angle, such as the cutting edge of a knife or the dangerous edge of a cliff.] **17.** pages /əz/ **18.** apples /z/, bananas /z/, strawberries /z/ . . . peaches /əz/ **19.** colleges /əz/ **20.** cockroaches /əz/ [The drawing shows a humorous view of cockroaches, which are insects that sometimes gather in dark corners of kitchens.]

CHART 4-5:   NOUNS: IRREGULAR PLURAL FORMS

• The most frequent irregular forms are given in this chart. Some others that fit into the category with (g) *fish* (no change for the plural) are *deer* and *sheep*.

• The word "people" seems difficult for many learners to use correctly. In English this is a plural word like "women," "children," or "men." It has no singular form. In the singular, one would say "a man, a woman, a child, a person."
   NOTE: The subject-verb agreement in the statement under Chart 4-5 might be confusing. "*People* is always plural" means the <u>word</u> *people*. The word *people* is one item; therefore, the verb in that sentence is singular. However, when we are really talking about people (many persons), then the verb must be plural.

• The spelling of *woman* and *women* changes in the second syllable. However, the pronunciation changes in the first syllable: *woman* /w<u>ʊ</u>mən/; *women* /w<u>ɪ</u>mən/. This strange phenomenon is the result of changes during the historical development of the English language.

□ **EXERCISE 11, p. 139.** *Irregular plural nouns.* *(Chart 4-5)*

Oral (books closed).
For variation, you could divide the class into two halves and have them alternate in responding to your cues, one half answering items 1, 3, 5, etc., and the other half answering 2, 4, 6, etc. Another possibility would be pair work or small groups with one student in each group acting as leader with book open.

ANSWERS: **1.** two children   **2.** two women   **3.** two teeth   **4.** two feet
5. two men   **6.** two mice   **7.** two fish   **8.** two pages   **9.** two places   **10.** two
bananas   **11.** two children   **12.** two desks   **13.** two sentences   **14.** two men
15. two oranges   **16.** two feet   **17.** two knives   **18.** two sexes   **19.** two girls
20. two exercises   **21.** two teeth   **22.** two women   **23.** two people OR two boys and
two women

☐ **EXERCISE 12, p. 139.** *Irregular plural nouns.* *(Chart 4-5)*

Open completion.
This game can challenge your more advanced and competitive students while still being fun for
the less advanced.
   Students should work alone. They can use their dictionaries or not, as you wish.
   During discussion, you could have the students simply call out answers. Or you could have
several students write their lists on the board. Another possibility would be to first have the
students work alone, then form groups where they pool their answers and try to come up with a
noun for as many letters of the alphabet as possible. The group that has the most answers
"wins."
   Be sure to stress that all the answers the students come up with are called "nouns." By this
point, the students should be quite familiar and comfortable with that term.

CHART 4-6:   NOUNS: COUNT AND NONCOUNT

• Countability (singular/plural/mass/collective nouns) is a peculiar feature of English, and it causes
problems for many learners whose languages do not have such categories. Do not expect students to
master this point now; they will meet it repeatedly in this course and in subsequent courses that use
other grammar books in this series.

• Noncount (also called "mass") nouns cannot be counted (*one money, *two moneys, etc.), so they
cannot use *a* or *one* or a plural form. A list of common noncount nouns is given to help the students get
an initial understanding and usage ability. The use of count vs. noncount nouns is difficult for all
learners and is the underlying cause of many article usage errors and singular-plural errors at all levels
of proficiency, from beginner to advanced.

• Dictionaries for non-native speakers identify the category of each noun as count or noncount.
However, most dictionaries written for native speakers of English usually do not note this point.

• In the chart, the word "(none)" means that there is no plural form for any noncount noun.

• For more information about count vs. noncount, see Chapter 8 in *Fundamentals of English Grammar*
and Chapter 5 in *Understanding and Using English Grammar* as well as the *Teacher's Guides* for those texts.

☐ **EXERCISE 13, p. 141.** *Count and noncount nouns.* *(Chart 4-6)*

Structure identification.
This exercise contrasts count and noncount nouns in sentence contexts so that learners can
begin to understand their differing features. There is a lot of information in Chart 4-6; it will
take time for it to make sense.

ANSWERS: **3.** coin = *count*   **4.** money = *noncount*   **5.** letters = *count*
6. mail = *noncount*   **7.** traffic = *noncount*   **8.** cars = *count*   **9.** fact = *count*

10. information = *noncount*   **11.** homework = *noncount*   **12.** assignment = *count*
13. music = *noncount*   **14.** coffee = *noncount*   **15.** library = *count*   **16.** peace = *noncount*   **17.** advice = *noncount*   **18.** job = *count*   **19.** work = *noncount*   **20.** water = *noncount*   **21.** jewelry = *noncount*   **22.** earrings, rings, necklaces, bracelets = *count*

☐ **EXERCISE 14, p. 142.**   *Count and noncount nouns.*   **(Chart 4-6)**

Oral; open completion.
This exercise intends to stress the idea of countability as well as to point out that the great majority of nouns are count nouns. Check a learner's dictionary if disagreements arise about a noun's category, but also be aware that many nouns have both count and noncount uses. For example, one can say *breads, cheeses, coffees, foods, fruits, meats,* etc., in certain contexts.

CHART 4-7:   USING *AN* vs. *A*

• The use of *an* before vowel sounds makes the words seem easier or smoother to pronounce, in the opinion of native speakers of English. For example, saying "an apple" smoothly together is easier than saying "a apple."

☐ **EXERCISE 15, p. 143.**   *AN vs. A.*   **(Chart 4-7)**

Controlled completion.
Exercises 15 and 16 could be done in pairs, with students checking each other's accuracy. You could lead a discussion of difficult items.

ANSWERS: **1.** an   **2.** a   **3.** an   **4.** an   **5.** a   **6.** a   **7.** an   **8.** a
9. an   **10.** an   **11.** an . . . a   **12.** An   **13.** A   **14.** a   **15.** an   **16.** A . . . an

☐ **EXERCISE 16, p. 144.**   *AN vs. A.*   **(Chart 4-7)**

Controlled completion.

ANSWERS: **1.** a   **2.** an   **3.** a   **4.** an   **5.** a   **6.** an   **7.** an   **8.** an
9. an . . . an   **10.** an . . . an   **11.** a   **12.** An   **13.** A   **14.** an   **15.** an . . . a

---

CHART 4-8:   USING *A/AN* vs. *SOME*

• If you want to understand what an amazingly complicated word *some* is, look it up in several dictionaries. It does not lend itself to easy definition or grammatical explanation. You might tell your students that the basic meaning of *some* is "an inexact amount." You could tell them that people use *some* when the exact amount is unknown or unimportant.

• Be sure students understand that *some* can be used with both plural count nouns and noncount nouns, but NOT with singular count nouns.

☐ **EXERCISE 17, p. 145.   *A/AN vs. SOME.*   *(Chart 4-8)***

Controlled completion.
Go slowly. Make sure the students understand that *some* is used with plural count nouns, but NOT with singular count nouns. This exercise contains only count nouns, not noncount nouns.

ANSWERS: **3.** a (desk = *a singular count noun*)   **4.** some (desks = *a plural count noun*)
5. some (students = *a plural count noun*)   **6.** a (student = *a singular count noun*)
7. a (apple = *a singular count noun*)   **8.** some (apples = *a plural count noun*)   **9.** Some
(children = *a plural count noun*)   **10.** A (child = *a singular count noun*)   **11.** an (exercise =
a singular count noun)   **12.** some (exercises = *a plural count noun*)

☐ **EXERCISE 18, p. 145.   *A/AN vs. SOME.*   *(Chart 4-8)***

Controlled completion.
This exercise contrasts singular count nouns and noncount nouns. In Exercise 17, the students
learned that *some* is used with plural count nouns. In this exercise, they learn that it is also used
with noncount nouns, which are grammatically singular, but again — NOT with singular count
nouns.
     NOTE: For the students' sake, one cannot help but regret that English has this very confusing
and difficult feature known as countability. Tell the students not to get frustrated; countability
will eventually become less of a problem as they gain experience with English. Make sure they
know that this feature of English is difficult for <u>all</u> learners.

ANSWERS: **3.** some (mail = *a noncount noun*)   **4.** a (letter = *a singular count noun*)
5. some (fruit = *a noncount noun*)   **6.** an (apple = *a singular count noun*)   **7.** some (food =
a noncount noun)   **8.** a (sandwich = *a singular count noun*)   **9.** some (water = *a noncount
noun*)   **10.** a (glass = *a singular count noun*)   **11.** some (milk = *a noncount noun*)
12. some (sugar = *a noncount noun*)   **13.** a (sandwich = *a singular count noun*)
14. some . . . some (bread = *a noncount noun;* cheese = *a noncount noun*)   **15.** some (soup =
a noncount noun)

☐ **EXERCISE 19, p. 146.   *A/AN vs. SOME.*   *(Chart 4-8)***

Controlled completion.
This exercise combines the grammar in the previous two exercises by including singular count
nouns, plural count nouns, and noncount nouns.

ANSWERS: **2.** a . . . a . . . some   **3.** some   **4.** some   **5.** some   **6.** some
7. a . . . a   **8.** an   **9.** some . . . some   **10.** some   **11.** some   **12.** some . . . a . . .
some . . . some   **13.** some . . . some . . . a [Note that *bowl* is countable, but *soup* is noncount. The first
noun is the one that carries the article: *a bowl of soup.* This allows us to count things that are normally
noncountable: *two bowls of soup*, as is explained in Chart 4-9.]

☐ **EXERCISE 20, p. 146.   *A/AN vs. SOME.*   *(Chart 4-8)***

Fill-in-the-blanks.
This exercise focuses on the nouns again: which ones are count and which noncount. It also
includes irregular noun plurals.
     All the sentences use the word "some," so the task is to decide whether the nouns following
some are plural count nouns or noncount nouns.
     The other point to stress is that noncount nouns do NOT have a final *-s*.

ANSWERS: **4.** music   **5.** flowers   **6.** information   **7.** jewelry   **8.** furniture
9. chairs   **10.** children   **11.** homework   **12.** advice   **13.** suggestions   **14.** help
15. tea   **16.** food   **17.** sandwiches   **18.** animals   **19.** bananas   **20.** fruit
21. weather   **22.** pictures   **23.** rice . . . beans

☐ **EXERCISE 21, p. 148.   A/AN vs. SOME.   (Chart 4-8)**

Transformation.
In this exercise, students can see how a change from singular to plural requires grammatical changes in a sentence. They also encounter again the fact that noncount nouns cannot be plural.

ANSWERS: **3.** some coins   **4.** *(none)*   **5.** *(none)*   **6.** are some letters   **7.** *(none)*
8. are some cars   **9.** *(none)*   **10.** *(none)*   **11.** *(none)*   **12.** *(none)* . . . *(none)*
13. are some dictionaries   **14.** *(none)* . . . *(none)*   **15.** *(none)*

☐ **EXERCISE 22, p. 149.   A/AN vs. SOME.   (Chart 4-8)**

Oral (books closed).
Lead this exercise in a lively manner, moving quickly from one student to the next. If someone challenges an answer, let that person produce the correct form. It may not be necessary to include all 52 items, but select some of the more difficult ones from the end of the list as well as the easier ones at the beginning.

ANSWERS: **1.** a desk   **2.** some desks   **3.** an animal   **4.** some animals
5. a chair   **6.** some chairs   **7.** some furniture   **8.** a child   **9.** some children
10. some music   **11.** some homework   **12.** a flower   **13.** some information
14. an apple   **15.** a man   **16.** an old man   **17.** some men   **18.** some bananas
19. a banana   **20.** some fruit   **21.** an island   **22.** some jewelry   **23.** a university
24. an uncle   **25.** some rice   **26.** some boys   **27.** a window   **28.** a horse
29. an hour   **30.** some dishes   **31.** some women   **32.** some oranges   **33.** an
orange   **34.** a place   **35.** some places   **36.** some water   **37.** some mail
38. a letter   **39.** some letters   **40.** some bread   **41.** an office   **42.** some food
43. a table   **44.** some cheese   **45.** some matches   **46.** an adjective   **47.** some
advice   **48.** a house   **49.** some people   **50.** some potatoes   **51.** a potato
52. some sugar

☐ **EXERCISE 23, p. 149.   A/AN vs. SOME.   (Chart 4-8)**

Error analysis.
Incorrect singular-plural usage of nouns is common among learners at all proficiency levels. This exercise reviews the grammar your students now know about noun usage and asks them to apply it. Attention to grammatical number is an important part of the self-monitoring skills all learners need to develop.

    To make a kind of game, you could announce in advance the number of errors and have students compete to find them all as fast as possible.

ANSWERS: **3.** horses   **4.** *(no change)*   **5.** children   **6.** stories   **7.** minutes
8. countries   **9.** toys   **10.** *(no change)*   **11.** shelves   **12.** women . . . men
13. *(no change)*   **14.** *(no change)*   **15.** islands   **16.** glasses   **17.** Tomatoes
18. *(no change)*   **19.** dishes, spoons, forks, knives . . . napkins   **20.** friends . . . enemies

CHART 4-9:

CHART 4-9:   **MEASUREMENTS WITH NONCOUNT NOUNS**

• This is a lesson in vocabulary as well as the grammar of counting quantities. Take time to connect the pictures on page 150 with the list of common expressions in the chart.

• When speakers say these expressions at normal speed, the word *of* becomes just a vowel sound /ə/. The sound of *a* and *of* are then the same: a bag of rice = /ə bæg ə rais/.

• NOTE: a *loaf* of bread refers to the whole bread, but one piece of bread cut from the loaf with a knife is often called a *slice* of bread. Similarly, one piece of cut cheese or meat is called a *slice*. Since the text neglects to introduce the term *slice*, you might want to do so.

• The expressions of quantity in this chart are called "partitives."

☐ **EXERCISE 24, p. 151.   Measurements.   (Chart 4-9)**

Controlled completion.
This exercise and the next are designed to reinforce the learning of vocabulary.
   The partitives students choose may reflect cultural differences. For example, some cultures typically use glasses, not cups, for tea.

EXPECTED ANSWERS: **2.** a piece of/a slice of   **3.** a glass of/a cup of   **4.** a cup of
5. a piece of/a slice of   **6.** a cup of/a bowl of   **7.** a piece of/a slice of   **8.** a glass of
9. a piece of   **10.** a cup of/a bowl of

☐ **EXERCISE 25, p. 151.   Measurements.   (Chart 4-9)**

Open completion.
The purpose of this exercise is to explore common noncount nouns used with the given expressions of quantity. See how many completions the students can come up with.
   EXPANSION: With quick learners, you might turn this into a game of memory. The first student answers the second item by first repeating the first item, then adding the answer to the second. The next student must repeat items 1 and 2 before adding the response to item 3. As the game continues, the responses get longer and harder to remember. No writing is allowed. The last student has the most difficult answer.

POSSIBLE COMPLETIONS: **2.** toothpaste . . . soap   **3.** peas . . . peanut butter
4. bread . . . matches   **5.** lettuce   **6.** wine . . . pickles

☐ **EXERCISE 26, p. 151.   A/AN or measurement vs. SOME.   (Charts 4-6 → 4-9)**

Oral (books closed).
This is a cumulative review exercise. The pace should be lively. If your students can do this exercise easily, be sure to congratulate them heartily. This seemingly simple exercise contains some difficult and complicated grammar.

ANSWERS: **1.** some coffee/a cup of coffee   **2.** some money   **3.** a dollar   **4.** some paper/a piece of paper   **5.** a new book   **6.** some new books   **7.** some fruit/a piece of fruit   **8.** a banana   **9.** an apple   **10.** some oranges   **11.** some water   **12.** a new pencil   **13.** some information   **14.** some help   **15.** some advice/a piece of advice   **16.** some food   **17.** a sandwich   **18.** some meat/a piece of meat   **19.** some roast beef/a slice of roast beef   **20.** some soup/a bowl of soup   **21.** some salt   **22.** some sugar   **23.** some fish [also possible but unlikely: a fish]   **24.** a new car   **25.** a new shirt/blouse   **26.** some new shoes   **27.** some tea/a cup of tea   **28.** some cheese/a piece of cheese   **29.** some rice/a bowl of rice   **30.** some bread/a piece of bread/a slice of bread   **31.** some chicken/a piece of chicken   **32.** some new furniture

☐ **EXERCISE 27, p. 152.   *MANY or MUCH.   (Chart 4-6)***

Oral.

The text is backtracking a little here and picking up *many* and *much,* which are introduced in Chart 4-6. Each item in this exercise contains *a lot of* as the quantifier. Point out that *a lot of* is used with both plural count nouns and noncount nouns, but *many* is used only with plural count nouns and *much* only with noncount nouns.

ANSWERS: **2.** many problems   **3.** many cities   **4.** much sugar   **5.** many questions   **6.** much furniture   **7.** many people   **8.** much mail . . . many letters   **9.** many skyscrapers . . . many tall buildings   **10.** much work   **11.** much coffee   **12.** many friends   **13.** much fruit [An answer to this question might be "No, not much." or "Yes, quite a lot."]   **14.** much coffee [This answer could be the same as in item 13.]   **15.** many letters [answer: "No, not very many." OR "Yes, quite a few."]

☐ **EXERCISE 28, p. 152.   *MANY or MUCH.   (Chart 4-6)***

Controlled completion.

After one student has formed the complete question, that student could ask another student to give a truthful answer, including "I don't know. Do you?"

ANSWERS: **3.** many   **4.** much   **5.** much   **6.** much   **7.** many   **8.** much

☐ **EXERCISE 29, p. 153.   *HOW MANY or HOW MUCH.   (Chart 4-9)***

Oral.

The purpose of this exercise is to give students practice forming a typical question pattern with *how many* and *how much.* These questions require students to be aware of the countability of the noun and to make subjects and verbs agree in number (singular or plural), as well as to put *is there/are there* in the correct place in the sentence. Not easy!

ANSWERS: **1.** How many restaurants are there in this city?   **2.** How many desks are there in this room?   **3.** How much furniture is there in this room?   **4.** How many letters are there in your mailbox today?   **5.** How much mail is there in your mailbox today?   **6.** How much cheese is there in the refrigerator?   **7.** How many bridges are there in this city?   **8.** How much traffic is there on the street right now?   **9.** How many cars are there on the street?   **10.** How many people are there in this room?

☐ **EXERCISE 30, p. 153.   *A FEW/A LITTLE.   (Chart 4-9)***

Transformation.

Some learners cannot understand why the article *a* is used with *few* and plural nouns. This is just a strange development in the English language. This exercise gives practice in the expression of small quantities with common count and noncount nouns.

ANSWERS: **2.** a little salt   **3.** a few questions   **4.** a little help . . . a few problems . . . a little advice   **5.** a few clothes   **6.** a little homework   **7.** a little mail   **8.** a few letters   **9.** a little cheese   **10.** a few oral exercises

☐ **EXERCISE 31, p. 154.   *Count and noncount nouns.   (Charts 4-1 → 4-9)***

Controlled completion.

This is a review exercise that puts the grammar and vocabulary the students have been working with into sentence-level contexts. (A context does not have to be long to be a context. "Contextualized grammar" comes in many forms.) Be sure to include spelling and pronunciation in the discussion of the correct answers.

ANSWERS: **2.** money   **3.** sexes   **4.** cities   **5.** knives   **6.** information   **7.** paper   **8.** countries   **9.** bushes   **10.** homework   **11.** monkeys   **12.** traffic   **13.** pages   **14.** pieces   **15.** help   **16.** children   **17.** edges   **18.** furniture   **19.** feet   **20.** fruit

☐ **EXERCISE 32, p. 155.   *Count and noncount nouns.   (Charts 4-1 → 4-9)***

Controlled completion.

ANSWERS: **1.** Leaves   **2.** potatoes   **3.** weather   **4.** horses   **5.** dishes   **6.** women   **7.** Thieves   **8.** Strawberries   **9.** trays   **10.** work   **11.** sizes   **12.** advice   **13.** men   **14.** valleys   **15.** fish   **16.** glasses   **17.** centimeters [BrE: centime<u>tres</u>]   **18.** inches   **19.** feet   **20.** sentences

---

CHART 4-10:   USING *THE*

- For learners, *the* is perhaps the most difficult word in the English language. It is also possibly the most difficult word for teachers to teach. This chart simply scratches the surface. It provides a beginning point.

- Emphasize the idea that when the speaker uses *the,* s/he knows that the listener has the same thing or person in mind. Students may well ask if they have to be mind-readers in order to use *the* correctly!

☐ **EXERCISE 33, p. 157.   *THE or A/AN.   (Chart 4-10)***

Controlled completion.
Learners need time to understand the uses of articles. This exercise, which is confined to the use of *the* for second mention, allows you to clarify some of the information in Chart 4-10. Go slowly. Make up additional examples from the classroom context or things you draw on the board. For example, for item 1 use an actual notebook and a grammar book in the classroom to demonstrate the use of *a* vs. *the.*

The student who reads an item aloud is the speaker. Everyone else is a listener. In item 1, for example, the speaker uses *the* when s/he knows that the listeners know which notebook and grammar book s/he is talking about: s/he's talking about the ones that s/he has.

ANSWERS: **1.** a notebook . . . a grammar book . . . The notebook . . . The grammar book
2. a woman . . . a man . . . The woman . . . The man   **3.** a ring . . . a necklace . . . The ring
4. a magazine . . . a newspaper . . . the newspaper . . . the magazine   **5.** a circle . . .
a triangle . . . a square . . . a rectangle . . . The circle . . . the triangle . . . The square . . . the
triangle . . . the rectangle   **6.** an apartment . . . an old building . . . the apartment . . . The
building   **7.** a card . . . a flower . . . The card . . . the card . . . the flower   **8.** a hotel . . .
The hotel

☐ **EXERCISE 34, p. 158.   THE or A/AN.   (Chart 4-10)**

Controlled completion.
This exercise, which gives the context of a picture to help students practice the use of articles, is
confined to the use of *the* for second mention, contrasting it with the use of *a/an*.

ANSWERS: **(2)** a chair . . . a desk . . . a window . . . a plant   **(3)** the chair
(4) The chair . . . the window   **(5)** the plant   **(6)** The plant . . . the chair
(8) a man . . . a woman . . . The man . . . The woman   **(10)** a dog . . . a cat . . .
a bird . . . a cage   **(11)** the dog   **(13)** the cat   **(14)** The cat . . . the bird

☐ **EXERCISE 35, p. 159.   THE or A/AN.   (Chart 4-10)**

Controlled completion.
In addition to the use of *the* for second mention, this exercise includes the use of *the* for
something that is "one of a kind," e.g., *the sun, the weather, the moon.*

   Students could work in pairs for this conversational exercise. They can discuss any difficult
answers or ask you for help. In item 2, you might want to explain the use of exclamation
points (!); they indicate expressions of greeting, surprise, or strong feeling. They are not used in
formal writing and are found mostly in conversational writing, such as letters to friends or family.

ANSWERS: **1.** A: a coat   B: an umbrella   **2.** B: The weather   A: the coat . . . the
umbrella . . . the kitchen   **3.** a good job . . . an office . . . a computer   **4.** the computer
5. a stamp   **6.** A: an egg   B: a glass of juice   **7.** the floor   **8.** the moon . . . The moon
9. a telephone   **10.** the telephone

**CHART 4-11:   USING Ø (NO ARTICLE) TO MAKE
              GENERALIZATIONS**

- This grammar is not easy for learners. A beginning, or even advanced, textbook cannot cover all the
contingencies of article usage. Be aware that you are just giving your students a small introduction to
articles.

- Don't expect proficiency in article usage from your students in their creative language use. Learning
how to use articles in English takes a long time. Tell your students not to get frustrated. Articles are just
one small part of English.

- A typical error students from diverse language groups make is to use *the* in generalizations: ★*The life is
hard.* ★*We need the food to live.*

- Explain as best you can the meaning of the word "generalization." Basically, a generalization says that
something is usually or always true, e.g., *Sugar is sweet.*

- Be sure that students understand that the symbol Ø is never written in English. This textbook uses it
to call attention to the absence of an article before a noun.

☐ **EXERCISE 36, p. 160.** *THE or Ø.* *(Chart 4-11)*

> *Controlled completion.*
> You might mention in item 1 that the "s" in *sugar* should be capitalized because it is the first word in the sentence. Note in example 2, *the sugar* means that there is a bowl of sugar on the table where the speaker and listener are eating.
>
> *ANSWERS:* **3.** Ø **4.** the bananas **5.** Ø **6.** The food **7.** Ø ... Ø
> **8.** the salt ... the pepper **9.** Ø **10.** The coffee ... the tea **11.** Ø ... Ø
> **12.** the fruit ... the vegetables **13.** The pages **14.** Ø ... Ø

CHART 4-12: USING *SOME* AND *ANY*

- Note that *any* is not used with singular count nouns. One would say, "I don't have *a* pencil."

- The text purposely does not make a distinction between *any* and *some* in examples (c) and (d). The distinction is subtle and difficult for beginning students to understand as well as for teachers and textbooks to explain.

☐ **EXERCISE 37, p. 161.** *SOME or ANY.* *(Chart 4-12)*

> *Controlled completion.*
> This exercise requires learners to recognize noncount and plural count nouns, then decide whether a statement is negative or affirmative. In a question, either *some* or *any* can be used.
>
> *ANSWERS:* **4.** some/any **5.** any **6.** some **7.** any **8.** any ... any ... any ...
> any **9.** any **10.** some ... some/any **11.** any **12.** any **13.** some ...
> some/any **14.** any **15.** any **16.** some

☐ **EXERCISE 38, p. 162.** *SOME or ANY.* *(Chart 4-12)*

> *Oral (books closed).*
> Students can have fun with this exercise because some of the items are completely unexpected. Discuss any confusion about expressing quantities in the answers.
> In item 20, *light bulbs* are the glass globes in electric fixtures that produce light.

☐ **EXERCISE 39, p. 162.** *ANY or A.* *(Chart 4-12)*

> *Controlled completion.*
> This exercise gives practice with negative statements. Students must recognize noncount and plural count nouns, then add *any* or *a* correctly.
>
> *ANSWERS:* **4.** any **5.** any **6.** any ... any **7.** a **8.** any **9.** any
> **10.** any **11.** a **12.** any **13.** a **14.** any **15.** any **16.** a

---

CHART 4-13: INDEFINITE PRONOUNS: *SOMETHING,*
**   *SOMEONE, ANYTHING, ANYONE***

- You could also introduce indefinite pronouns with *-body* if you wish: *somebody* and *anybody*.
- Note the parallel uses in Charts 4-12 and 4-13. Point this out to your students.

☐ **EXERCISE 40, p. 163.** *SOMETHING, SOMEONE, ANYTHING, or ANYONE.* *(Chart 4-13)*

Controlled completion.
Note the information at the bottom of page 163 about *someone/somebody* and *anyone/anybody*.

ANSWERS: **2.** something/anything **3.** anything **4.** something **5.** anything
6. something/anything **7.** someone **8.** anyone **9.** someone
10. someone/anyone **11.** something **12.** anything **13.** something/anything
14. someone **15.** anyone **16.** anything **17.** anyone **18.** Someone
19. anyone **20.** anything

CHART 4-14: INDEFINITE PRONOUNS: *NOTHING* AND *NO ONE*

• Learners must understand that there are often two or more correct ways to state an idea. This chart presents one example of this.

• It might be useful to point out that only one *"no*-word" can be used in a correct sentence in English: either *not* or *nothing/no one/nobody,* but not both.

• Strange developments in historical English produced the following: *no* is pronounced /no/ in *no one* and *nobody,* but *nothing* is pronounced /nəθɪŋ/.

• In AmE, *no one* is written as two words; in BrE, it is usually hyphenated: *no-one.*

☐ **EXERCISE 41, p. 164.** *ANYTHING, NOTHING, ANYONE or NO ONE.* *(Chart 4-14)*

Controlled completion.
You might lead the whole class through items 1–6, then have them continue in pairs, discussing any problems that might arise.

ANSWERS: **1.** anything **2.** nothing **3.** anyone/anybody **4.** no one/nobody
5. nothing **6.** anything **7.** anything **8.** nothing **9.** nothing
10. anyone/anybody **11.** No one/Nobody **12.** nothing **13.** No one/Nobody
14. anyone/anybody **15.** A: anything B: nothing

☐ **EXERCISE 42, p. 165.** *Review.* *(Chapter 4)*

Structure identification.
You could call out the grammatical term and a student could say the word(s) that have that function in the sentence.

ANSWERS:

2.	Anita	carries	her books	in	her bookbag
	subj.	verb	obj.	prep.	obj. of prep.

3.	Snow	falls	(none)	(none)	(none)
	subj.	verb	obj.	prep.	obj. of prep.

4.	Monkeys	sleep	(none)	in	trees
	subj.	verb	obj.	prep.	obj. of prep.

5.	The teacher	is writing	words	on	the chalkboard
	subj.	verb	obj.	prep.	obj. of prep.

6.	I	like	apples	(none)	(none)
	subj.	verb	obj.	prep.	obj. of prep.

☐ **EXERCISE 43, p. 166.** *Review.* *(Chapter 4)*

Transformation.
The students have been learning all along what a "complete sentence" in English is. Now they have a term for it. Define the word "complete" for your students.

ANSWERS: **4.** Rain falls.   **5.** Inc.   **6.** This class ends at two o'clock.   **7.** Do the students go to class on Saturdays?   **8.** Inc.   **9.** My mother works in an office. **10.** Inc.   **11.** Inc.   **12.** Does your brother have a job?   **13.** Inc.   **14.** Where do you work?   **15.** My brother lives in an apartment.   **16.** Inc.   **17.** The apartment has two bedrooms.   **18.** Inc.   **19.** Inc.   **20.** Inc.

☐ **EXERCISE 44, p. 167.** *Review.* *(Chapter 4)*

Controlled completion; multiple choice.
This is a review of subject and object pronouns (Chart 4-3).

ANSWERS: **2.** B   **3.** C   **4.** C   **5.** C   **6.** A   **7.** D   **8.** B   **9.** B **10.** A

☐ **EXERCISE 45, p. 168.** *Review.* *(Chapter 4)*

Error analysis.
Most students enjoy the challenge of using their knowledge of English grammar to correct mistakes in this kind of exercise.

ANSWERS: **2.** Our teacher gives <u>difficult tests</u>.   **3.** I need <u>some advice</u> from you. **4.** Alex helps Mike and <u>me</u>.   **5.** I like rock <u>music</u>. I listen to <u>it</u> every day.   **6.** <u>Babies</u> cry. **7.** Mike and Tom <u>live in an apartment</u>.   **8.** There are seven <u>women</u> in this class. **9.** I don't like hot <u>weather</u>.   **10.** I usually have <u>an</u> egg for breakfast.   **11.** There are nineteen <u>people</u> in my class.   **12.** <u>The sun</u> rises every morning.   **13.** Olga and Ivan <u>have</u> three <u>children</u>.   **14.** The students in this class do a lot of <u>homework</u> every day.   **15.** How many <u>languages</u> do you know?   **16.** I don't have <u>much/any</u> money.   **17.** There <u>are</u> twenty <u>classrooms</u> in this building.   **18.** I don't know <u>anything</u> about ancient history. OR I know <u>nothing</u> about ancient history.

☐ **EXERCISE 46, p. 169.** *Review.* *(Chapter 4)*

Oral/written.
You could ask some students to read their lists aloud while the rest of the class listens carefully for correct uses of nouns and their markers.

☐ **EXERCISE 47, p. 169.** *Review.* *(Chapter 4)*

Oral/written.
Students could compare their lists.

☐ **EXERCISE 48, p. 169.** *Review.* *(Chapter 4)*

Oral.
The purpose of this exercise is for the students to use the target structures in this chapter in semi-structured conversation. The students should also have fun.

Chapter 5: EXPRESSING PAST TIME

ORDER OF CHAPTER	CHARTS	EXERCISES
Past of *be: was* and *were*	5-1 → 5-3	Ex. 1 → 6
Simple past: using *-ed*	5-4	Ex. 7
Yesterday, last, ago	5-5	Ex. 8 → 9
Pronunciation and spelling of *-ed*	5-6 → 5-8	Ex. 10 → 18
Simple past: irregular verbs	5-9	Ex. 19 → 21
Simple past: negative	5-10	Ex. 22 → 24
Simple past: yes/no questions	5-11	Ex. 25 → 30
More irregular verbs	5-12	Ex. 31 → 35
Simple past: information questions	5-13 → 5-16	Ex. 36 → 48
More irregular verbs	5-17	Ex. 49 → 50
Before, after, when in time clauses	5-18 → 5-19	Ex. 51 → 57
Review		Ex. 58 → 67

General Notes on Chapter 5

As with the other chapters, this one contains far more information than the title suggests. The focus is first on the past-tense forms of the verb *be* in statements, negatives, and questions. Then other verbs are introduced along with simple adverbs of past time. Attention is given to the pronunciation and spelling of past-tense verb forms, then some commonly used irregular forms are introduced. Many additional exercises with negatives and questions are provided. The final section introduces dependent time clauses, giving learners a means of expressing more complex ideas in their sentences.

CHART 5-1:   USING *BE:* PAST TIME

- The chart uses the adverbs *today* and *yesterday* to show the meanings of the verb forms. The text consistently uses adverbs of time with verb tenses because the adverbs establish the time period more clearly for learners than the verbs alone.

- The bottom half of the chart organizes the forms of *be* in the past tense in two ways: on the left is the traditional list of first, second, and third person pronouns in singular and plural; on the right is a list of pronouns associated with the two past forms of *be*. Your learners may have a preference for one list or the other to help them remember the forms.

- Point out that noun subjects require *was* if singular or *were* if plural. The chart includes some noun subjects in examples (c)–(f).

☐ **EXERCISE 1, p. 171.   *Past of BE.   (Chart 5-1)***

Oral.
This exercise is simply a quick check on the students' understanding of the forms presented in Chart 5-1.
   Although it is natural to use contractions *(I'm, we're, she's,* etc.*)* in the present tense, they are not used with past tense forms of *be*. However, in normal, rapid, contracted speech, the form *was* has the unstressed pronunciation /wz/.

ANSWERS: **3.** Mary was at the library yesterday.   **4.** We were in class yesterday.
5. You were busy yesterday.   **6.** I was happy yesterday.   **7.** The classroom was hot yesterday.   **8.** Ann was in her office yesterday.   **9.** Tom was in his office yesterday.
10. Ann and Tom were in their offices yesterday.

☐ **EXERCISE 2, p. 172.   *Past of BE.   (Chart 5-1)***

Oral (books closed).
Add the names of your students in the blank spaces. Adapt or add more examples to fit the classroom situation.

SAMPLE RESPONSES: **1.** We're in class today. We were in class yesterday too.   **2.** I'm in class today. I was in class yesterday too.   **3.** Talal is in class today. He was in class yesterday too.   **4.** Fumiko and Pedro are in class today. They were in class yesterday too.   **5.** Rita is here today. She was here yesterday too.   **6.** Sue is absent. She was absent yesterday too.
7. I'm tired today. I was tired yesterday too.   **8.** Olga and Mustafa are in the third row today. They were in the third row yesterday too.   **9.** The door is closed. The door was closed yesterday too.   **10.** It's cold today. It was cold yesterday too.

CHART 5-2:   PAST OF *BE:* NEGATIVE

- The text introduces *was* and *were* slowly, with each of the three basic patterns (statement, negative, question) having its own chart—just to make sure information does not get lost or buried. In all likelihood, you can cover these three charts quite quickly.

- The learners should try to use the negative contractions in their speaking. Their pronunciations: *wasn't* /wəznt/; *weren't* /wə-nt/

- Remind students that a noun subject requires *wasn't* if it is singular or *weren't* if it is plural.

☐ **EXERCISE 3, p. 172.** *Past of BE: negative.* *(Chart 5-2)*

Controlled completion.

The main point of this exercise is to ensure understanding of the information in Chart 5-2 on *wasn't* and *weren't.*

Another purpose is to introduce a few adverbs of time (prior to a fuller presentation in Chart 5-5). Students should understand that in the box with the adverbial time phrases, each item on the left in the present is equivalent to the item on the right in the past. The oddity is that English speakers use *yesterday* with *morning, afternoon,* and *evening,* but use *last* with *night.*

A third possible point of discussion in this exercise is the use of *but.* You could point out that the conjunction *but* requires a contrast between the fact in the first clause and the fact in the second clause. You might show that the sentences in the previous exercise (Exercise 2) could be joined by *and* because there is no contrast: for example, *John is in class today, and he was in class yesterday too.*

Students also have to pay attention to antecedents for their pronoun usage.

This is an easy exercise—but fertile ground for the aware teacher. The students are focusing on past-tense main verb *be* negative contractions. But they're also learning or reviewing adverbial time phrases, being passively introduced to the meaning and use of *but,* and having to demonstrate control of personal pronoun reference.

ANSWERS: **3.** she wasn't busy yesterday.   **4.** we weren't in class yesterday morning.
5. he wasn't at the library last night.   **6.** it wasn't cold last week.   **7.** they weren't at work yesterday afternoon.   **8.** they weren't at home last night.   **9.** you weren't in class yesterday.   **10.** she wasn't in her office yesterday afternoon.

CHART 5-3:   PAST OF *BE:* QUESTIONS

- You might review Charts 1-9 and 1-10 with the students. Then they can see the similarities between questions with *be* in the present and in the past. The word order is the same.

- In short answers, the verb *was* is stressed and must have its full pronunciation: /waz/ or /wəz/.

- In questions, the verb *was* is unstressed and is pronounced /wz/.

- Speakers of some languages, e.g., Japanese, may have difficulty answering with *Yes* and *No* as speakers of English expect. They often say "Yes" and mean "What you just asked is true"—something like the old song "Yes, We Have No Bananas." In English the *yes* or *no* must express the truth of the situation: "No, we don't have any bananas." Also in Japanese, a way of saying "No, thank you" is to say something that roughly translates as "Yes, that's perfect."

☐ **EXERCISE 4, p. 173.** *Past of BE: questions.* *(Chart 5-3)*

Transformation.
Students could work in pairs to complete the dialogues, then you could ask pairs to speak the dialogues without looking at their books (or maybe just peeking a little).

Occasionally students have difficulty following *Yes* or *No* with an appropriate short answer. Be prepared to deal with this, as explained in the note to Chart 5-3. *Yes* must be followed by an affirmative verb and *no* by a negative verb.

ANSWERS: **2.** A: Was Mr. Yamamoto absent from class yesterday? B: Yes, he was.
3. A: Were Alex and Sue at home last night? B: Yes, they were. **4.** A: Were you nervous the first day of school? B: No, I wasn't. **5.** A: Was Ahmed at the library last night? B: Yes, he was. **6.** A: Was Mr. Shin in class yesterday? B: No, he wasn't. A: Where was he? **7.** A: Were you and your wife in Canada last year? B: No, we weren't. A: Where were you?

☐ **EXERCISE 5, p. 174.** *Questions with BE.* *(Charts 1-9, 1-10, and 5-3)*

Transformation.
In this exercise, both present and past answers are required. Students have to pay attention to the adverbs of time.

ANSWERS: **3.** A: Were you tired last night? B: Yes, I was. **4.** A: Are you hungry right now? B: No, I'm not . . . . **5.** A: Was the weather hot in New York City last summer? B: Yes, it was. **6.** Is the weather cold in Alaska in the winter? B: Yes, it is. **7.** A: Were Yoko and Mohammed here yesterday afternoon? B: Yes, they were. **8.** A: Are the students in this class intelligent? B: Of course they are! **9.** A: Is Mr. Tok absent today? B: Yes, he is. A: Where is he? B: *(free response)* **10.** A: Were Tony and Benito at the party last night? B: No, they weren't. A: Where were they? B: *(free response)* **11.** A: Are Mr. and Mrs. Rice in town this week? B: No, they aren't. OR No, they're not. A: Oh? Where are they? B: *(free response)* **12.** A: Was Anna out of town last week? B: Yes, she was. A: Where was she? B: *(free response)*

☐ **EXERCISE 6, p. 176.** *Past of BE: questions.* *(Chart 5-3)*

Oral (books closed).
Set up this exercise carefully. First, decide who will be "A" with book open and who will be "B" with book closed. Note that students change roles after item 8 so that each has practice with asking and answering.

The note at the bottom of page 176 brings up grammar that is introduced in Chart 6-4 on page 239. You probably don't need to explain at this point that present and past tenses can be used with the same adverbial time phrases depending on the relation of the adverb to the moment of speaking. The footnote should be sufficient to allow the student to use the appropriate tense with the adverbial phrase *this morning.*

CHART 5-4: THE SIMPLE PAST TENSE: USING *-ED*

• After practicing forms of *be,* students now learn about other verbs in the past tense. This chart presents the regular form, the *-ed* ending.

☐ **EXERCISE 7, p. 177.** *Simple present vs. simple past.* *(Chart 5-4)*

Controlled completion.
The purpose of this exercise is to convey the idea that *-ed* signifies past time. You could limit the exercise to that purpose, or expand it by discussing pronunciation and spelling of *-ed* endings even though the text delays that discussion until Chart 5-6. Only you can decide how much information your students are ready for at this point.

ANSWERS: 2. walk . . . walked /wɔkt/ 3. asks . . . asked /æskt/ 4. watched /wɔčt/ . . . watch 5. cooked /kʊkt/ . . . cooks 6. stay . . . stayed /steid/ 7. work . . . worked /wɚkt/ 8. dream . . . dreamed /drimd/ OR dreamt /drɛmt/ 9. waits . . . waited /weitəd/ 10. erased /ɪreist/ 11. smiles 12. shaved /šeivd/ . . . shaves

---

CHART 5-5:	**PAST TIME WORDS: *YESTERDAY, LAST,* AND *AGO***

● These adverbs of time are very useful for students learning the past tense system. Help them understand that the lists are separate; elements from one list cannot be mixed with the other. For example, it is not possible to say *yesterday night* or *last afternoon*. (There is one exception the text chooses not to mention: *last evening* is also correct.)

● As a pedagogical note, the text continually connects adverbs of time with verb tenses—present, past or future—so that students are learning both at once; learning one helps students learn the other.

☐ **EXERCISE 8, p. 179.** *YESTERDAY or LAST.* *(Chart 5-5)*

Controlled completion.
This exercise and the next one will help students learn the separate uses of the adverbs in Chart 5-5. (Make sure they do not use the article *the* with *last* in their answers. *Last* has various uses and meanings. When used with *the, last* usually means "final": *Tom arrived the last week in April.* The meaning of *last* in the adverbial phrases in Chart 5-5 is more or less "the most recent one" or "the previous one." In *I saw her last week,* the phrase *last week* means "the week previous to this one" or "the week most recent to this week.")

ANSWERS: 2. yesterday 3. last 4. last 5. yesterday/last 6. last 7. last 8. yesterday 9. last 10. last 11. yesterday/last 12. last 13. last 14. last 15. yesterday

☐ **EXERCISE 9, p. 179.** *AGO.* *(Chart 5-5)*

Open completion.
Items 3 and 4 might not be suitable for your students' situation. You could substitute other items that mention events that occurred at a specific time in the past, such as visiting a museum, graduating from high school, or working at a part-time job.

SAMPLE COMPLETIONS: 2. two days ago 3. two years ago 4. Caracas a week ago 5. fifteen years ago 6. one month ago 7. two weeks ago 8. a day ago 9. four hours ago 10. a week ago

CHART 5-6: PRONUNCIATION OF -ED: /t/, /d/, AND /əd/

- Refer to Chart 2-4 to review the difference between voiced and voiceless sounds.

- Have the students emphasize the final -ed sounds as they repeat after you.

- In (a), point out that the -gh in *laugh* is pronounced /f/, which is a voiceless sound.
  NOTE: for teachers who are not native speakers of English: *laughed* = BrE /laft/; AmE /læft/.

- A vowel is a voiced sound, so any verb that ends in a vowel sound will follow rule (b): for example, *play–played* /pleyd/ and other verbs that end in -y. As it happens, many of the verbs that end in a vowel sound have irregular past tense forms *(go–went, know–knew, say–said, see–saw, buy–bought).*

☐ **EXERCISE 10, p. 180.** *Pronunciation of -ED.* *(Chart 5-6)*

Pronunciation and controlled completion.
Lead the students through the Group A list to be sure they use a /t/ sound for all of the -ed endings. Then they can work in pairs and check each other's pronunciation. Tell them to say the endings loudly and clearly. Continue in this way for Groups B and C.

ANSWERS:

GROUP A:
16. walked **17.** washed **18.** erased **19.** kissed **20.** laughed **21.** stopped
22. finished **23.** touched **24.** worked **25.** coughed /kɔft/ **26.** cooked
27. asked **28.** helped

GROUP B:
13. snowed [For the meaning of *it* in these sentences, refer to Chart 2-16.] **14.** arrived . . . arrived
[Call attention to the note on prepositions at the bottom of p. 181.] **15.** played **16.** signed
[A credit card is a plastic card that can be used like money.] **17.** shaved [*used to* = habitually in the past, but not now] **18.** smiled **19.** enjoyed **20.** closed /klozd/ **21.** rained
22. sneezed [*Bless you* is a common phrase used when someone sneezes. *Gesundheit!* /gɛzʊnthait/ is a German word used by many Americans when someone sneezes. It means "good health."]
23. remembered **24.** killed [*going crazy* = getting very upset]

GROUP C:
9. wanted **10.** needed **11.** counted **12.** invited **13.** visited **14.** folded
15. waited **16.** added [*added* is a calculation; *counted* is not]

☐ **EXERCISE 11, p. 183.** *Pronunciation of -ED.* *(Chart 5-6)*

Oral (books closed).
This is an active exercise. You tell the students what to do, then they do it. This can lead to a lot of fun and laughter while they are learning to hear and pronounce past tense verbs. *Pantomime* means "pretend to do the activity, speaking no words."

ANSWERS: **1.** smile/d/ **2.** laugh/t/ **3.** cough/t/ **4.** sneeze/d/ **5.** shave/d/
6. erase/t/ **7.** sign/d/ **8.** open/d/ **9.** close/d/ **10.** ask/t/ **11.** wash/t/
12. touch/t/ **13.** point/əd/ **14.** fold/əd/ **15.** count/əd/ **16.** push/t/
17. pull/d/ **18.** yawn/d/ **19.** pick/t/ **20.** add/əd/ [*Add two and two* means "2 + 2 = 4."]

CHART 5-7: SPELLING OF -ED VERBS

- The addition of *-ed* causes some changes in the spellings of verbs. These six rules are best learned through understanding and then practice. Exercises 12, 13, and 14 provide practice, but spelling continues to be a problem for some learners.

☐ **EXERCISE 12, p. 184.**   *Spelling of -ED and -ING verbs.   (Chart 5-7)*

Spelling.
Give students time to write the answers, then review them. The *-ing* forms in items 3, 8, 11, and 13 may cause problems. The rule for 3 and 8 is to drop the final *-e* before adding *-ing*. The rule for 11 and 13 is NOT to change a consonant + *-y* before *-ing*. One of the all-time most common misspellings in student writing is *⋆studing* instead of *studying*.

ANSWERS: **2.** stopped, stopping   **3.** smiled, smiling   **4.** rained, raining
5. helped, helping   **6.** dreamed, dreaming   **7.** clapped, clapping   **8.** erased, erasing
9. rubbed, rubbing   **10.** yawned, yawning   **11.** studied, studying   **12.** stayed, staying
13. worried, worrying   **14.** enjoyed, enjoying

☐ **EXERCISE 13, p. 184.**   *Spelling of -ED verbs.   (Chart 5-7)*

Controlled completion.
You could lead students through the list to be sure they understand the meaning, pronunciation, and spelling of each verb, or discuss the verbs as you go through the exercise.

ANSWERS: **2.** learned   **3.** tasted   **4.** waited   **5.** stopped   **6.** enjoyed
7. clapped [*clap* = applaud]   **8.** carried   **9.** rubbed   **10.** stayed . . . cried   **11.** failed
12. smiled

☐ **EXERCISE 14, p. 185.**   *Spelling and pronunciation of -ED.   (Chart 5-7)*

Spelling and pronunciation.
Some teachers feel it is unimportant or unnecessary for students to use phonetic symbols to represent pronunciation. The text uses these three phonetic symbols as simply one more tool in the teacher's and text's repertoire. Some students will respond well and others won't; learning styles differ. The text seeks to make students aware of the different pronunciations of *-ed* as an aid to their learning how to use this somewhat complicated inflection, but testing the students on this material would not seem to be beneficial. If phonetic symbols help some students, that's good. If they don't help others, nothing is lost. Awareness of the three pronunciations helps most students, but learning to use *-ed* correctly comes with lots and lots of practice. Learning the "pronunciation rules" in no way guarantees students will consistently produce correct pronunciations in their own creative speech.

ANSWERS: **4.** planned, /d/   **5.** joined, /d/ [*join* = connect; become a member of a group]
6. hoped, /t/   **7.** dropped, /t/   **8.** added, /əd/   **9.** pointed, /əd/   **10.** patted, /əd/
[*pat* = touch lightly]   **11.** shouted, /əd/   **12.** replied, /d/   **13.** played, /d/
14. touched, /t/   **15.** ended, /əd/   **16.** mopped, /t/ [*mop* = clean with a wet mop, a long-handled, absorbent implement]   **17.** drooped, /t/ [*droop* = hang loosely, like a wet cloth; a person who is hot and tired may appear to droop]   **18.** coped, /t/ [*cope* = put up with; strive successfully under difficult circumstances]   **19.** ranted, /əd/ [*rant* = speak loudly, angrily, violently, and at length]

20. dated, /əd/ [*date* = establish the calendar date for an event; or, go out for the evening with a special friend of the opposite sex]   **21.** heated, /əd/   **22.** batted, /əd/ [*bat* = hit a ball with a wooden bat in baseball or cricket]   **23.** tricked, /t/   **24.** fooled, /d/   **25.** rewarded, /əd/
26. grabbed, /d/ [*grab* = reach out the hand suddenly and catch something]   **27.** danced, /t/
28. pasted, /əd/ [*paste* = attach two things together using paste, a sticky white substance]
29. earned, /d/   **30.** grinned, /d/ [*grin* = smile broadly]   **31.** mended, /əd/

CHART 5-8:   SPELLING OF -*ED* AND -*ING*: TWO-SYLLABLE VERBS

• There are certain common two-syllable verbs whose -*ed* and -*ing* forms are frequently misspelled, by both native and non-native speakers of English. This chart attempts to show learners the underlying spelling pattern. Some students will get it and be glad to know the rules, and some won't.

• Spelling errors such as *★happenned, visitting, openning, occured,* and *begining* are exceedingly common.

• This chart should be titled "SPELLING OF -*ed* AND -*ing*: TWO-SYLLABLE VERBS THAT DO NOT END IN -*Y*." If the question arises, point out again that verbs that end in -*y* follow their own rules, even those verbs that are two syllables such as *enjoy, study,* and *worry.*

☐ **EXERCISE 15, p. 187.**   *Spelling of -ED and -ING.   (Chart 5-8)*

Spelling.

ANSWERS: **2.** preferred, preferring   **3.** happened, happening   **4.** visited, visiting
5. permitted, permitting   **6.** listened, listening   **7.** offered, offering   **8.** occurred, occurring   **9.** opened, opening   **10.** entered, entering   **11.** referred, referring
12. *(none),* beginning

☐ **EXERCISE 16, p. 187.**   *Spelling of -ED.   (Chart 5-8)*

Controlled completion.

ANSWERS: **2.** visited   **3.** listened   **4.** permitted   **5.** opened
6. happened/occurred   **7.** happened/occurred   **8.** offered   **9.** admitted

☐ **EXERCISE 17, p. 188.**   *Spelling of -ED.   (Chart 5-8)*

Oral/written (books closed).
By this point, students should understand the spelling patterns underlying each one of the -*ed* as well as -*ing* forms of these verbs. More likely than not, however, some of your students will still be consistently making errors such as *★waitted, studing, smilled,* etc. Don't get upset with them. Rather, suspect that some kind of learning disability may be interfering—and let go. Cultural values could also be playing a part; in some cultures, spelling simply is not important.
   POSSIBLE EXPANSION ACTIVITY: One way to conduct a spelling test is called a "spelling bee." Everyone stands up. You pronounce a word and indicate which student should spell it. If the spelling is incorrect, the student must sit down and the next student spells it. At the end of the list, the students who are still standing are the winners. (You may have to add more items, or divide a large class into teams.)

ANSWERS: **1.** stopped   **2.** waited   **3.** studied   **4.** smiled   **5.** enjoyed
6. rained   **7.** permitted   **8.** listened   **9.** rubbed   **10.** visited   **11.** carried
12. opened   **13.** folded   **14.** offered   **15.** happened   **16.** occurred   **17.** stayed
18. helped   **19.** dropped   **20.** counted

☐ **EXERCISE 18, p. 188.** *Spelling of -ED and -ING.* *(Chart 5-8)*

Fill-in-the-blanks.
This is a review of verb tenses as well as spelling and pronunciation. Students may work in pairs, discussing any disagreements.

ANSWERS: **4.** finished **5.** studied **6.** study **7.** am studying **8.** is raining **9.** rained **10.** helped **11.** stopped **12.** are playing **13.** played **14.** brushed . . . washed . . . shaved **15.** is watching **16.** watches **17.** watched **18.** are doing . . . are using **19.** arrived **20.** listens **21.** A: is he doing B: is listening **22.** A: Do you listen B: like . . . listen . . . listened

---

CHART 5-9: THE SIMPLE PAST: IRREGULAR VERBS

• This chart is the students' introduction to the phenomenon of irregular verbs in English. This chart presents a selection of frequently used irregular verbs as a starting point. Others are introduced in subsequent charts and chapters, a dozen or so at a time. There is a complete list in APPENDIX 5.

• Many of the most commonly used verbs in English are irregular verbs. The students cannot avoid them.

• How best to learn them? Some teachers believe students should not try to learn these lists; they believe that it's better to do exercises and learn the forms in the context of sentences. Other teachers assign lists of irregular verbs for memorization; they believe it helps students to know the principal parts of all irregular verbs.
   Choose whatever way seems best to you—all the while understanding that your students have their own ideas of how best to learn irregular verbs and will probably adapt the lists and exercises to their own learning styles.

☐ **EXERCISE 19, p. 190.** *Simple past: irregular verbs.* *(Chart 5-9)*

Oral.
This exercise is books-open so that students can quickly check the chart if they need to as they are getting used to these new verb forms.
   In these sentences, students should change *every day* to *yesterday,* but *every night* becomes *last night* and *every week* becomes *last week.* In item 11, *every morning* can become either *yesterday* or *yesterday morning.* Refer students to Chart 5-5 if necessary.
   Changing the adverbs reinforces the idea that these strange verb forms communicate the idea of past time.

ANSWERS: **2.** They went downtown yesterday. **3.** We had lunch yesterday. **4.** I saw my friends yesterday. **5.** Hamid sat in the front row yesterday. **6.** I slept for eight hours last night. **7.** The students stood in line at the cafeteria yesterday. **8.** I wrote a letter to my parents last week. **9.** Wai-Leng came to class late yesterday. **10.** We did exercises in class yesterday. **11.** I ate breakfast yesterday morning. **12.** I got up at seven yesterday. **13.** Robert put his books in his briefcase yesterday.

☐ **EXERCISE 20, p. 190.** *Simple past: irregular verbs. (Chart 5-9)*

Oral (books closed).
This exercise is books-closed so that the students can discover whether or not they remember the past forms of the verbs in Chart 5-9. Repeat items as necessary or make up your own for additional practice.

All the adverbs change to *yesterday* except in item 10. The students need to concentrate on the verb forms in this exercise, but you can change *every day* in the cues to *every week, every morning,* and *every afternoon* as you wish.

ANSWERS: **1.** I ate lunch yesterday. **2.** I saw you yesterday. **3.** I sat in class yesterday. **4.** I wrote a letter yesterday. **5.** I did my homework yesterday. **6.** I had breakfast yesterday. **7.** I went downtown yesterday. **8.** I got up at eight yesterday. **9.** I stood at the bus stop yesterday. **10.** I slept for eight hours last night. **11.** I came to school yesterday. **12.** I put my pen in my pocket yesterday.

☐ **EXERCISE 21, p. 191.** *Verb tense review. (Chapters 2, 3, and 5)*

Fill-in-the-blanks.
This exercise mixes the three tenses the learners have studied thus far. The time expressions are the keys to the tenses.

ANSWERS: **2.** talked **3.** is talking **4.** talks **5.** ate **6.** eat **7.** went **8.** studied **9.** wrote **10.** writes **11.** is sitting **12.** did **13.** saw [Point out that adverbial time expressions can sometimes come at the beginning of a sentence.] **14.** had . . . dreamed/ dreamt . . . slept **15.** happened **16.** comes **17.** came **18.** is standing **19.** stood **20.** put **21.** puts **22.** sits . . . sat . . . is . . . was

---

CHART 5-10: THE SIMPLE PAST: NEGATIVE

• This chart introduces *did* as a helping verb. Relate these sentences to simple present sentences to show the relationship between the use of *do* and the use of *did.*
  Simple present: *I **do** not walk to school every day.*
  Simple past: *I **did** not walk to school yesterday.*

• Some grammarians call these sentences examples of "*do*-support." English adds the "helping verb (auxiliary) *do*" in order to support the verb tense which is not attached to the main verb. In other words, we could say that the *-ed* has moved from the main verb and attached itself to *do,* forming the word *did.*

• Learners often make the mistake of adding the past tense to both *do* and the main verb: for example, *★They didn't came yesterday.*

• Encourage students to use contractions when they speak.

☐ **EXERCISE 22, p. 192.** *Simple present and past: negative. (Charts 2-9 and 5-10)*

Oral (books closed).
This is an easy exercise, but remind yourself that at least some of your students have never used *didn't* before and it may seem an odd word to them. They need a little time to get used to it. The text prefers that initial practice with new grammar be simple and stress free.

At the same time, of course, you have to make sure you're not boring a large portion of the class. For more advanced students who are already familiar with *didn't,* you can make the items more challenging by following up with extemporaneous questions that involve them in a brief interchange in which they have to produce *didn't* creatively.

Students have to pay attention here to time adverbs, tense, and contractions, so give them as much time as they need to respond.

ANSWERS: **1.** I don't eat breakfast every day. I didn't eat breakfast yesterday.   **2.** I don't watch TV every day. I didn't watch TV yesterday.   **3.** I don't go shopping every day. I didn't go shopping yesterday.   **4.** I don't read the newspaper every day. I didn't read the newspaper yesterday.   **5.** I don't study every day. I didn't study yesterday.   **6.** I don't go to the library every day. I didn't go to the library yesterday.   **7.** I don't visit my friends every day. I didn't visit my friends yesterday.   **8.** I don't see my sister every day. I didn't see my sister yesterday.   **9.** I don't do my homework every day. I didn't do my homework yesterday.   **10.** I don't shave every day. I didn't shave yesterday.

☐ **EXERCISE 23, p. 192.**   *Simple present and past: negative.*   *(Charts 2-9 and 5-10)*

Oral (books closed).

This can be fun and challenging. The students need to speak loudly enough for their classmates to hear, and everyone needs to listen carefully. You could stand behind one student and ask another about the first student's response, then move to another student and continue. This allows everyone to focus on the student seated in front of him/her rather than looking at you in another part of the classroom.

ANSWERS: **1.** A: I don't eat breakfast every morning. I didn't eat breakfast yesterday morning.   B: She/He doesn't eat breakfast every morning. She/He didn't eat breakfast yesterday morning.   **2.** A: I don't watch TV every night. I didn't watch TV last night.   B: She/He doesn't watch TV every night. She/He didn't watch TV last night.   **3.** A: I don't talk to Roberto every day. I didn't talk to Roberto yesterday.   B: She/He doesn't talk to Roberto every day. She/He didn't talk to Roberto yesterday.   **4.** A: I don't play soccer every afternoon. I didn't play soccer yesterday afternoon.   B: She/He doesn't play soccer every afternoon. She/He didn't play soccer yesterday afternoon.   **5.** A: I don't study grammar every evening. I didn't study grammar yesterday evening.   B: She/He doesn't study grammar every evening. She/He didn't study grammar yesterday evening.   **6.** A: I don't dream in English every night. I didn't dream in English last night.   B: She/He doesn't dream in English every night. She/He didn't dream in English last night.   **7.** A: I don't visit my aunt and uncle every year. I didn't visit my aunt and uncle last year.   B: She/He doesn't visit her/his aunt and uncle every year. She/He didn't visit her/his aunt and uncle last year.   **8.** A: I don't write to my parents every week. I didn't write to my parents last week.   B: She/He doesn't write to her/his parents every week. She/He didn't write to her/his parents last week.   **9.** A: I don't read the newspaper every morning. I didn't read the newspaper yesterday morning.   B: She/He doesn't read the newspaper every morning. She/He didn't read the newspaper yesterday morning.   **10.** A: I don't pay all of my bills every month. I didn't pay all of my bills last month.   B: She/He doesn't pay all of her/his bills every month. She/He didn't pay all of her/his bills last month.

☐ **EXERCISE 24, p. 193.**   *Verb tense review.*   *(Chapters 2, 3, and 5)*

Fill-in-the-blanks.

The learners must think about the verb tenses that match the adverbs of time, some irregular forms, and using *is/are/do/does/did* with negatives. Assign this and other review exercises as homework whenever possible. If that is not practical, be sure to give the students time to think before they respond. There is no benefit to the students going through a fill-in-the-blanks review exercise by writing in the correct answers they hear other students give. It's important for the students to come up with their own completions before the correct answers are discussed.

ANSWERS: **3.** didn't finish . . . went   **4.** isn't standing . . . is sitting   **5.** isn't raining . . . stopped   **6.** isn't . . . was   **7.** didn't go . . . went   **8.** went . . . didn't enjoy . . . wasn't   **9.** wrote . . . didn't write   **10.** is reading . . . isn't watching   **11.** didn't come   **12.** went . . . are sleeping   **13.** were . . . started . . . didn't arrive   **14.** asked . . . didn't answer   **15.** doesn't eat . . . doesn't have   **16.** ate . . . didn't eat

---

CHART 5-11:   THE SIMPLE PAST: YES/NO QUESTIONS

- The students are now aware of the use of *did* as a helping verb in the simple past negative. You might tell them that in forming a question in the simple past, the helping verb *did* moves to the beginning of the sentence. The subject and main verb do not change positions.

- Perhaps write the following on the board and ask the students what's wrong:
  Did Mary walked to school?
  Did Mary walks to school?
  Did Mary to walk to school?
  Did Mary walking to school?

☐ **EXERCISE 25, p. 194.   *Simple past: yes/no questions.   (Chart 5-11)***

   Transformation.
   Give students time to work out their responses, then have them go through the exercise with a partner before you select some items for some students to present to the whole class.
      NOTE: You may wish to point out that Olga, Yoko, and Gina /jǐnə/ are feminine names, while Benito and Ali are masculine names.

   ANSWERS: **3.** A: Did you eat lunch at the cafeteria?   B: Yes, I did.   **4.** A: Did Mr. Kwan go out of town last week?   B: No, he didn't.   **5.** A: Did you have a cup of tea this morning?   B: Yes, I did.   **6.** A: Did Benito and you/you and Benito go to a party last night? B: Yes, we did.   **7.** A: Did Olga study English in high school?   B: Yes, she did.   **8.** A: Did Yoko and Ali do their homework last night?   B: No, they didn't.   **9.** A: Did you see Gina at dinner last night?   B: Yes, I did.   **10.** A: Did you dream in English last night? B: No, I didn't. [A learner's first dream in English is a significant milestone!]

☐ **EXERCISE 26, p. 195.   *Simple past: yes/no questions.   (Chart 5-11)***

   Controlled completion.
   In this exercise, students need to recognize the main verb. If it is *be*, they must use *was/were;* if it is some other verb, they must use *did.*

   ANSWERS: **2.** was . . . did   **3.** A: Was . . . Did   B: was   **4.** A: Were . . . Did B: was . . . Were   **5.** A: were   B: was   A: Did   B: was . . . were . . . was . . . did

☐ **EXERCISE 27, p. 196.   *Simple past: yes/no questions.   (Charts 5-3 and 5-11)***

   Transformation.
   Here the students must use simple present or simple past, the correct form of *be* or *do,* and the correct word order. Give them time to work out the answers, perhaps with partners or as homework, then lead a discussion of difficult items.
      EXPANSION: Pair the students and ask them to write a dialogue by completing something like the following: A: Do . . . ?   B: *(answer)*   A: Did . . . ?   B: *(answer)*   A: Was . . . ? B: *(answer)*   A: Were . . . ?   B: *(answer)*

ANSWERS: **2.** A: Is it cold today? B: No, it isn't. **3.** A: Do you come to class every day? B: Yes, I do. **4.** A: Was Roberto absent yesterday? B: Yes, he was. **5.** A: Did Roberto stay home yesterday? B: Yes, he did. **6.** A: Do you watch television every day? B: No, I don't. **7.** A: Is Mohammed in class today? B: No, he isn't. A: Was he here yesterday? B: Yes, he was. A: Did he come to class the day before yesterday? B: Yes, he did. A: Does he usually come to class every day? B: Yes, he does. **8.** A: Do you live in an apartment? B: Yes, I do. A: Do you have a roommate? B: No, I don't. A: Do you want a roommate? B: No, I don't. A: Did you have a roommate last year? B: Yes, I did. A: Was he difficult to live with? B: Yes, he was. A: Did you ask him to keep the apartment clean? B: Yes, I did. [Perhaps point out that in *he never **did** it, did* means "kept the apartment clean."] A: Were you glad when he left? B: Yes, I was.

☐ EXERCISE 28, p. 197.   *Simple past: yes/no questions.*   *(Chart 5-11)*

Oral (books closed).
Tell students that they must answer truthfully. To make a kind of game, tell them not to answer any question that is not grammatically correct.

The phrase "this morning" is intended to refer to a time before now, even if it is still before noon at this moment. *This morning* should be interpreted to mean "before you came to class today." Change the adverbial phrasing to suit your circumstances.

☐ EXERCISE 29, p. 198.   *Simple past: yes/no questions.*   *(Chart 5-11)*

Oral (books closed).
After you say the cue, Student A asks a question about the present and Student B answers. They continue with a question about the same situation in the past. To keep other students alert, you could occasionally ask Student C, "What did Student B answer?" or "Do you think that's the truth?"

Explore interesting responses and engage your students in short conversations. This exercise is not intended to be approached as a cut-and-dried drill.

Items 14 and 15 passively introduce the structure *go + -ing (go shopping, go swimming, go dancing, go fishing, go camping,* etc.). This structure is not presented in a chart in this text. You may want to mention it briefly.

☐ EXERCISE 30, p. 198.   *Simple past: yes/no questions.*   *(Chart 5-11)*

Oral (books closed).
Here the students must answer "yes," not necessarily the truth. They must also listen carefully to your question so they can repeat it in their answer. This is a drill. The students practice understanding spoken English and responding appropriately, consciously utilizing learned patterns. It is not and is not intended to be practice in meaningful personal communication (as the previous exercise can easily be if you so choose). You can, of course, make it more personally communicative by drawing the students into conversation about the topics raised in the items, leading your students into spontaneous simple-past production of the target verbs.

You may want to choose students in random order so they cannot predict when they have to speak. Always remind yourself to include both slower and quicker students; sometimes teachers neglect one or the other. Repeat items until you're sure everyone in the class has recalled and has control of the previously taught irregular verbs. Students can work in pairs if you so choose.

CHART 5-12: MORE IRREGULAR VERBS

- The concept of irregular verbs was introduced in Chart 5-9. Additional irregular verbs are introduced in charts in this chapter and then in Chapters 6, 7, and 8. The text asks students to learn only a few irregular verbs at a time, rather than expecting them to learn all at once the 76 irregular verbs listed in the APPENDIX.

- Each irregular verb chart is followed by an oral (books-closed) exercise, such as Exercise 31 following this chart. These exercises only suggest a way for you to help your students learn the given irregular verbs. You don't have to follow the "script" verbatim. The idea is for you to put the verbs in meaningful contexts, demonstrating their use and eliciting usage from your students. The script is written out simply because sometimes teachers find a little priming useful to get a drill flowing.

  Remind yourself that these are odd, unfamiliar words for your students. Try to put your students into situations where they have to use these words, and then make sure they know they have communicated a meaning by assuring them you understood perfectly what they said.

- The words *brought, bought, thought, caught,* and *taught* have the same pronunciation after the first sound: /ɔt/. Unfortunately for learners, the historical development of English has produced some odd spellings.

- Go through the list with the class, pronouncing each word clearly after your model.

☐ **EXERCISE 31, p. 199.** *Irregular verbs.* *(Chart 5-12)*

> *Oral (books closed).*
> Be sure to read the note above about this kind of exercise. In this exercise, you serve as a sort of living dictionary for the students. (You might want to practice before the class period.) SUGGESTION: Copy this exercise on a piece of paper so you don't have to hold the somewhat large book.
>
> First pronounce the verb forms and have the students repeat after you. Then use them in the given contexts. The whole class or an individual student can answer your question. Then ask a followup question of just one student, who should answer truthfully, trying to use the same verb. Keep the pace lively and interesting.
>
> Items 6 and 12 require students to remember what has just been discussed in the classroom. The items are intended as another way of eliciting irregular verb usage in a meaningful classroom context.
>
> In item 4, the idiom "catch the bus" = get on the bus.

☐ **EXERCISE 32, p. 199.** *Irregular verbs.* *(Chart 5-12)*

> *Fill-in-the-blanks.*
> This exercise contextualizes the irregular verbs. The dialogues are models of how these verbs are used. Make the models more memorable for your students by asking them to say the dialogues without looking at their texts. Assign pairs to memorize particular dialogues and say them for the class. Don't make this too stressful. Students can peek at the text if they need to. Make it a fun activity.
>
> Alternatively, students can work with partners, discussing any difficult items, including spelling and pronunciation. Or, if class time is limited or your students advanced, assign it for out-of-class completion and quickly give the answers in class.
>
> ANSWERS: **1.** B: ran [idiom "out of breath" = unable to take enough air into the lungs (after exercise)] **2.** A: Did Ms. Carter teach   B: taught   **3.** A: rode   B: drove   **4.** thought **5.** A: Did you go   B: bought   **6.** A: Did you study   B: read . . . went   **7.** drank . . . was **8.** brought   **9.** caught

☐ **EXERCISE 33, p. 200.** *Irregular verbs.* *(Chart 5-12)*

Fill-in-the-blanks.
These items are more complex than those in Exercise 32, but again the purpose is to contextualize the irregular verbs. When you go through the items with the class, first establish the correct completions to an item, and then follow up with extemporaneous questions about the item. For example, follow up item 1 by asking "What did you and Ann do yesterday?" For item 2, ask Student B what Student A (the one who read the item aloud and supplied the answers) did yesterday. For item 3, ask a student what s/he ate or drank the last time s/he went to a movie. These are ways in which a teacher makes a grammar text come alive and provides her/his students with valuable communicative practice in the classroom context.

ANSWERS: **1.** went . . . bought **2.** caught . . . rode . . . got off . . . was [idiom "had to" = it was necessary (past of *have to*)] **3.** ate . . . drank . . . didn't eat [idiom "be on a diet" = try to lose weight, eat less] **4.** asked . . . thought **5.** wanted to go . . . stayed **6.** read . . . was **7.** taught . . . taught **8.** went . . . bought . . . didn't buy **9.** didn't pass . . . failed **10.** drove . . . visited . . . camped . . . went . . . caught . . . didn't catch . . . enjoyed . . . was **11.** had . . . ran . . . slammed . . . missed [idiom "slam on the brakes" = try to stop a car very suddenly by pushing the foot hard on the brake pedal; idiom "just missed" = almost hit it. Students should, at this point, be able to understand why the "m" is doubled in *slammed* even if they've never seen the word before.] **12.** played . . . caught . . . dropped

☐ **EXERCISE 34, p. 202.** *Irregular verbs.* *(Chart 5-12)*

Oral (books closed).
This is a review of simple past verb forms. Students can use any adverbs about the past, not just *this morning*.

If you assign this for pair work, one student has the book open, the other has it closed. If teacher-led, you give the cue, and Students A and B speak their dialogue for the whole class to hear. Follow up on interesting responses with extemporaneous conversation with your students.

☐ **EXERCISE 35, p. 202.** *Irregular verbs.* *(Chart 5-12)*

Oral (books closed).
To save yourself some time, you could have students exchange their lists with partners and make corrections before you see them. Alternatively, you could mark only mistakes with the verbs, paying no attention to other words in the sentences.

CHART 5-13:   THE SIMPLE PAST: USING *WHERE, WHEN, WHAT TIME,* AND *WHY*

- You could point out the similarity with present tense questions in Charts 2-11 and 2-12.

- It's useful to point out that learners need to listen to the first word of a question. If they can't hear that word (*When, Where, Why,* etc.), they can't answer the question meaningfully.

☐ **EXERCISE 36, p. 203.** *WHERE, WHEN, WHAT TIME, and WHY.* *(Chart 5-13)*

Open completion.
Give students time to think about these items because they have to work with word order and the correct question word. If they work in pairs, they should exchange "A" and "B" roles after 10 items.

ANSWERS: **2.** When did Jason arrive in Canada?   **3.** When/What time did your plane arrive?   **4.** Why did you stay home last night?   **5.** Where did you study last night?   **6.** Why did you turn on the light?   **7.** Where did Sara go for her vacation?   **8.** When did you finish your homework?   **9.** When did you come to this city?   **10.** Why did you laugh?   **11.** Where did you get your sandals?   **12.** Where is Kate?   **13.** Where does Ben live?   **14.** Where did you go yesterday afternoon?   **15.** Why is Bobby in bed?   **16.** Why did Bobby stay home?   **17.** When/What time does the movie start?   **18.** When did Sara get back from Brazil?   **19.** Why did Tina call?   **20.** Why does Jim lift weights?

☐ **EXERCISE 37, p. 205.   *WHERE, WHEN, WHAT TIME, and WHY.*   (Chart 5-13)**

Oral (books closed).

You are giving the answer and expecting someone to ask the question that produced your answer. This is a kind of "backward conversation," just for practice. It's a language game. Many people enjoy language games. Such games are a useful tool in a language classroom.

For many of the items in this exercise, there is more than one possible correct response. Accept any correct question a student generates.

EXPECTED ANSWERS: **1.** Where did you go?   **2.** When did you go to the zoo? [also possible: Where did you go yesterday? (Accept any correct question.)]   **3.** Why did you go to the zoo yesterday?   **4.** Where did (. . .) go?   **5.** When did (. . .) go to the park?   **6.** Why did (. . .) go to the park yesterday?   **7.** Where are you?   **8.** When did you come to class?   **9.** Where is (. . .)?   **10.** When did (. . .) come to class?   **11.** Where did (. . .) study last night?   **12.** When/What time did (. . .) finish his/her homework?   **13.** When/What time did (. . .) go to bed last night?   **14.** Why did (. . .) go to bed early?   **15.** Where did (. . .) go?   **16.** When did (. . .) go to the park?   **17.** Why did (. . .) go to the park yesterday?   **18.** Why is (. . .) absent today?   **19.** Where is (. . .)?   **20.** Why did (. . .) stay home?

☐ **EXERCISE 38, p. 205.   *WHY DIDN'T.*   (Chart 5-13)**

Open completion.

The use of negative verbs in questions is a grammatical can of worms, but negative verbs after *why* are relatively straightforward and common, so the pattern merits some attention. In *why didn't* questions, the speaker knows that something didn't happen and wants to know the reason. Typical errors with this pattern:
    ★*Why you didn't come to class?*
    ★*Why you not come to class?*
    This is an open-completion exercise, so students need to use their imaginations for the questions.

SAMPLE QUESTIONS: **2.** Why didn't you study for the test?   **3.** Why didn't you call me?   **4.** Why didn't you come to class?   **5.** Why didn't you eat breakfast?   **6.** Why didn't you come to Yoko's party?

☐ **EXERCISE 39, p. 206.   *Information questions.*   (Chart 5-13)**

Open completion.

Students can use their imaginations and perhaps some humor in their questions. You could have them work with partners, then ask each group to repeat their best question and answer for the whole class.

SAMPLE RESPONSES: **2.** What time does class begin?   **3.** Why didn't you come to the party last night?   **4.** When did your parents visit?   **5.** Where is Pedro from?   **6.** Why didn't you meet me at the mall?   **7.** Where did you go yesterday?   **8.** When did you start your new job?   **9.** Where did you eat last night?

CHART 5-14:   QUESTIONS WITH *WHAT*

- In examples (c) and (d), a form of *be* is a helping (auxiliary) verb, not the main verb. The helping verb is part of the present progressive tense. (See Chart 3-1.)

- Compare Chart 1-15 for questions with *what* and *be* as the main verb.

- In (a) and (b), a form of *do* is a helping verb because the main verb is not *be* and not in a progressive tense.

- Learners frequently make this mistake: ★*What Carol bought?*

☐ **EXERCISE 40, p. 207.** *Questions with WHAT.*   *(Chart 5-14)*

Transformation.
There is a lot to think about in this exercise and Exercise 41: the kind of question, the verb tense, helping verbs, irregular forms, and word order. Give students time to work out their answers.

ANSWERS: **3.** Is Mary carrying a suitcase?   **4.** What is Mary carrying?   **5.** Do you see that airplane?   **6.** What do you see?   **7.** What did Bob eat for lunch?   **8.** Did Bob eat a hamburger for lunch?   **9.** What does Bob usually eat for lunch?   **10.** Does Bob like salads?

☐ **EXERCISE 41, p. 207.** *Questions with WHAT.*   *(Chart 5-14)*

Transformation.
This exercise extends the grammar presented in Chart 5-14 by introducing question words used as the objects of prepositions. The depth of the grammatical explanation you give to your class is up to you. The question pattern with *what* is the same whether it is used as the object of a verb or of a preposition.
   NOTE: The pattern of formal questions that begin with a preposition (e.g., *About what did John talk?)* is not useful for students at this level. Questions in which *what* is the subject are relatively infrequent and are dealt with in subsequent texts in this series.

ANSWERS: **3.** What are you looking at?   **4.** Are you looking at that bird?
5. Are you interested in science?   **6.** What are you interested in?   **7.** What are you thinking about?   **8.** What did you dream about last night?   **9.** What is the teacher pointing at?   **10.** Are you afraid of snakes?

☐ **EXERCISE 42, p. 208.** *Questions with WHAT.*   *(Chart 5-14)*

Oral (books closed).
This may be very difficult for some learners. You could write an example from Chart 5-14 on the chalkboard for them to refer to. Perhaps they could work with partners before speaking in front of you and the whole class.

CHART 5-15:   QUESTIONS WITH *WHO*

- This is not an easy chart for the students. Those who understand the basic S–V–O structure of a simple sentence will have a much easier time than those who don't. Give ample additional examples when you present this chart. Draw arrows and circles around words on the board to show relationships and ordering.

- Some teachers and grammar books insist that (d) is correct and that (b) and (c) are incorrect. Most people today, however, rarely or never use *whom* at the beginning of a question. For this reason, (e) shows the letter "m" as optional: *who(m)*.

- Many learners have difficulty understanding the difference between (b) and (h). They need to practice a lot and make the connection in meaning between (a) and (b).

☐ **EXERCISE 43, p. 209.   Questions with WHO.   (Chart 5-15)**

Transformation.
You could lead the class slowly through this exercise, then let them work in pairs on the answers to Exercise 44. It is helpful for students to explain grammar to each other.

ANSWERS: **1.** Who(m) did you see at the party?   **2.** Who came to the party?
3. Who lives in that house?   **4.** Who(m) did you call?   **5.** Who(m) did you visit?
6. Who visited you?   **7.** Who helped Ann?   **8.** Who(m) did Bob help?   **9.** Did Bob help Ann?   **10.** Are you confused?

☐ **EXERCISE 44, p. 210.   Questions with WHAT.   (Chart 5-15)**

Transformation.

ANSWERS: **1.** Who(m) did you see?   **2.** Who(m) did you talk to?   **3.** Who(m) did you visit?   **4.** Who(m) are you thinking about?   **5.** Who called?   **6.** Who answered the question?   **7.** Who taught English class?   **8.** Who helped you?   **9.** Who(m) did you help?   **10.** Who carried your suitcase?

☐ **EXERCISE 45, p. 211.   Information questions.   (Charts 5-13 → 5-15)**

Transformation.
These items are ordered to contrast different questions about similar information. Lead students through items 1–3 as examples, and then, if and as time permits, let them work out the rest of the answers with partners prior to class discussion.

ANSWERS: **1.** Where did Ann go?   **2.** When did Ann go to the zoo?   **3.** Who went to the zoo yesterday?   **4.** Who(m) did you see?   **5.** Where did you see Ali?   **6.** When did you see Ali at the zoo?   **7.** Why did you go to the zoo yesterday?   **8.** Who(m) did you talk to?   **9.** Who called?   **10.** When did Dr. Jones call?   **11.** Where were you yesterday afternoon?   **12.** Where are you living?   **13.** What is the teacher talking about?
14. What does Annie have in her pocket?

```
┌─────────────────────────────────────────────────────────┬──────────────┐
│  CHART 5-16:   ASKING ABOUT THE MEANING OF              │              │
│                A WORD                                   │              │
├─────────────────────────────────────────────────────────┴──────────────┤
│                                                                         │
│  ● This is one of the most useful questions for students to learn, and  │
│  one with which many of them have problems. The incorrect example       │
│  represents a very common error.                                        │
│                                                                         │
└─────────────────────────────────────────────────────────────────────────┘
```

☐ **EXERCISE 46, p. 212.** *Meanings of words.* *(Chart 5-16)*

Oral.
Learners enjoy this vocabulary-building exercise. Encourage them to give their own definitions of the words (in any form they choose, including gestures or pictures), but allow them to consult their dictionaries if they are stuck. Also, make sure they use either (a) or (b) from Chart 5-16 as the question.

ANSWERS: **1.** humid; damp   **2.** disagreeable; dreadful   **3.** making little or no sound or noise   **4.** 100 years   **5.** make an end to something   **6.** give attention with the ear; obey   **7.** a big store; a large self-service retail store that sells food and other household goods   **8.** a large group of people   **9.** give something to someone for a short time, not forever   **10.** the unlawful killing of a person   **11.** find or realize something   **12.** easy to understand   **13.** containing nothing   **14.** take pleasure in; like a lot   **15.** sick   **16.** a large area of land covered with trees   **17.** own   **18.** ask; request the presence of someone in a courteous way   **19.** of the present time; new; not old-fashioned   **20.** *pretty* = an informal intensifier indicating an intensity less than *very; difficult* = hard, not easy

☐ **EXERCISE 47, p. 212.** *Review.* *(Charts 5-1 → 5-16)*

Open completion.

SAMPLE RESPONSES: **1.** When did you buy your new raincoat?   **2.** Who is your best friend?   **3.** What did you buy downtown yesterday?   **4.** When did you meet Mark?   **5.** Where did you meet him?   **6.** When do you have your composition class?   **7.** Where do you live?   **8.** Who lives with you?   **9.** Why did you move into an apartment?   **10.** What's your roommate's name?   **11.** What's that?   **12.** Where did you go last Sunday?

☐ **EXERCISE 48, p. 213.** *Review.* *(Charts 5-1 → 5-16)*

Oral (books closed).
Some students will still be unsure about their answers. It takes time and a lot of practice to gain control of these questions, so don't expect perfection yet.

SAMPLE RESPONSES: **1.** Where does your family live?   **2.** When was your last English class?   **3.** What does *terrific* mean?   **4.** Who's sitting behind you?   **5.** When do you usually eat dinner?   **6.** What is (. . .) wearing?   **7.** What did you eat for lunch?   **8.** Do you own your own house?   **9.** Why did you come to class today?   **10.** What are you studying right now?   **11.** Do you attend class regularly?   **12.** What were you whispering just now?   **13.** Where do most students live?   **14.** Why didn't you wait up for me last night?   **15.** Who's sitting in front of you?   **16.** What time is your favorite TV program on?   **17.** What did you buy?   **18.** Where do you live?   **19.** Where is (name of this city) located?   **20.** When did you talk to (. . .)?

CHART 5-17: MORE IRREGULAR VERBS

- See the notes for Chart 5-12, page 84, for information on how to present irregular verbs.
- Pronunciation note: *flew* is either /flu/ or /fliu/; *paid* is /peid/.
- Vocabulary note: *wake up* = open your eyes after sleeping; *get up* = get out of bed.

☐ **EXERCISE 49, p. 213.** *Irregular verbs.* *(Chart 5-17)*

Oral (books closed).
See the notes for Chart 5-12 and Exercise 31 for ideas on how to present irregular verbs to your students.

☐ **EXERCISE 50, p. 214.** *Irregular verbs.* *(Chart 5-17)*

Controlled completion.
Students enjoy doing this exercise with partners. During subsequent class discussion of the correct answers, ask each pair to speak a dialogue without looking at their texts. Then follow up with questions about the dialogue, such as *What happened to (Speaker B)'s finger?*

ANSWERS: **1.** broke **2.** spoke **3.** left [incorrect: flew for Europe] **4.** sent
5. met **6.** heard **7.** took **8.** rang **9.** sang **10.** woke **11.** paid
12. flew

CHART 5-18: *BEFORE* AND *AFTER* IN TIME CLAUSES

- Time clauses give learners a way to combine information into complex sentences. This chart is the students' introduction to complex (as compared to simple) sentence structure in English.

- A time clause is a type of dependent clause usually called an adverb(ial) clause or a subordinate clause. *After* and *before* are called subordinating conjunctions. The text deems it preferable to minimize terminology.

- Call attention to the punctuation: In (d) and (f), a comma is necessary when the time clause comes at the beginning of the sentence. In speaking, there is a short pause where the comma appears. (See the note at the bottom of page 216 in the textbook.)

- Point out the prepositional phrases in (g) and (h). They do not contain a subject and verb as required in a clause.

☐ **EXERCISE 51, p. 216.** *BEFORE and AFTER in time clauses.* *(Chart 5-18)*

Structure identification.
In example 1, some students might ask about the pronoun *it*. They might want to say, "Before I ate it, I peeled the banana." It is more common, however, to give the noun in the first part of the sentence and the pronoun later.

You might ask one student to analyze a sentence for the class. Ask him/her about the placement of commas.

2. *main clause* = We arrived at the airport; *time clause* = before the plane landed
3. *main clause* = I went to a movie; *time clause* = after I finished my homework
4. *time clause* = After the children got home from school; *main clause* = they watched TV
5. *time clause* = Before I moved to this city; *main clause* = I lived at home with my parents

☐ **EXERCISE 52, p. 217.** *BEFORE and AFTER in time clauses.* *(Chart 5-18)*

Structure identification; error analysis.
A common error is for students to write adverb clauses as though they were complete sentences. Learners need to understand that time clauses must be connected to main (or independent) clauses.

ANSWERS: **4.** Inc. **5.** We went to the zoo. **6.** We went to the zoo before we ate our picnic lunch. **7.** The children played games after they did their work. **8.** The children played games. **9.** Inc. **10.** The lions killed a zebra. **11.** Inc. **12.** They ate it. **13.** After the lions killed a zebra, they ate it.

☐ **EXERCISE 53, p. 217.** *BEFORE and AFTER in time clauses.* *(Chart 5-18)*

Sentence construction.
Understanding variations increases a student's creative usage repertoire.

ANSWERS: **1.** Before she went to work, she ate breakfast. She ate breakfast before she went to work. After she ate breakfast, she went to work. She went to work after she ate breakfast.
2. Before he went to bed, he did his homework. He did his homework before he went to bed. After he did his homework, he went to bed. He went to bed after he did his homework.
3. Before we entered the theater, we bought tickets. We bought tickets before we entered the theater. After we bought tickets, we entered the theater. We entered the theater after we bought tickets.

☐ **EXERCISE 54, p. 219.** *BEFORE and AFTER in time clauses.* *(Chart 5-18)*

Open completion.
When you check these sentences, watch for comma placement as well as logical combinations of ideas.

CHART 5-19: *WHEN IN TIME CLAUSES*

- *When* basically means "at that time." It has variations of meaning that students at this level probably aren't ready for. For example, in (a) it means "as soon as" or "immediately after," compared to (b) where it means "for the same period of time."

☐ **EXERCISE 55, p. 219.** *WHEN in time clauses.* *(Chart 5-19)*

Sentence construction and transformation.
The list on the left (1–8) must be combined with the list on the right (A–H) to make good sentences. Students can do this alone or with partners.

ANSWERS: **2.** When I was in Japan, I stayed in a hotel in Tokyo. I stayed in a hotel in Tokyo when I was in Japan.   **3.** Maria bought some new shoes when she went shopping yesterday. When Maria went shopping yesterday, she bought some new shoes.   **4.** I took a lot of photographs when I was in Hawaii. When I was in Hawaii, I took a lot of photographs.   **5.** When a stranger grabbed Ann's arm, she screamed. Ann screamed when a stranger grabbed her arm.   **6.** Jim was a wrestler when he was in high school. When Jim was in high school, he was a wrestler.   **7.** When the rain stopped, I closed my umbrella. I closed my umbrella when the rain stopped.   **8.** The antique vase broke when I dropped it. When I dropped the antique vase, it broke.

□ **EXERCISE 56, p. 220.   *WHEN in time clauses.   (Chart 5-19)***

Structure identification.

After the students complete this exercise, they can compare their answers with partners and discuss any differences.

ANSWERS: **3.** Inc.   **4.** When were you in Iran?   **5.** When did the movie end?   **6.** Inc.   **7.** Inc.   **8.** Inc.   **9.** Inc.   **10.** When does the museum open?

□ **EXERCISE 57, p. 220.   *WHEN in time clauses.   (Chart 5-19)***

Open completion.

Praise your students heartily for their ability to complete these sentences. The underlying grammar is quite complicated. You could tell them that they have shown that they can distinguish between the use of *when* as a subordinating conjunction and its use as an interrogative pronoun—just to impress them with their good knowledge of English grammar. They know and can correctly use the grammar whether they know the terminology or not—just like native speakers.

You could include items like this on a test.

□ **EXERCISE 58, p. 220.   *Review.   (Chapter 5)***

Fill-in-the-blanks.

This should be assigned as homework prior to class discussion.

ANSWERS: **(1)** was   **(2)** went . . . overslept   **(3)** didn't ring   **(4)** woke   **(5)** heard   **(6)** got   **(7)** ran   **(8)** was   **(9)** was   **(10)** went   **(11)** had   **(12)** dropped   **(13)** broke . . . dropped   **(14)** looked   **(15)** went   **(16)** got   **(17)** paid   **(18)** sat   **(19)** ate   **(20)** drank   **(21)** went . . . sat   **(22)** saw   **(23)** called   **(24)** joined   **(25)** talked   **(26)** relaxed   **(27)** stood   **(28)** stepped   **(29)** broke   **(30)** drove   **(31)** went   **(32)** took   **(33)** put   **(34)** paid . . . left   **(35)** took   **(36)** helped   **(37)** got   **(38)** looked . . . looked   **(39)** rang   **(40)** thought   **(41)** wasn't   **(42)** sat   **(43)** waited   **(44)** came   **(45)** got . . . ate   **(46)** went   **(47)** slept

□ **EXERCISE 59, p. 222.   *Review.   (Chapter 5)***

Oral.

Go through the example with the class. Learners can help each other if everyone is friendly and able to accept correction.

☐ EXERCISE 60, p. 223.   *Review.*   *(Chapter 5)*

Written.
When you check this writing, mark only the verbs. If other mistakes exist, just underline them, but don't count them in your marks.

If some students say they can't remember the story, tell them to make one up.

☐ EXERCISE 61, p. 223.   *Review.*   *(Chapter 5)*

Written.
When you check this writing, add an encouraging comment about the content—how interesting or unusual or humorous it is. Build your students' confidence whenever you can.

☐ EXERCISE 62, p. 223.   *Review.*   *(Chapter 5)*

Written.
If possible, students should interview native speakers of English or very good speakers of English. If this is impractical, they will have to translate into English the information they are given.

☐ EXERCISE 63, p. 223.   *Review.*   *(Chapter 5)*

Spelling.
Lead the class through the list, asking them to spell the words to you as you write them on the chalkboard. You should write exactly what they tell you, then let them catch any mistakes.

ANSWERS: **3.** went   **4.** worried   **5.** spoke   **6.** rode   **7.** stood   **8.** turned
9. heard   **10.** paid   **11.** caught   **12.** happened   **13.** listened   **14.** planned
15. rained   **16.** brought   **17.** took   **18.** wrote   **19.** broke   **20.** stopped
21. hoped   **22.** sang   **23.** thought   **24.** drove   **25.** rang   **26.** met   **27.** left
28. occurred   **29.** taught   **30.** read

☐ EXERCISE 64, p. 224.   *Review.*   *(Chapter 5)*

Oral.
Encourage relaxed conversation. Don't necessarily pair a more advanced student with a less advanced one. Sometimes less advanced students can teach each other better because they are more comfortable with each other, and more advanced students benefit from challenging each other.

☐ EXERCISE 65, p. 224.   *Review.*   *(Chapter 5)*

Error analysis.

ANSWERS: **1.** Did you <u>go</u> downtown yesterday?   **2.** Yesterday I <u>spoke</u> to Ken before he <u>left</u> his office and <u>went</u> home.   **3.** I <u>heard</u> a good joke last night.   **4.** Pablo <u>finished</u> his work.   OR   When Pablo <u>finished</u> his work, he <u>went</u> home.   OR   When <u>did</u> Pablo <u>finish</u> his work?   **5.** I <u>visited</u> my relatives in New York City last month.   **6.** Where <u>did you</u> go yesterday afternoon?   **7.** Ms. Wah <u>flew</u> from Singapore to Tokyo last week.   **8.** When I <u>saw</u> my friend yesterday, he didn't <u>speak</u> to me.   **9.** Why <u>didn't</u> Mustafa <u>come</u> to class last week?   **10.** Where <u>did</u> you <u>buy</u> those shoes? I like them.   **11.** Mr. Adams <u>taught</u> our class last week.   **12.** I <u>wrote</u> a letter last night.   **13.** Who <u>did</u> you <u>write</u> a letter to?
14. Who <u>opened</u> the door? Jack <u>opened</u> it.

□ **EXERCISE 66, p. 225.** *Review.* *(Chapter 5)*

Fill-in-the-blanks.
You might want to lead the whole class in this review of verb tenses and sentence types. You will then see where they still have difficulty.

ANSWERS: **2.** is walking   **3.** Does Tom walk   **4.** Do you walk   **5.** walked
6. saw   **7.** didn't see   **8.** Did you see   **9.** doesn't walk . . . takes   **10.** don't walk
[*either* indicates agreement in a negative sentence]

□ **EXERCISE 67, p. 225.** *Review.* *(Chapter 5)*

Fill-in-the-blanks.
Don't make this exercise a test or work. It's supposed to be fun and interesting. It's sort of a reward. Expand upon this exercise as time allows. Students can do role-plays, write summaries, discuss the meaning of the story in small groups, do artwork as a basis for retelling the story, continue the story (Will Bear eventually eat Fish?), etc.

ANSWERS: **(1)** was . . . saw   **(2)** are you   **(3)** am doing   **(4)** Would you like
(5) sit . . . need   **(6)** don't need   **(7)** are you doing   **(8)** am getting
(9) is   **(9)** + **(10)** don't trust   **(10)** do you want   **(11)** want   **(12)** had
(13) saw   **(14)** love . . . stopped   **(15)** reached   **(16)** came   **(17)** was
(18) don't believe   **(19)** don't believe   **(20)** are . . . aren't   **(21)** is   **(22)** is it
(23) did the bee sting   **(24)** are you doing   **(25)** are you holding   **(26)** am holding
(27) tricked   **(28)** happened   **(29)** got   **(30)** wanted to catch   **(31)** caught
(32) looks   **(33)** don't believe   **(34)** is . . . is coming   **(35)** don't see
(36) dropped   **(37)** fooled   **(38)** tricked . . . taught   **(39)** learned
(40) am . . . have   **(41)** Would you like

Chapter 6: EXPRESSING FUTURE TIME

ORDER OF CHAPTER	CHARTS	EXERCISES
Future time: Using *be going to*	6-1	Ex. 1 → 6
Words used for past and future time	6-2	Ex. 7 → 9
A couple of or *a few* with *ago* and *in*	6-3	Ex. 10 → 11
Today, tonight, and *this + morning, afternoon, evening, week, month, year*	6-4	Ex. 12 → 15
Future time: using *will*	6-5	Ex. 16
Asking questions with *will*	6-6	Ex. 17
Verb summary: present, past, and future	6-7	Ex. 18
Verb summary: forms of *be*	6-8	Ex. 19 → 21
Using *what* + a form of *do*	6-9	Ex. 22 → 23
May/might vs. *will*	6-10	Ex. 24 → 26
Maybe vs. *may be*	6-11	Ex. 27 → 31
Future time clauses with *before, after* and *when*	6-12	Ex. 32 → 34
Clauses with *if*	6-13	Ex. 35 → 37
Habitual present with time clauses and *if*-clauses	6-14	Ex. 38 → 43
More irregular verbs	6-15	Ex. 44 → 46
More irregular verbs	6-16	Ex. 47 → 49
Review		Ex. 50 → 53

General Notes on Chapter 6

Some grammarians say that English has no future tense because there is no single verb form like -*ed* for the past tense or -*s* for the present tense. This chapter introduces the phrases that express future time in English. The first of these is *be going to*, which is especially common in conversation. Simple adverbial phrases with future meanings are also introduced and practiced. The next section introduces *will* in verb phrases with future meanings. Then there is a review of all verb tenses studied in the textbook so far and forms of the verb *be*. The use of *do* as a main verb is contrasted with *do* as a helping verb or auxiliary. Then *may, might,* and *maybe* are contrasted with *will*. A section on time clauses focuses on expressions of future time and predictions with *if*. This is followed by an explanation of using such clauses to express habitual present actions. The chapter concludes by introducing a few more irregular past tense verbs and providing a variety of exercises on all of the verb forms introduced in the textbook so far.

CHART 6-1: FUTURE TIME: USING *BE GOING TO*

• Contractions with both *be* and *going to* are the most common use of these forms in spoken English. Thus, *I am going to go downtown* is spoken like "I'm gonna go downtown." *gonna* = /gənə/. It is unusual for a speaker to speak this phrase without contractions, but *gonna* is not a written form.

• Model *gonna* for the class, but don't teach it as the only way of speaking *be going to*. Learners pick up natural use of *gonna* as they gain experience with English.

• When students learn to say *gonna* for *going to*, they sometimes make the mistake of adding *to* again: ★"I'm gonna to go downtown." This is like saying ★"I am going to to go downtown."

• The general meaning of *be going to* is expressing a plan or intention.

• Chart 6-1 includes negative statements and questions that use *be going to*. Lead students through these forms, pointing out parallels with the word order in present progressive sentences (compare with Charts 3-3 and 3-4).

☐ **EXERCISE 1, p. 231.** *BE GOING TO.* **(Chart 6-1)**

Oral.
Set up the exercise so that students are in pairs, one with an open book. Model the examples for them, and tell them to change A and B roles after 10 items. As the pairs work, walk around the classroom listening to their efforts. Interrupt as little as possible, but make mental notes on items that need discussion after everyone is finished.

☐ **EXERCISE 2, p. 232.** *BE GOING TO.* **(Chart 6-1)**

Oral (books closed).
Lead this exercise as a kind of natural conversation. (Perhaps pretend that you are a bit hard of hearing.)

☐ **EXERCISE 3, p. 232.** *BE GOING TO.* **(Chart 6-1)**

Controlled and/or open completion.
Lead the students through the list of phrases to be sure they know the meanings and pronunciations. Note that the instructions suggest adding their own words to make their answers more real and truthful. Allow about 10 minutes of quiet time for everyone to write the answers, then go over the exercise together.

ANSWERS: **2.** am going to ('m gonna) go to bed   **3.** is going to get something to eat
4. am going to take them to the laundromat   **5.** am going to see a dentist [*toothache* /tuθeik/]
6. am going to look it up in my dictionary   **7.** is going to take it to the post office   **8.** is
going to call the landlord [*plumbing* /pləmɪŋ/ = pipes that bring water into a house]   **9.** are going to
go to the beach   **10.** am going to lie down and rest for a while [*headache* /hɛdeik/]   **11.** am
going to call the police [*burglar* /bɚglɚ/ = a thief who breaks into a home]   **12.** am going to major
in psychology [*psychologist* /saikaləǰɪst/; *psychology* /saikaləǰi/]   **13.** am going to stay in bed today
[*the flu* = a cold in the head and chest, sometimes with an upset stomach]   **14.** are going to go to an
Italian restaurant   **15.** are going to take a long walk in the park

☐ **EXERCISE 4, p. 234.**   *BE GOING TO.*   *(Chart 6-1)*

Oral (books closed).
You might ask students to close their eyes and picture in their minds the situation that your
words describe. Then ask one student to answer your question. Substitute names of your
students and perhaps other teachers between parentheses ( ).

In item 6, a *laundromat* /lɔndrəmæt/ is a kind of shop with many washing machines where
people can wash their clothes for a few coins.

In item 9, an *engagement ring* is given by a man to the woman he is planning to marry. In the
United States, this ring is worn on what is called the "ring finger" of the left hand (the finger
next to the little finger), and the wedding ring will also be worn on that finger.

In item 10, *swimming suits* are worn for swimming in the water or sunbathing on the beach;
sandals are shoes that are open at the toes and heels.

☐ **EXERCISE 5, p. 234.**   *BE GOING TO.*   *(Chart 6-1)*

Oral.
Students could work with partners. They should change roles after item 5.

☐ **EXERCISE 6, p. 235.**   *BE GOING TO.*   *(Chart 6-1)*

Oral.
You lead this exercise, following the instructions. Keep the pace lively with a little humor. In
item 14, you should substitute a local food if pizza is not appropriate.

**CHART 6-2:   WORDS USED FOR PAST TIME AND
FUTURE TIME**

• You might begin with the sentences on the right side of the chart, asking students what differences
they see in each pair.

• You might divide the class in half and have one group say a word from the "Past" list followed by the
other group saying the contrasting word from the "Future" list. Note that we do not use the article *the*
before *last* or *next* in these time phrases. Also note that we can say "last night" but not *"next night"; we
must say "tomorrow night."

☐ **EXERCISE 7, p. 236.**   *YESTERDAY, LAST, TOMORROW, or NEXT.*   *(Chart 6-2)*

Controlled completion.
Students must identify the verb tense before completing each sentence correctly. Give them
time to look back at the list in Chart 6-2 if necessary while completing their answers. Then
review the whole exercise. Make sure they don't use *the* before *last* or *next*.

ANSWERS: **3.** next   **4.** last   **5.** yesterday   **6.** Tomorrow   **7.** next   **8.** last
9. next   **10.** Last   **11.** next   **12.** last   **13.** tomorrow   **14.** Last
15. Tomorrow   **16.** yesterday

☐ **EXERCISE 8, p. 237.   *AGO or IN.   (Chart 6-2)***

Controlled completion.
Again, students must identify the verb tense before they can complete the sentence correctly.
They should be able to do this exercise orally without writing their answers first.

ANSWERS: **3.** an hour ago   **4.** in an hour   **5.** in two more months
6. two months ago   **7.** a minute ago   **8.** in half an hour   **9.** in one more week
10. a year ago

☐ **EXERCISE 9, p. 237.   *YESTERDAY, LAST, TOMORROW, NEXT, IN, or AGO.   (Chart 6-2)***

Controlled completion.
This is similar to Exercise 8. You may wish to use some of the items for a test.

ANSWERS: **2.** ago   **3.** next   **4.** in   **5.** yesterday   **6.** tomorrow   **7.** last
8. next   **9.** tomorrow   **10.** ago   **11.** in   **12.** Tomorrow   **13.** Last
14. Yesterday   **15.** ago   **16.** next   **17.** tomorrow   **18.** last   **19.** in
20. Next

CHART 6-3: USING *A COUPLE OF* OR *A FEW* WITH *AGO* (PAST) AND *IN* (FUTURE)	

• This is a usage expansion lesson.

☐ **EXERCISE 10, p. 238.   *AGO or IN with A COUPLE OF or A FEW.   (Chart 6-3)***

Semi-controlled completion.
Students should give truthful answers to make the exercise more realistic.

SAMPLE ANSWERS: **3.** a few hours ago   **4.** in a couple of hours   **5.** a few minutes ago
6. in thirty (more) minutes   **7.** twenty years ago   **8.** thirty years ago
9. in a couple of years   **10.** ten weeks ago . . . in a few months

☐ **EXERCISE 11, p. 239.   *AGO or IN with A COUPLE OF or FEW.   (Chart 6-3)***

Open completion.
This should be done as seatwork or homework. Then students can read their answers aloud to
the whole class or a group, correcting each other if necessary.

   In this exercise and others in this unit, the present progressive is possible in some instances.
The present progressive is used for a future meaning when the speaker is expressing a planned
activity. For example, item 2 could be completed with *I am leaving in a few days* OR *My sister is
arriving in a few days.* This text does not present the use of the present progressive for a future
meaning, but some of your students may ask about it or use it spontaneously.

**CHART 6-4: USING *TODAY, TONIGHT,* AND *THIS +
MORNING, AFTERNOON, EVENING, WEEK,
MONTH, YEAR***

- It is difficult for some learners to understand that the time expressions in this list can be used with present, past, or future verb forms. The tense depends on the relationship between the time of the event or activity and the moment of speaking.

- Make up additional examples from the class context. For instance, if you are teaching an afternoon class, show how *this morning* refers to a past time and *this evening* to a future time. Show how past, present, and future tenses can truthfully be used with *this afternoon.*

    Examples: *I ate breakfast this morning. I'm going to eat dinner this evening.*
    I saw Pedro before class this afternoon. We're in class this afternoon.
    I'm going to go to the bookstore after class this afternoon.

☐ **EXERCISE 12, p. 240. *TODAY, TONIGHT, etc.* (Chart 6-4)**

Open completion.
Students should answer truthfully. They can work with partners or as a whole class.

SAMPLE ANSWERS: **4.** I ate breakfast earlier today.   **5.** I am sitting in English class right now.   **6.** I am going to meet my friends later today.   **7.** I brushed my teeth earlier this morning.   **8.** I am going to read the newspaper later this evening.

☐ **EXERCISE 13, p. 240. *TODAY, TONIGHT, etc.* (Chart 6-4)**

Open completion.
Pairs of students can cooperate to discuss various good sentences for each item, or you could lead a general discussion in which students call out various completions.

☐ **EXERCISE 14, p. 241. *TODAY, TONIGHT, etc.* (Chart 6-4)**

Oral.
Divide the class into groups of three and lead them through the example. All sentences will include *be going to.* The group should change roles after each item so that everyone gets a chance to be Students A, B, and C. In other words, the role of Student A rotates.

☐ **EXERCISE 15, p. 241. *TODAY, TONIGHT, etc.* (Chart 6-4)**

Oral.
This gives more practice with past and future verb phrases related to time adverbs. Partners should change roles after item 9.

CHART 6-5: FUTURE TIME: USING *WILL*

• In most cases, there is little difference in meaning between *will* and *be going to;* both are used to make predictions about the future.

• This text does not present the differences between *will* and *be going to*, but some questions may arise. *Be going to* (but not *will*) is used to express a preconceived plan (e.g., *I bought some wood because I'm going to build a bookcase*). *Will* (but not *be going to*) is used to volunteer or express willingness (e.g., *This chair is too heavy for you to carry alone. I'll help you.*). In this case, the use of *will* is related to its historical meaning of willingness or promise.

• This text does not present *shall* either, but you may be asked questions about it. *Shall* is used instead of *will* (with *I* and *we* as subjects) far more frequently in British English than American English. The use of *shall* to express future time is infrequent in American English.

   Shall has another meaning besides future. In expressions such as *Shall I call you tomorrow?* or *Shall we leave at eight?*, *shall* is not synonymous with *will*; rather, it expresses a polite offer of help or an invitation.

• *Won't* is pronounced /wount/.

☐ **EXERCISE 16, p. 242.** *Future time: using WILL.* *(Chart 6-5)*

   Oral; transformation.
   Be sure the students understand that they have not changed the meaning of the sentence by using *will* instead of *be going to*. (There are some very subtle distinctions between *will* and *be going to* that the students will come to understand much, much later in their experience with English. They cannot understand these distinctions at this point.)
   Model spoken contractions of *will* with nouns (e.g., "Fred'll") as well as pronouns.

   ANSWERS: **2.** Fred will not/won't come to our party.   **3.** He'll be out of town next week.   **4.** Sue will be in class tomorrow.   **5.** She has a cold, but she will not/won't stay home.   **6.** Jack and Peggy will meet us at the movie theater.   **7.** They will be there at 7:15.   **8.** Tina will stay home and watch TV tonight.   **9.** I will send this letter by express mail. [Note: *is* in the first sentence does not change to *will* because the sentence does not express a future meaning.]   **10.** My parents will stay at a hotel in Honolulu.   **11.** Hurry up, or we'll be late for the concert.   **12.** I will not/won't be at home this evening.   **13.** I'll wash the dishes and clean the kitchen after dinner. [Call the learners' attention to the parallel verbs, pointing out that the helping verb *will* is usually omitted from the second of the two verbs.]   **14.** You'll hurt yourself!

CHART 6-6: ASKING QUESTIONS WITH *WILL*

• You might ask students to compare these questions with those in Chart 6-1, looking for similarities in word order.

☐ **EXERCISE 17, p. 243.** *Asking questions with WILL.* *(Chart 6-6)*

   Transformation.
   The words in parentheses ( ) should not be spoken. They give the information necessary for completing the questions and answers. For additional practice, you might have students repeat part of this exercise, using *be going to*.

ANSWERS: **4.** A: Will the plane be on time?   B: Yes, it will.   **5.** A: Will dinner be ready in a few minutes?   B: Yes, it will.   **6.** When/What time will dinner be ready? **7.** When will you graduate?   **8.** Where will Mary go to school next year?   **9.** A: Will Jane and Mark be at the party?   B: No, they won't.   **10.** A: Will Mike arrive in Chicago next week?   B: Yes, he will.   **11.** Where will Mike be next week?   **12.** A: Will you be home early tonight?   B: No, I won't.   **13.** When/What time will Dr. Smith be back? **14.** A: Will you be ready to leave at 8:15?   B: Yes, I will.

CHART 6-7:   VERB SUMMARY: PRESENT, PAST, AND FUTURE

• This is a good review of the verb forms studied so far. You might divide the class into three groups, then have one group say the statement, one the negative, and one the question. Another possibility is to hand out a grid of the chart with the vertical and horizontal labels but no examples, then ask the students to make up their own examples or place those you dictate into the proper place in the grid.

• Discuss any questions students have about these forms.

☐ **EXERCISE 18, p. 245.   *Verb review.   (Chart 6-7)***

Fill-in-the-blanks.

ANSWERS: **2.** isn't doing [*do* is the main verb] . . . is writing   **3.** writes   **4.** doesn't write   **5.** don't expect   **6.** wrote . . . started   **7.** rang . . . was [*was writing* is past progressive; see Chart 10-8.]   **8.** didn't finish . . . talked . . . went   **9.** is going to write/will write   **10.** isn't going to write/won't write   **11.** Do you write   **12.** Did you write **13.** Are you going to write/Will you write

---

CHART 6-8:   VERB SUMMARY: FORMS OF *BE*

• *Be* is the main verb in these sentences. It is also the helping verb (auxiliary) in the present progressive and *be going to.* Help learners understand the difference.

• It is difficult to explain the meaning of *be* as a main verb. It may mean "exist" or "occupy a specific place" or "occur." Sometimes it is like the equals sign (=) in an equation: *Ann was late. (Ann = late)*

• You might divide the class into three groups, then have one group say the statement, one the negative, and one the question. Or you could make a grid, as suggested in the notes above for Chart 6-7, and have the students fill it in.

☐ **EXERCISE 19, p. 247.   *Review of BE.   (Chart 6-8)***

Fill-in-the-blanks.
Give students time to read the complete item before answering, because they have to relate the verb form to the time adverb as well as to the singular or plural subject.

ANSWERS: **1.** am . . . wasn't . . . was . . . Were you . . . Was Carmen   **2.** were . . . weren't **3.** are going to be/will be . . . am going to be/will be . . . Are you going to be/Will you be . . . Is Yuko going to be/Will Yuko be   **4.** isn't . . . is . . . aren't . . . are [*whale* /hweil/ or /weil/; *dolphin* /dɔlfən/]

☐ **EXERCISE 20, p. 247.** *Verb review.* *(Chart 6-8)*

Fill-in-the-blanks.
Note in the example: The main verb is *have*. In British English, this question is sometimes "Have you a bicycle?" and the answer is "Yes, I have." But in American English, the auxiliary *do* is required in the question and the short answer.

Assign as homework or seatwork. Students can correct their work in pairs if you wish.

ANSWERS: **2.** A: Did you walk   B: didn't . . . rode   **3.** A: Do you know   B: do
A: did you meet   B: met [incorrect: I knew Mr. Park yesterday. (Note: First you must meet someone, then you know him/her.)]   **4.** Do you get up . . . are you going to get up/will you get up [also correct: At six-thirty.]   **5.** A: do you usually study . . . Do you go   B: don't like   **6.** A: Are you going to be/Will you be   B: am/will . . . am not going to be/won't be [*the day after tomorrow* = two days from now; similar expressions: *the week after next, the month after next,* etc.]   **7.** A: Did Yuko call
B: did . . . talked   A: Did she tell   B: didn't . . . didn't say   A: was . . . ran . . . didn't want . . . tried . . . ran [Note: A dog *walks* or *runs*; we use the same verbs for humans. The bike *ran into* a truck, which means they collided or hit together.]   B: Is he   A: isn't . . . is   **8.** A: Do whales breathe
B: do   A: Does a whale have [*lungs* /ləŋz/= two organs in the body that pull in and push out air]
B: does   A: Is a whale   B: isn't . . . is   **9.** A: Did you watch . . . is . . . is . . . Do you like
B: do . . . read . . . is *Star Trek* going to be/will *Star Trek* be . . . am going to try/will try . . .
does "trek" mean   A: means   B: does "journey" mean   A: means

☐ **EXERCISE 21, p. 250.** *Verb review.* *(Chart 6-8)*

Oral/written.
You could assign this as homework or use it as a test. Students have to use verb forms, tenses, and time adverbs correctly together. Most sentences should include *because*.

Students should write Description #1 as a connected discourse paragraph, then do the same for the other two descriptions.

CHART 6-9:   USING *WHAT* + A FORM OF *DO*

- Questions with *what* + a form of *do* are common and useful, especially in everyday conversation.

- Examples (a) and (c) show the use of *do* as both main verb and helping (auxiliary) verb.

☐ **EXERCISE 22, p. 251.** *Using WHAT + a form of DO.* *(Chart 6-9)*

Fill-in-the-blanks.
This exercise gives learners practice in using the verb *do* in the present, past, and future. Give them time to work out the verb tense, the word order, and the singular or plural forms. You could divide the class in half, with one part saying the sentence together and the other saying the "B" response. Change roles after item 6.

ANSWERS: **2.** A: did you do   B: came   **3.** A: are you going to do/will you do   B: am going to come/will come [*Be going to,* not *will,* would be the idiomatic usage in this item and others in this exercise, but both *be going to* and *will* are correct. Students will pick up subtle distinctions between the usage of these two future forms as they gain experience with the language. In the experience of the author, involved explanations of these subtle, idiomatic distinctions are usually not helpful.]   **4.** A: did you do
B: watched   **5.** A: do you do   B: watch   **6.** A: are you going to do/will you do
B: am going to watch/will watch   **7.** A: are you doing   B: am doing   **8.** A: does Maria do
B: goes   **9.** A: are the students doing   B: are working   **10.** A: are they going to do/will
they do   B: are going to take/will take   **11.** A: did Boris do   B: went   **12.** A: does the
teacher do   B: puts . . . looks . . . says

□ **EXERCISE 23, p. 252.** *Using WHAT + a form of DO.* *(Chart 6-9)*

> *Oral.*
> After the control of Exercise 22, this one gives learners a chance to use their own words. Students may work with a partner. They should change roles after item 7.

CHART 6-10: *MAY/MIGHT* vs. *WILL*

- *May, might,* and *will* are some of the many modal auxiliaries in English. By focusing on just a few, learners should not become confused. Modals give special qualities to the meaning of main verbs, such as possibility, necessity, or advisability.

- Stress that *might* and *may* have the same meaning here. Sometimes students have been taught that *might* is the past tense of *may*. *Might* is used as a past form of *may* only in noun clauses introduced by a past tense verb (e.g., *He said, "I may come"* can become *He said he might come* in reported speech). *May* has additional meanings that are not presented in this lesson.

- For an explanation of *may be* (verb) and *maybe* (adverb), see Chart 6-11.

□ **EXERCISE 24, p. 253.** *MAY/MIGHT vs. WILL.* *(Chart 6-10)*

> *Semi-controlled completion.*
> These modals add meaning to the main verbs. They express the speaker's opinion as to degree of certainty or uncertainty. Students should complete these sentences with real information. You might change some of the sentences to suit the local situation better.
>
> Items 14 and 15 are included more as a good topic for a spontaneous classroom discussion involving the target structures than as good, clear examples of the use of *will* vs. *may/might*. Downplay the grammar and engage the class in expressing their opinions about the possibility of beings in the universe besides ourselves.

□ **EXERCISE 25, p. 254.** *MAY/MIGHT vs. WILL.* *(Chart 6-10)*

> *Written.*
> Some students may be confused by the directions (which is the fault of the directions, to be sure). The students are to use either *be going to* or *may/might* (not both) in any particular sentence. The directions intend for the students to switch back and forth as they wish: e.g., 2. *Then I'm going to go to the computer lab.* 3. *After that I may go to the library, or I might go back to my apartment for lunch.* Etc.
>
> You might suggest that the students may use other verb forms besides *be going to* and *may/might,* as they wish, but encourage them to try to practice with those forms as much as they can.
>
> The meaning of *be going to* is similar to *will/won't* in the examples in Chart 6-10. They express certainty.

□ **EXERCISE 26, p. 254.** *Review of Past Tense.*

> *Written.*
> This exercise is a review of past tense forms. The answers cannot include *may, might,* or *will/won't.* Be sure students understand this before they try to complete the sentences. Point out that they're writing about past events that they are sure happened, compared to future events, which there is no way to be absolutely sure will occur.

CHART 6-11: *MAYBE* (ONE WORD) *vs. MAY BE* (TWO WORDS)

- The historical development of English has produced these two forms with similar meanings. *Maybe* is an adverb written as a single word and placed only at the beginning of a sentence. *May be* is a modal auxiliary + a main verb.

- In speaking, *may be* is longer with two equally stressed syllables. *Maybe* is stressed on the first syllable: /ˈmeybi/.

☐ **EXERCISE 27, p. 255.** *MAYBE vs. MAY BE.* *(Chart 6-11)*

Structure identification.
Items 1 and 2 have exactly the same meaning. Items 4 and 5 have almost the same meaning. Help learners understand this.

ANSWERS: **3.** may = part of the verb *may go*   **4.** Maybe = adverb   **5.** may = part of the verb *may like*   **6.** may = part of the verb *may be;* Maybe = adverb

☐ **EXERCISE 28, p. 255.** *MAYBE vs. MAY BE.* *(Chart 6-11)*

Controlled completion.
The adverb *maybe* can be a complete short answer, as in item 1. *May/might* must follow a subject in a short answer: "I don't know. I might."
    Items 2 and 3 show the difference in forms with the same meanings. Items 4 and 5 also show this.

ANSWERS: **3.** Maybe   **4.** may/might   **5.** Maybe   **6.** Maybe   **7.** may/might
8. Maybe . . . may/might   **9.** Maybe . . . maybe   **10.** Maybe . . . maybe   **11.** Maybe
(also correct: I might/I may.)   **12.** Maybe . . . maybe . . . may/might . . . may/might

☐ **EXERCISE 29, p. 256.** *MAYBE vs. MAY BE.* *(Chart 6-11)*

Controlled completion.
Students should practice pronouncing these two forms. (See the comments above for Chart 6-11.)

ANSWERS: **3.** may be   **4.** may be   **5.** Maybe   **6.** may be . . . Maybe

☐ **EXERCISE 30, p. 257.** *MAYBE vs. MAY/MIGHT.* *(Charts 6-10 → 6-11)*

Oral (books closed).
Keep the pace moving from one student to another, giving them just enough time to think of a truthful answer.

☐ **EXERCISE 31, p. 257.** *MAYBE vs. MAY/MIGHT.* *(Charts 6-10 → 6-11)*

Oral (books closed).
This is intended to be a fun and challenging exercise after the control of the preceding exercises. Now the students get to use what they've been learning so that they can express their own ideas. Don't rush through this exercise. Slowly and gently encourage your students to express their opinions.

CHART 6-12: FUTURE TIME CLAUSES WITH *BEFORE,*
**   *AFTER,* AND *WHEN***

- This feature of English seems completely illogical—a future time clause does not permit the use of *will* or *be going to* with its verb.

- Emphasize that the examples in (b) are incorrect. Make sure the students understand which parts of the sentences are the errors (the boldface type indicates the errors). These examples represent extremely common (and logical, it should be said) errors made by all levels of learners.

☐ **EXERCISE 32, p. 258.   *Future time clauses.   (Chart 6-12)***

> *Structure identification.*
> After students identify the time clauses, you could review word order in sentences with time clauses and the use of commas, as presented in Chart 5-18, page 90. Change the positions of the adverb clauses (i.e., time clauses) and note the difference in punctuation in the new sentence.

> *ANSWERS:*   **2.** After I get home tonight   **3.** before he leaves the office today
> **4.** when I go to the market tomorrow   **5.** Before I go to bed tonight   **6.** after I graduate next year

☐ **EXERCISE 33, p. 259.   *Future time clauses.   (Chart 6-12)***

> *Fill-in-the-blanks.*
> This exercise forces students to pay attention to the differences in verb forms in the main clause and the future time clause. Give them time to see and discuss these differences.

> *ANSWERS:*   **2.** am going to buy/will buy . . . go   **3.** finish . . . am going to take/will take
> **4.** see . . . am going to ask/will ask   **5.** go . . . am going to meet/will meet   **6.** is going to change/will change [*change clothes* = take off some clothes and put on different clothes] . . . works

☐ **EXERCISE 34, p. 260.   *Future time clauses.   (Chart 6-12)***

> *Oral (books closed).*
> You should lead this exercise like a conversation. Keep a lively pace, but pay attention to the students' verb forms, especially in future time clauses. You may want to photocopy this exercise on a single page so you can walk around the room without carrying your textbook.

CHART 6-13:   CLAUSES WITH *IF*

- An *if*-clause states a condition, and the main clause states the effect or result of that condition.

- Point out the use of commas, which is the same for other adverb clauses. (See the footnote on p. 216 in Chapter 5 of the textbook.)

- In (c) and (d) students learn that *if*-clauses are like future time clauses—they do not permit the use of *will* or *be going to.*

☐ **EXERCISE 35, p. 261.** *Clauses with IF.*   *(Chart 6-13)*

Fill-in-the-blanks.
Give students time to think about verb tenses, singular/plural forms, helping verbs, etc., before they answer. This exercise is intended to clarify the information in Chart 6-13 and let you, the teacher, know if your students have understood what you intended them to understand. In this way, this exercise is typical of every other exercise that immediately follows a chart.

Note on the illustration: The body of water is a large lake or freshwater inland sea, not an ocean. Hence the sign about not drinking the water. The purpose of the illustration is to generate brief spontaneous discussion with *if*-clauses about what will happen to our world if we continue to pollute it.

ANSWERS: **2.** is . . . am going to go/will go   **3.** am not going to stay/won't stay . . . is
4. don't feel . . . am not going to go/won't go [Both *feel well* and *feel good* are acceptable in current usage.]
5. is going to stay/will stay . . . doesn't feel   **6.** am going to stay/will stay . . . go
7. are . . . am going to go/will go   **8.** continue . . . are going to suffer/will suffer

☐ **EXERCISE 36, p. 262.**   *Clauses with IF.*   *(Chart 6-13)*

Oral (books closed).
Students should work in pairs, listening carefully to each other. They should help each other produce correct sentences.

☐ **EXERCISE 37, p. 262.**   *Clauses with IF.*   *(Chart 6-13)*

Oral and written.
Both students should fill out the calendar in their books on page 263. Then one of them takes Student A's part in the activity, and they follow the instructions. Then they can switch roles.

Lead everyone carefully through the instructions, then walk around as they work. Clarify the instructions as needed so that every student produces a written paragraph based on an interview.

**CHART 6-14:   EXPRESSING HABITUAL PRESENT WITH
TIME CLAUSES AND *IF*-CLAUSES**

- *Habitual* means "repeated frequently as part of a routine." In words that beginning students understand, you could say that habitual means "something you do again and again and again" or "something you usually do Monday, Tuesday, Wednesday, Thursday, Friday, Saturday, and Sunday."

- Lead students through the examples so they see the differences between (a) and (b) and between (c) and (d). Help them understand the notion of an habitual activity.

- In (d) it may be helpful to add the word *always* or *usually* before *wear.*

- The grammar of present vs. future verb forms in the result clause of a factual conditional sentence may be too difficult for students at this level. The author is unsure. Use your own judgment as to how much emphasis you place on this chart. Keep in mind that all the grammar in this text is revisited again and again in other texts in this series. If your students don't understand this grammar right now, they'll have another chance in other texts.

☐ **EXERCISE 38, p. 264.** *Time clauses and IF-clauses.* **(Chart 6-14)**

Fill-in-the-blanks.
Items 1 and 2 show the difference between habitual and future forms of the same sentence. Items 3 and 4, 5 and 6, and 7 and 8 are related in the same way. After these sentences are discussed, students could work in pairs to complete the rest of the exercise.

ANSWERS: **1.** go . . . usually stay   **2.** go . . . am going to stay/will stay   **3.** go . . . am going to have/will have   **4.** go . . . usually have   **5.** am . . . usually stay . . . go   **6.** am . . . am going to stay/will stay . . . (am going to) go/ (will) go [Note: The helping verb is not usually repeated after *and*.]   **7.** get . . . usually sit . . . read   **8.** get . . . am going to sit/will sit . . . (am going to) read/(will) read   **9.** are going to go/will go . . . is   **10.** like . . . is   **11.** often yawn . . . stretch . . . wake   **12.** am going to buy/will buy . . . go   **13.** walks . . . is   **14.** go . . . am going to stay/will stay . . . leave . . . am going to go/will go   **15.** goes . . . is . . . likes . . . takes

☐ **EXERCISE 39, p. 265.** *Time clauses and IF-clauses.* **(Chart 6-14)**

Oral (books closed).
This exercise is intended to suggest topics for teacher-student interaction; it's not intended as a script to be read verbatim. The idea is for you to get your students talking about their lives and interests—using present and future time clauses.

☐ **EXERCISE 40, p. 265.** *Time clauses and IF-clauses.* **(Chart 6-14)**

Open completion.
Take a silent moment to look at this exercise and pretend that it's in a language you don't know: Tagalog, Navaho, Greek, whatever. Understand that you could not possibly make meaningful statements from these structure hints. Then understand what an accomplishment you and your students have made to get to this point. Congratulate your students (and yourself)!

☐ **EXERCISE 41, p. 265.** *Review.* **(Chapter 6)**

Oral/written.
Some students will be able to make longer lists than others. Perhaps suggest a minimum of three predictions and a maximum of six.

☐ **EXERCISE 42, p. 266.** *Review.* **(Chapter 6)**

Oral/written.
This is a sort of "fortune-teller" exercise. Your students don't know each other well, but do have impressions of each other. Tell them to use their powers of observation and intuition to predict the future, to pretend to be fortune tellers. Maybe they want to read each other's palms? The exercise should be light-hearted and fun.

EXPANSION: Follow this exercise with an assignment for the students to write a composition about what is going to happen in their own lives in the next 50 years. When you return the papers, make sure to tell the students to save these compositions in a special place and look at them when they are past 60.

☐ **EXERCISE 43, p. 266.** *Review.* *(Chapter 6)*

    Oral/written.

You can raise the interest of the students in this exercise by the way you introduce it. Tell them about the mysterious letter, and have them decide how much money it contains. Then ask for suggestions about what they would do with so much money. After a short discussion, tell them to read about all six letters and choose the one they want. Tell them how long their description should be (perhaps 3 to 6 sentences).

CHART 6-15: MORE IRREGULAR VERBS

• The rest of this chapter has review exercises using the verb tenses that have been presented so far in this textbook. Prior to those review exercises, more irregular verbs are introduced. The text asks students to learn only a few irregular verbs at a time, not the entire list in the APPENDIX at once. See the comments in this *Teacher's Guide* for Chart 5-12 for ways of handling Charts 6-15 and 6-16 and their accompanying exercises.

• Using Exercise 44, lead the class through the list of verbs, having them pronounce both forms. Discuss any meanings that are not clear.

• There are two verbs *hang* in English. The one in this chart means "to suspend, or to fasten something above with no support below." The other verb *hang* means "to kill a person by suspending with a rope around the neck"; the past tense of this verb is *hanged*.

☐ **EXERCISE 44, p. 266.** *Review.* *(Chapter 6)*

    Oral (books closed).

Lead the class through the exercise, perhaps writing the verb forms on the chalkboard as you read out the sentences. When you ask the questions, you could allow the whole class to call out short answers, or you could ask individuals to respond. (You might want to copy this exercise in advance on a single page so you don't have to hold the textbook.)

    Some pronunciations:

    In item 2, *lose* is pronounced /luz/. This should not be confused with the adjective *loose*, which is pronounced /lus/.

    In item 8, *wear* /wɛr/; *wore* /wɔr/ (the same as *war*).

    In item 9, *steal* /stil/.

    In item 10, *said* /sɛd/.

☐ **EXERCISE 45, p. 267.** *More irregular verbs.* *(Chart 6-15)*

    Semi-controlled and open completion.

Students can work in pairs. Some of the items contain phrases and situations that could lead to discussions about cultural traditions.

    ANSWERS: **1.** began   **2.** told [*tell a lie* = say an untruth; *be upset* = be angry or very sad]
   3. found   **4.** lost   **5.** hung   **6.** tore   **7.** sold   **8.** said   **9.** stole   **10.** wore

☐ **EXERCISE 46, p. 268.** *More irregular verbs.* *(Chart 6-15)*

    Fill-in-the-blanks.

Students must be alert to important cues in each sentence to help them use the correct verb forms and tenses.

ANSWERS: **1.** A: Are you going to be/Will you be   B: am going to be/will be   **2.** lost . . . think . . . left   **3.** is improving [*getting along* = adjusting to a new situation]   **4.** A: Did she tell . . . did she tell [*honest* /anəst/ (The letter "h" is not pronounced.)]   B: told   **5.** A: Did you write   B: sent   **6.** want to look . . . need to find [The classified section lists short advertisements of things for sale or for rent and jobs that are available.]   **7.** A: did you go   B: went . . . saw . . . talked . . . met [*cousin* /kəzən/]   **8.** A: Are you going to study? [*Will you study* can be considered grammatically correct, but *are you going to study* is idiomatically correct.]   B: will watch . . . will listen [*Will*, not *be going to*, is usually used in noun clauses introduced by *think* and in clauses with *maybe*.] . . . don't want to study [Use the present tense because this is what you don't want now.]   **9.** A: Did you do   B: was . . . went . . . slept   **10.** A: said   B: didn't understand [*at first* = in the beginning]   **11.** woke up . . . went . . . stole . . . took . . . got . . . tore . . . borrowed . . . lost . . . found

---

CHART 6-16: MORE IRREGULAR VERBS	

- Note that *cost, cut, hit,* and *hurt* have no change in their past tense forms.
- Use Exercise 47 to lead the students through this list of verb forms.

☐ **EXERCISE 47, p. 270.   *More irregular verbs.   (Chart 6-16)***

Oral (books closed).
Follow the suggestions for Exercise 44 above. You might point out that *give* is the opposite of *receive; lend* is the opposite of *borrow; forget* is the opposite of *remember; spend* is the opposite of *save;* and *shut* is the same as *close* and the opposite of *open.*

☐ **EXERCISE 48, p. 271   *More irregular verbs.   (Chart 6-16)***

Fill-in-the-blanks.
After assigning this exercise as homework, you should lead the class through it leisurely, answering any and all questions while checking their understanding of the irregular verb forms, tenses, and singular/plural agreement.

ANSWERS: **1.** A: does a new car cost   B: costs   **2.** cost [past tense]   **3.** gave   **4.** hit   **5.** B: forgot   A: forgot   **6.** made   **7.** puts   **8.** put [past tense]   **9.** spent   **10.** lent   **11.** cuts   **12.** cut [past tense]

☐ **EXERCISE 49, p. 272.   *More irregular verbs.   (Chart 6-16)***

Oral (books closed).
Students can work in groups of two or three, taking turns in responding and checking each other's correctness. Their books can be open. Give them a time limit of about 10 minutes to finish all 54 items.
   This exercise can be returned to again and again as a quick review of irregular verbs.

□ **EXERCISE 50, p. 272.**   *Review.   (Chapter 6)*

Fill-in-the-blanks.
Some of these items contain idioms and cultural information that may need some discussion.

ANSWERS: **1.** am going to cut/will cut [*cut class* = not go to class]   **2.** took [*take a plane/taxi/bus* = use public transportation] . . . flew   **3.** usually walk . . . take   **4.** A: did you meet   B: met   **5.** hit   **6.** began . . . got [*get to* = arrive at a place]   **7.** A: did the movie begin . . . Were you   B: made [*make it* = arrive just in time, but almost too late]   **8.** Are you listening?   **9.** lost . . . forgot . . . gave . . . lost . . . stole . . . didn't have [*actually* = really, truthfully; *I see* = I understand]   **10.** A: stole   B: is   **11.** A: Are you going to stay/Will you stay   B: am going to take/will take . . . am going to visit/will visit [also possible: Are you staying . . . am taking . . . am visiting (In these cases, the present progressive is used to express a planned future activity. This use of the present progressive is not taught in this textbook.)]   A: are you going to be/will you be   **12.** A: are you wearing [*cast* = a strong plaster covering to protect a bone while it heals]   B: broke . . . stepped   **13.** A: Do you want to go [present tense because you want something now]   B: Are you going to go/Will you go   A: want to get [*get* = be able to go] . . . enjoy   **14.** A: Did you see   B: spoke . . . called   **15.** B: isn't . . . left   A: Is she going to be/Will she be . . . did she go   B: went

□ **EXERCISE 51, p. 275.**   *Review.   (Chapter 6)*

Controlled completion; multiple choice.
It's a good idea to lead the class through a discussion of these items because some of them contain adverbs and other signals that learners often overlook.

ANSWERS: **1.** D   **2.** B   **3.** C   **4.** B   **5.** C   **6.** B   **7.** C   **8.** C   **9.** A   **10.** D

□ **EXERCISE 52, p. 276.**   *Error analysis.   (Chapter 6)*

Error analysis.

ANSWERS: **1.** Is Ivan <u>going to go</u> to work tomorrow? OR <u>Will</u> Ivan go to work tomorrow?   **2.** When <u>will you</u> call me?   **3.** Will Tom <u>meet</u> us for dinner tomorrow?   **4.** We went to a movie <u>last</u> night.   **5.** If <u>it's</u> cold tomorrow morning, my car won't start.   **6.** We <u>may be</u> late for the concert tonight.   **7.** Did you <u>find</u> your keys?   **8.** What time <u>are you</u> going to come tomorrow?   **9.** My brother <u>won't be</u> there.   **10.** Fatima will call us tonight when she <u>arrives</u> home safely.   **11.** Mr. Wong will <u>sell</u> his business and <u>retire</u> next year.   **12.** <u>Will you be</u> in Venezuela next year?   **13.** Emily <u>may be</u> at the party. OR Emily <u>will be</u> at the party.   **14.** I'm going to return home in a couple of <u>months</u>.   **15.** When <u>I</u> see you tomorrow, I'll return your book to you.   **16.** I saw Jim three <u>days</u> ago.   **17.** I <u>may not</u> be in class tomorrow.   **18.** Ahmed puts his books on his desk when he <u>walks</u> into his apartment. OR Ahmed <u>put</u> his books on his desk when he walked into his apartment.   **19.** A thief <u>stole</u> my bicycle.   **20.** I'll see my parents when I <u>return</u> home for a visit next July.

☐ **EXERCISE 53, p. 277.** *Review.* *(Chapter 6)*

Fill-in-the-blanks.

This is a long exercise in the form of a story. Give students time to complete it as homework or seatwork, then lead them through the whole thing carefully. Perhaps one student could read a paragraph, then you can discuss any mistakes or questions. Check the spelling of some verb forms.

Discuss the moral of the story with your students. Do our fears bring about our own misfortunes? Do we call bad luck to us?

EXPANSION: Have the students retell the story in writing and then apply the moral, as they understand it, to their own lives.

ANSWERS: **(1)** are   **(2)** are staying   **(3)** like . . . always makes   **(4)** tells
(5) go   **(6)** went   **(7)** asked . . . agreed   **(8)** put . . . brushed   **(9)** sat
(10) are you going to tell/will you tell   **(11)** begin . . . am going to give/will give
(12) love   **(13)** am going to tell/will tell   **(14)** was   **(15)** was   **(16)** saw
(17) was . . . ran   **(18)** stayed   **(19)** was . . . got   **(20)** stayed   **(21)** found . . .
needed   **(22)** to eat   **(23)** put   **(24)** didn't smell   **(25)** didn't see
(26) hopped . . . found   **(27)** saw   **(28)** looked   **(29)** heard   **(30)** didn't see
(31) decided   **(32)** wanted to rest   **(33)** said   **(34)** heard . . . spotted
(35) flew . . . picked   **(36)** didn't know   **(37)** ate   **(38)** are   **(39)** expect
(40) Do you understand   **(41)** have   **(42)** am going to go/will go . . . to get
(43) is going to be/will be   **(44)** are we going to do/will we do   **(45)** have . . . are going
to go/will go   **(46)** are   **(47)** are going to see/will see   **(48)** are going to see/will see
(49) see . . . are going to have/will have   **(50)** are going to have/will have

Chapter 7: EXPRESSING ABILITY

ORDER OF CHAPTER	CHARTS	EXERCISES
Can	7-1 → 7-2	Ex. 1 → 5
Know how to	7-3	Ex. 6 → 7
Could: past of *can*	7-4	Ex. 8 → 11
Very and *too* + adjective	7-5	Ex. 12 → 14
Too many and *too much* + noun	7-6	Ex. 15 → 16
Too + adjective + infinitive	7-7 → 7-8	Ex. 17 → 19
Enough	7-9 → 7-11	Ex. 20 → 26
Be able to	7-12	Ex. 27 → 28
Polite questions: *may I, could I,* and *can I*	7-13	Ex. 29 → 30
Polite questions: *could you* and *would you*	7-14	Ex. 31 → 33
Imperative sentences	7-15	Ex. 34 → 36
Two, too, and *to*	7-16	Ex. 37
Using *at* and *in* for locations	7-17	Ex. 38 → 40
Review		Ex. 41 → 45
More irregular verbs	7-18	Ex. 46 → 48

General Notes on Chapter 7

English has many ways to express ability. This chapter begins with the most common: *can/can't.* Less familiar in grammar books but very useful is a short section on the phrase *know how to.* Then *could* is introduced as the past tense form of *can.* Some modifiers that often accompany statements of ability are *very, too,* and *enough,* which are presented next. The quantifiers *too many, too much,* and *more* are also introduced. Then a section compares *can/could* with the phrase *be able to.* Since *could, can,* and *may* have already been introduced with other meanings, they now return in polite questions and requests. The final structure in this chapter is imperative sentences, also called "commands." The chapter ends with more practice with prepositions of location and irregular verbs as well as exercises to review the whole chapter.

CHART 7-1:   USING *CAN*

- Lead the students through the examples, allowing them to notice and explain the meanings and important features.

- In listening to English speakers, learners often misunderstand the words *can* and *can't*. This is usually because of the pronunciation. In a short answer, *can* is pronounced /kæn/, as expected. However, in a statement or question, *can* is pronounced with no stress and almost no vowel sound: /kn/ or /kən/. The negative form *can't* is pronounced with more stress but almost no final *t* sound: /kæn'/. The final /n'/ sound is very short and almost like a voiceless "ng" sound.

☐ **EXERCISE 1, p. 281.**   *Using CAN.   (Chart 7-1)*

Oral.
Remind students not to stress the word *can,* but to stress *can't.* Thus, sentence 1 will have stress on *bird* and *sing,* and sentence 2 will have three stresses: *cow, can't,* and *fly.*

ANSWERS: **1.** can   **2.** can't   **3.** can't   **4.** can   **5.** can't   **6.** can't
7. can   **8.** can't   **9.** can't   **10.** can   **11.** can't   **12.** can   **13.** can
14. can't

☐ **EXERCISE 2, p. 282.**   *Using CAN.   (Chart 7-1)*

Oral.
This exercise can be fun if students tell the truth about themselves. It also introduces some new vocabulary, so it's good for the whole class to discuss the items together. In their answers, make sure no one uses an infinitive with *to* after *can.*
 In item 1, *whistle* = make music by blowing air through the lips.
 In item 6, *lift* = raise up in your arms.
 In item 7, *a stick-shift car* = an automobile that has a lever for changing (shifting) gears as the car goes faster.
 In item 8, *fix* = repair; *a flat tire* = a tire (BrE: tyre) that has lost air pressure.
 In item 10, *float* = lie on the water without moving arms or legs.
 In item 11, *ski* = move over snow or water while standing on flat wooden or plastic skis.
 In item 12, *arithmetic* = basic adding, subtracting, multiplying, and dividing numbers.
 In item 14, *sew* = use a needle and thread.
 In item 15, *chopsticks* = round sticks of wood held in the hand and used for putting food into one's mouth.
 In item 16, *wiggle* = move rapidly back and forth.

CHART 7-2:   USING *CAN:* QUESTIONS

- Ask students to compare these examples with those using *will* in Chart 6-6. They should be able to tell you the similarities in word order.

- *Can* refers either to the present or to the future. There is no difference in form. The context of the sentence or conversation gives the necessary information about the time.

□ **EXERCISE 3, p. 282.** *Using CAN: questions.* *(Chart 7-2)*

Transformation.

Remind students to pronounce *can* with no stress and almost no vowel. The words in parentheses are not to be spoken; they only provide information for the response.

ANSWERS: **3.** A: Can Jim play the piano? B: No, he can't. **4.** A: Can you whistle? B: Yes, I can. **5.** A: Can you go shopping with me this afternoon? B: Yes, I can. **6.** A: Can Carmen ride a bicycle? B: No, she can't. **7.** A: Can elephants swim? B: Yes, they can. **8.** A: Can the students finish this exercise quickly? B: Yes, they can. **9.** A: Can you stand on your head? B: Yes, I can. **10.** A: Can the doctor see me tomorrow? B: Yes, he/she can. **11.** A: Can we have pets in the dormitory? B: No, we can't.

□ **EXERCISE 4, p. 283.** *Using CAN: questions.* *(Chart 7-2)*

Oral.

Students can work in pairs while you walk around and listen to them. They should change roles A and B after item 10.

In items 7 and 13 they should use the name of a nationality or a language in the parentheses.

□ **EXERCISE 5, p. 284.** *Using CAN: questions.* *(Chart 7-2)*

Oral.

In this exercise, students are combining repetitive pattern practice with the communication of real information in a dialogue with a classmate.

Lead the class through the example, then let them work in pairs, changing A and B roles after item 8.

In items 2, 4, and 12, *get* = obtain, buy.

In item 3, *a window fan* = an electric fan that fits into a window to move air and cool the room.

In item 10, *a hammer* = a metal tool for pounding nails into wood in order to fasten two pieces of wood together.

In item 11, *a zebra* = an African animal, similar to a horse, with black and white stripes.

In item 13, *an encyclopedia* /ɛnsaikləpidiə/ = a volume of articles on many topics arranged in alphabetical order.

In item 15, *a sandwich* /sændwɪč/ = some meat, cheese, or fresh greens between two slices of bread.

In item 16, *cash a check* = get money from a bank or a shop by writing a check.

CHART 7-3: USING *KNOW HOW TO*	

• Using *do you know how to* to express ability in a question is much more common than using *can*.

• The basic pattern for using the helping verb *do* in questions is presented in Chart 2-10 on page 61 of the textbook.

☐ **EXERCISE 6, p. 284.** *Using KNOW HOW TO.* *(Chart 7-3)*

> *Oral.*
> Lead the class through the example, then let them work in pairs, changing A and B roles after item 8.
>> In items 4, 10, and 11, *get to (a place)* = find your way there.
>> In item 13, *a screwdriver* = a slender metal tool for turning screws into wood or metal in order to fasten two pieces together.
>> In item 16, *the square root of a number* = a number that, multiplied by itself, produces the original number (for example, 3 is the square root of 9 because 3 x 3 = 9, or $3^2 = 9$).

☐ **EXERCISE 7, p. 285.** *Using KNOW HOW TO.* *(Chart 7-3)*

> *Oral/written.*
> This is a kind of interview. If it is not convenient for your students to walk around in the classroom, you could have them interview some English speakers outside of class and bring back their reports later. Or they could form groups of four to six classmates and find out the abilities represented in a group.

CHART 7-4: USING *COULD*: PAST OF *CAN*

- This is only one meaning of the word *could*. *Could* is a complicated word; in fact, all of the modals are complicated words with nuances and idiomatic usages that do not lend themselves to easy explanations.

- When *could* is used to mean past ability, it is usually used in the negative. Other expressions are more commonly used to express affirmative past ability: for example, *managed to* or *was/were able to*. (Examples: *I managed to finish my homework before midnight last night. Fred was able to fix my radio for me.*) For this reason, Exercises 8, 9, and 10 focus on negative *could*. It's best to avoid affirmative *could* for ability at this stage in the learners' experience.

- It is important to show how the time/tense relationship is established in each pair of examples. A period of time in the past must be established (e.g., *last month, yesterday,* or another verb in the past tense) so that the word *could* may be used appropriately.

☐ **EXERCISE 8, p. 285.** *Using COULD: past of CAN.* *(Chart 7-4)*

> *Controlled and/or open completion.*
> Students are gaining experience with *because*-clauses as well as the target structure of *couldn't*. This exercise prepares the learners for the next exercise, in which they have to make up their own *because*-clauses.
>
> *POSSIBLE RESPONSES:* **2.** couldn't call you **3.** couldn't watch TV **4.** couldn't light the candles **5.** couldn't come to class **6.** couldn't listen to music **7.** couldn't wash his clothes **8.** couldn't go swimming **9.** couldn't get into my car **10.** couldn't go to the movie

☐ **EXERCISE 9, p. 286.** *Using COULD: past of CAN.* *(Chart 7-4)*

> *Oral (books closed).*
> Ask each question with a tone and facial expression that show that you are truly interested in each student's response. If you wish, you might follow up a response with an additional comment such as "Oh, I'm so sorry" or "Oh? I didn't know that," etc.

□ **EXERCISE 10, p. 286.** *Using COULD: past of CAN.* *(Chart 7-4)*

Oral (books closed).
Give students a few seconds to think of a good response. Perhaps ask for volunteers to answer.

□ **EXERCISE 11, p. 287.** *Using COULD: past of CAN.* *(Chart 7-4)*

Error analysis.
Students can work individually or with partners. You might make it a kind of contest to see who can find and correct all the mistakes first.

ANSWERS: **1.** Could you <u>drive</u> a car when you were thirteen years old? **2.** If your brother goes to the graduation party, he can <u>meet</u> my sister. **3.** He <u>couldn't</u> understand spoken English before he moved to Canada, but now he <u>speaks</u> and <u>understands</u> English very well. **4.** I couldn't <u>open</u> the door because I didn't have a key. **5.** When Ernest arrived at the airport last Tuesday, he <u>couldn't</u> find the right gate. **6.** I <u>can't</u> hear it.

CHART 7-5: USING *VERY* AND *TOO* + ADJECTIVE

• The words *very* and *too* are often called intensifiers. They give a stronger meaning to the adjectives that follow.

• It is difficult for some learners to remember that the intensifier *too* gives a negative meaning to the adjective. You might demonstrate the natural tendency for a speaker to frown and shake his or her head from side to side negatively when using *too* in this way.

• The drawings illustrate the meanings of examples (a) and (b) very clearly.

□ **EXERCISE 12, p. 288.** *Using TOO + adjective.* *(Chart 7-5)*

Controlled and/or open completion.
This exercise gives practice with the negative meaning of *too* + adjective. Give students a few minutes to work out the answers, then lead the class through all the items.

ANSWERS: **1.** eat it. **2.** buy it. **3.** go swimming. **4.** reach the cookie jar. **5.** do his homework. **6.** take a break. **7.** sleep. **8.** lift it.

□ **EXERCISE 13, p. 288.** *Using TOO + adjective.* *(Chart 7-5)*

Controlled and/or open completion.
Again, this exercise gives practice with the negative meaning of *too* + adjective.

ANSWERS: **1.** too heavy. **2.** too young. **3.** too noisy. **4.** too cold. **5.** too tired. **6.** too expensive. **7.** too small/too tight. **8.** too tall.

□ **EXERCISE 14, p. 289.** *Using VERY and TOO + adjective.* *(Chart 7-5)*

Controlled completion.
After Exercises 12 and 13, learners should know that *too* before an adjective implies a negative result. In this exercise they must decide whether *too* or *very* is correct in the context. Items 11 and 12 give a good contrast between the meanings.

ANSWERS: **3.** too **4.** very . . . very **5.** too **6.** very **7.** very **8.** too **9.** too **10.** very **11.** very **12.** too **13.** too **14.** very **15.** too **16.** very **17.** too **18.** too

CHART 7-6:   USING *TOO MANY* AND *TOO MUCH* + NOUN

- You may want to begin with a brief review of some of the information in Chart 4-6 on count and noncount nouns.

- *Too + much/many* has a negative meaning. It is the speaker's opinion that the situation is impossible or undesirable.

- You might mention that *too* can also mean "in addition." In this case, *too* comes at the end of a sentence or clause: *Tom wants to go to the beach. Mary wants to go too.* See Chart 7-16.

☐ **EXERCISE 15, p. 290.**   *Using TOO MANY and TOO MUCH.*   (Chart 7-6)

Controlled completion.
You might lead the class through the first 4–6 items, then have them work in pairs to figure out the answers.

ANSWERS: **3.** too much   **4.** too many   **5.** too much . . . too many   **6.** too much
7. too many   **8.** too many   **9.** too much   **10.** too much   **11.** too much
12. too many   **13.** too much   **14.** too many . . . too much

☐ **EXERCISE 16, p. 292.**   *Using TOO MANY and TOO MUCH.*   (Chart 7-6)

Oral (books closed).
The class will have to listen very carefully to your rather long cues. You may have to repeat some. Wait a few seconds for one or two students to produce a good answer. Discuss alternatives.

CHART 7-7:   USING *TOO* + ADJECTIVE + INFINITIVE

- This chart introduces yet another use of an infinitive.

- Again, the word *too* before an adjective gives the speaker's negative opinion.

☐ **EXERCISE 17, p. 293.**   *Using TOO + adjective + infinitive.*   (Chart 7-7)

Controlled completion and transformation.
Give students time to write the answers to items 1–4, then go over them with the whole class. Continue orally with you or a student reading the cue and another student giving the response.

ANSWERS:

2. Susie is | too | tired | to go | to the party.

3. Robert is | too | short | to touch | the ceiling.

4. I was | too | sleepy | to finish | my work.

5. Jackie is | too | young | to get | married.

6. Sam was | too | busy | to go | to the zoo.

7. I'm | too | full | to eat | another sandwich.

8. I'm | too | lazy | to clean up | my apartment today.

[*Clean up* is a bit more intensified than *clean;* the speaker intends to do a thorough job of cleaning on another day.]

CHART 7-8:   USING *TOO* + ADJECTIVE + *FOR* (SOMEONE) + INFINITIVE

- This structure puts three concepts into one sentence with few words:

    The box is too heavy. Someone can't lift the box. Someone is Bob. → *The box is too heavy for Bob to lift.*
    Therefore, it is an economical, efficient sentence pattern to use.

- Point out that if the preposition *for* is followed by a pronoun, it must be the objective form of a pronoun *(me, him, her, us, them)*.

☐ **EXERCISE 18, p. 294.   *Using TOO + adjective + FOR (SOMEONE) + infinitive.   (Chart 7-8)***

Controlled completion and transformation.
Lead the class through items 1–4, then ask individuals to respond to items 5–8.

ANSWERS:

2.   The homework is | too | difficult | for me | to do.

3.   The coffee is | too | hot | for Rosa | to drink.

4.   It's | too | late | for us | to go | to the movie.

5.   The suitcase is | too | heavy | for Ann | to carry.

6.   This book is | too | expensive | for me | to buy.

7.   The weather is | too | cold | for us | to go swimming.

8.   The pill is | too | big | for Mrs. Rivers | to swallow.

☐ **EXERCISE 19, p. 295.   *Using TOO + adjective + FOR (SOMEONE) + infinitive.   (Chart 7-8)***

Oral (books closed).
Lead the class through the example, reminding them to answer "no" to all items in this exercise. Substitute students' names in parentheses. You may omit item 5 if none of your students is married.

In item 6, *Antarctica* /æntˈarktɪkə/ is the name of the continent at the South Pole.

In item 10, *a fist* is a hand with all the fingers closed into the center of the palm.

CHART 7-9: USING ADJECTIVE + *ENOUGH*

- The notion of adjective + *enough* is that someone or something meets a qualification, reaches an acceptable level, is satisfactory or adequate.

- Learners now have two ways to say the same idea in different words:

  too + adjective = *not* + adjective + *enough*

  Point out that *not . . . enough* shows the negative meaning of *too* + adjective.

□ **EXERCISE 20, p. 295.** *Using adjective + ENOUGH.* *(Chart 7-9)*

Controlled completion and fill-in-the-blanks.
Point out that the adjectives listed in the exercise are opposites. Give students time to think about each item; it's not easy to use *too* and *enough* correctly.

ANSWERS: **2.** too soft . . . loud enough **3.** too small . . . big enough **4.** too short . . . tall enough **5.** too cold . . . hot enough **6.** strong enough . . . too weak **7.** too sour . . . sweet enough **8.** too old . . . fresh enough **9.** old enough . . . too young **10.** too weak . . . strong enough **11.** big enough . . . too small **12.** too uncomfortable . . . comfortable enough **13.** too narrow . . . wide enough . . . too large . . . small enough **14.** warm enough . . . too cold

□ **EXERCISE 21, p. 297.** *Using adjective + ENOUGH.* *(Chart 7-9)*

Oral (books closed).
This exercise can be fun because it generates talk about strange situations.

SAMPLE ANSWERS: **1.** No, the door isn't big enough for an elephant to walk through. [*elephant* = a large animal with a long trunk for a nose] **2.** No, ten-year-old children aren't old enough to go to college. **3.** No, I'm not close enough to touch (. . .) without standing up. [*without standing up* = if I do not stand up] **4.** No, I can't. My shirt pocket isn't big enough for my grammar book. **5.** No, a dog isn't smart enough to learn to read. **6.** No, I'm not hungry enough to eat (four hamburgers) right now. **7.** No, I can't. Moonlight isn't bright enough for me to read a book. [*by moonlight* = at night with only the moon's light] **8.** No, I don't know enough English to understand every word an English-speaking TV newscaster says. [*newscaster* = a news reader, a reporter on radio or television] **9.** No, a turtle isn't fast enough to win a race with a rabbit. [*turtle* = a slow-moving animal with a very hard shell] **10.** No, those letters aren't big enough for me to read. **11.** No, this room isn't big enough to hold (200) people. **12.** No, my fingernail isn't sharp enough to cut a piece of paper. [*fingernail* = the hard shell that grows at the end of a finger]

CHART 7-10:   USING *ENOUGH* + NOUN AND *MORE* + NOUN

• Ask students to compare the sentences in Charts 7-9 and 7-10. They should see that *enough* follows an adjective but comes in front of a noun.

• *More* and *enough* are opposites here. Needing more of something means you don't have enough. Having enough of something means you don't need more.

• Other languages have very different structures for expressing these concepts of *more* and *enough*. You might have students demonstrate how their languages express them. Tell them to think of a way to remember the English patterns—perhaps with a clever phrase or a drawing to aid their memories.

☐ **EXERCISE 22, p. 297.   *Using ENOUGH + noun.*   (Chart 7-10)**

Open completion.
Again, the students are working with *because*-clauses. Ask students to think of good results for the reasons in each item. They must pay attention to the verb tenses as well as to the meanings of the sentences.

SAMPLE COMPLETIONS: **1.** buy a new car   **2.** go to the poetry reading   **3.** pay the rent yesterday   **4.** do my laundry yesterday   **5.** go to the park this afternoon   **6.** pay for your dinner

☐ **EXERCISE 23, p. 298.   *Using ENOUGH + noun and MORE + noun.*   (Chart 7-10)**

Controlled completion.
Students could work with partners to complete these sentences. Then you can lead a review of the exercise with the whole class.

ANSWERS: **3.** more minutes   **4.** enough time   **5.** more sugar   **6.** more desks   **7.** enough vocabulary   **8.** enough light   **9.** enough gas [BrE: petrol]   **10.** more tea

CHART 7-11:   USING *ENOUGH* + INFINITIVE

• Ask students to compare Charts 7-7 and 7-11. They should note differences in word order. Also, example (c) in Chart 7-7 is the opposite in meaning of sentence (b) in Chart 7-11.

• Be sure students understand that the pairs of sentences in Chart 7-11 have the same meanings.

☐ **EXERCISE 24, p. 299.   *Using ENOUGH + infinitive.*   (Chart 7-11)**

Transformation.
Give students time to think of their responses; they must consider word order. Take time in item 6 to discuss the idioms at the bottom of page 299 in the textbook.

ANSWERS: **2.** I don't have enough time to finish my work.   **3.** Mustafa has enough money to buy a new car.   **4.** Johnny isn't old enough to get married.   **5.** Mr. and Mrs. Forest don't earn enough money to feed their family.   **6.** I'm hungry enough to eat a horse.   **7.** Sally bought enough food to feed an army.   **8.** Did you have enough time to finish your homework last night?   **9.** Do you have enough money to buy a ticket to the show?   **10.** I don't know enough vocabulary to understand this article in the newspaper.

□ **EXERCISE 25, p. 300.** *Using ENOUGH + infinitive.* *(Chart 7-11)*

Open completion.
Students can work with partners, each suggesting a response to each item. Then you can ask for interesting items to be reported to the class.

SAMPLE COMPLETIONS: **1.** drive a car.   **2.** lift a chair.   **3.** lift a sofa.
4. eat a large dinner.   **5.** go to the movies.   **6.** buy new furniture.   **7.** cook dinner.
8. read a magazine.   **9.** carry on a conversation.   **10.** read a novel in English.

□ **EXERCISE 26, p. 300.** *Using ENOUGH + infinitive.* *(Chart 7-11)*

Oral (books closed).
Give students time to think of good responses. Keep the pace lively, with your gestures and voice showing interest.

SAMPLE ANSWERS: **1.** No, she's not old enough to go to school./No, she's too young to go to school.   **2.** No, it's too soft to hear./No, it's not loud enough to hear.   **3.** No, he's not old enough to get married./No, he's too young to get married.   **4.** No, you can't put (my purse) in your (pants pocket). Your (pocket) is too small/not big enough.   **5.** No, I can't understand everything on the front page of a newspaper. I don't know enough English.
6. No, an elephant can't sit in that chair. An elephant is too big. The chair is too small/not large enough.   **7.** No, I don't like winters in this city. The winters are too cold/not warm enough. OR No, I don't like summers in this city. The summers are too hot.   **8.** No, I didn't have enough time to finish my homework last night.   **9.** No, I don't have enough time to go on a picnic Saturday.   **10.** No, I don't want to eat my lunch on the floor of this room. The floor is too dirty/not clean enough.   **11.** No, I don't have enough money to buy a hotel.
12. No, it's too difficult to multiply 673 by 897 without a calculator in three seconds.

CHART 7-12:   USING *BE ABLE TO*

- The modal *can* has the same form for present and future. *Be able to* has different forms for the tenses.

□ **EXERCISE 27, p. 301.** *Using BE ABLE TO.* *(Chart 7-12)*

Oral.
This exercise asks students to see the relationships between *can/could* and *be able to*. Students need to pay special attention to the tense forms of *be* used in the transformed sentences.

ANSWERS: **3.** Mark is able to speak two languages.   **4.** Sue will be able to get her own apartment next year. [*get* = obtain, find]   **5.** Animals aren't able to speak.   **6.** Are you able to touch your toes without bending your knees? [*without __ing* = if you do not __]   **7.** Jack wasn't able to describe the thief.   **8.** Were you able to do the homework?   **9.** I wasn't able to sleep last night because my apartment was too hot.   **10.** My roommate is able to speak four languages.   **11.** I'm sorry that I wasn't able to call you last night.   **12.** I'm sorry that I won't be able to come to your party next week.   **13.** Will we be able to take vacations on the moon in the 22nd century?

> *Open completion.*
> Encourage students to use their imaginations to make interesting sentences. Perhaps they could work as partners; then you could ask each pair to tell the class their most interesting answers.
>
> *SAMPLE COMPLETIONS:*   **1.** sleep . . . there was too much noise   **2.** fly to other planets
> **3.** take you shopping Saturday   **4.** fly   **5.** speak several languages   **6.** speak two
> languages   **7.** finish Exercise 5 . . . they didn't have enough time   **8.** call me
> **9.** Toshi . . . come to class . . . he was sick   **10.** Jim . . . fix your car today . . . he doesn't have
> enough time   **11.** We . . . come to your party Saturday . . . we live too far away

---

CHART 7-13:   POLITE QUESTIONS: *MAY I, COULD I,*
**   AND** *CAN I*

- This chart explains the language functions of asking permission and giving permission.

- You may wish to discuss the notion of politeness and informality. The ranges and uses of such forms are different in many cultures, so discussing them can be very interesting and useful to learners of English.

- Some people consider requests with *Can I* to be informal or too direct to be polite. Many people use *Can I* in most situations, adding *please* to be polite.

☐ **EXERCISE 29, p. 303.**   *Polite questions.*   (Chart 7-13)

> *Open completion.*
> The pictures give a different kind of cue—visual instead of written. Students can work in pairs to construct the dialogues. You might ask them to stand up and perform as the people in the pictures.
>
> *SAMPLE DIALOGUES:*
> May I please have another cup of coffee? *Certainly.*
> Can I have this apple? *Yes.*
> Could I make an appointment to see you outside of class? *Of course.*
> May I come in? *Yes, of course.*

☐ **EXERCISE 30, p. 304.**   *Polite questions.*   (Chart 7-13)

> *Oral (books closed).*
> Lead the class through the example, then continue by reading a cue while you indicate which student you are talking about and whom you are talking to.

CHART 7-14:   POLITE QUESTIONS: *COULD YOU* **AND**
**   *WOULD YOU***

- The word *please* is optional but very frequently used in such requests. (Some learners feel that speakers of English use *please* and *thank you* too much!)

- *I'd be glad to* = I would be happy to do what you requested.

- *Could you* is more often used than *Would you* in requests.

□ **EXERCISE 31, p. 305.** *Polite questions.* *(Chart 7-14)*

> *Open completion.*
> Note that *sir* in item 1 is used only in speaking to a male person; for females the polite word is either *ma'am* /mæm/ or *miss*.
>
> In item 2, "Excuse me?" is spoken with rising intonation; also possible is the word "Pardon?" These questions are different in meaning from the sentence "Excuse me, sir." or "Pardon me, sir." in item 1, which is a way to catch someone's attention.
>
> *SAMPLE COMPLETIONS:*
>
> **1.** A: Excuse me, sir. Could you please open the door for me?
> B: Of course. I'd be happy to.
>
> **2.** A: Would you please shut the window?
> B: Excuse me? I didn't understand what you said.
> A: I said, "Would you please shut the window?"
> (Some students might spontaneously use an infinitive in reported speech: "I asked you to shut the window.")
> B: Certainly. I'd be glad to.

□ **EXERCISE 32, p. 306.** *Polite questions.* *(Chart 7-14)*

> *Oral (books closed).*
> Lead the class through the example. You should substitute Student B's name in the parentheses when you speak to Student A. You could break the class into groups of three, with one student giving the cues to the other two.

□ **EXERCISE 33, p. 306.** *Polite questions.* *(Chart 7-14)*

> *Oral.*
> Students can use their imaginations here, especially if you ask them to perform their dialogues for the class. Lead them through the examples, then give them time to work out the conversations. In the first example, *(Knock, knock)* indicates that the student should make the sound of someone knocking on a door, perhaps by knocking on a desk top with his/her knuckles. Other appropriate sound effects could be added to the dialogues.

CHART 7-15:   IMPERATIVE SENTENCES

- Imperative sentences make much stronger requests than the polite questions in Charts 7-13 and 7-14. The sound of the speaker's voice can make an imperative either a very strong order or a softer request. Also, as in (i), the use of *please* will soften the imperative. Imperative sentences have several uses. Discuss the different effects of (f)–(i). Students might be able to compare the English variants with how their own language expresses them.

- Point out the negative examples (d) and (e). The meaning of *don't* is "You must not."

- The "understood subject" of imperative sentences is *you*. The speaker directs an imperative sentence to a second person or persons.

□ EXERCISE 34, p. 307. *Imperative sentences.* *(Chart 7-15)*

Structure identification.

This exercise gives contextualized examples of imperative sentences for you to discuss with the class. You might ask students to identify which type of imperative meaning is used in each dialogue—orders, directions, advice, or requests. In item 1, *wait for me* is probably more of a request than an order; *hurry up* is advice.

Item 1 uses *Let's,* which is presented in Chart 10-2, student book page 423. It could probably be analyzed as a type of imperative sentence. The author didn't think of that when writing the exercise and apologizes if its inclusion causes unnecessary confusion and discussion in class. It's not intended that students identify it as an imperative. If any students push, tell them it's a periphrastic modal with a meaning close to *shall* when used in a question, such as "Shall we go?"

ANSWERS: **2.** Come in . . . have [*have/take a seat* = sit down]   **3.** Don't forget
4. Hold . . . Drink . . . Breathe . . . Eat [*hiccups* (also spelled *hiccoughs*) = a series of uncontrollable gulps that the body makes to get air into the lungs. (The speakers are giving Jim some traditional advice on how to cure the hiccups. You might ask your students what technique they use.)]   **5.** Read . . . answer
6. Walk . . . turn . . . Go . . . turn   **7.** Wait . . . Do . . . Hang . . . Make . . . Put . . . Empty
8. close . . . hand . . . Take care . . . Take care . . . Don't worry [*the remote control for the TV* = a device for turning the TV on/off or changing channels from across the room]

□ EXERCISE 35, p. 309. *Imperative sentences.* *(Chart 7-15)*

Open completion.
Students should be able to offer answers quickly without writing them down. Discuss alternatives.

SAMPLE COMPLETIONS:
Open wide. (Open your mouth wide, please.)
Watch out! / Look out!
Stop! Don't eat that dirt!

□ EXERCISE 36, p. 310. *Imperative sentences.* *(Chart 7-15)*

Oral.
Several students should volunteer different responses for each situation. Students can work in groups.

SAMPLE RESPONSES:
1. Study Chart 7-16 before you come to class. (Please) do Exercise 37.
2. Hold your breath. Blow into a paper bag.
3. Come straight home after school. Put on your jacket.
4. Get more exercise. Eat healthful foods.
5. Use 1 cup of rice and 2 cups of water. Add a little salt to the water. Bring the water to a boil, then turn the heat down. Etc.
6. Visit the (. . .). Go downtown and see (. . .). Eat at (. . .).

CHART 7-16:	USING *TWO, TOO,* AND *TO*

- Point out the positions of *too* in examples (b) and (c). When *too* means "also," the word is usually at the end of the sentence or clause. (In rather formal speech, you might hear "I too saw the movie"; however, in that position the word *also* is preferred: "I also saw the movie.")

- In speaking, the word *to* is not stressed. The words *two* and *too* are stressed (spoken with a higher pitch and more sound).

☐ **EXERCISE 37, p. 310.** *Using TWO, TOO, and TO.* *(Chart 7-16)*

> *Controlled completion.*
> It's impossible to tell which word students are saying when they read their answers to this exercise aloud, so you might have them make a set of three cards. Each card has one word on it in large letters, either *too, two,* or *to.* They hold up the correct card for everyone to see as they read the answer. You could ask all students to hold up a card so that you can quickly check their answers.
>
> *ANSWERS:*   **2.** two   **3.** too . . . too . . . to   **4.** to . . . to . . . to . . . too
> **5.** to . . . to . . . too   **6.** to . . . to   **7.** to . . . to   **8.** too   **9.** too . . . to . . . to
> **10.** two . . . to . . . two . . . too

CHART 7-17:	MORE ABOUT PREPOSITIONS: *AT* AND *IN* FOR LOCATIONS

- These are idiomatic uses. They must be memorized because there is no clear logic to predict their forms.

- In (a) no article *(a/an/the)* is used. However, with other nouns an article is usually necessary: *at the office, sitting at a table, working at his desk.*

- In example (d) you might point out that proper nouns (names) do not usually have an article *(a/an/the)* in English. In example (c), *the* is used to identify a unique or specific room. (See Charts 4-10 and 4-11.)

- The difference between *at* and *in* is not easy to understand, so take some time to discuss (e) and (f) with your learners.

- Perhaps review prepositions of location in Charts 1-7 and 3-14.

☐ **EXERCISE 38, p. 312.** *AT and IN.* *(Chart 7-17)*

> *Controlled completion.*
> Call attention to the footnote for item 1, and check the students' understanding that *at* is not correct in item 2.
>
> *ANSWERS:*   **3.** at   **4.** in   **5.** in . . . at   **6.** in . . . in   **7.** in [*conferenc*e = a convention; a large meeting]   **8.** in [*fire extinguisher* = a device for putting out a small fire]
> **9.** at . . . at   **10.** at   **11.** in   **12.** at   **13.** at   **14.** in . . . in [*jewelry* /jūlri/ or /juwəlri/]   **15.** in   **16.** at   **17.** in   **18.** At   **19.** in [AmE: elevator = BrE: lift]
> **20.** in

☐ **EXERCISE 39, p. 313.** *AT and IN.* *(Chart 7-17)*

> *Oral (books closed).*
> This is a quick check of students' use of these prepositions. Substitute any names you wish in parentheses.
>
> *ANSWERS:*   **1.** in   **2.** at/in   **3.** in   **4.** at   **5.** in   **6.** at/in   **7.** at
> **8.** in   **9.** at/in   **10.** in   **11.** in   **12.** at/in

☐ **EXERCISE 40, p. 313.** *AT and IN.* *(Chart 7-17)*

> *Oral (books closed).*
> Select two students for each item. Give the cue to Student A. Then A asks a question and B answers.

☐ **EXERCISE 41, p. 314.** *Review.* *(Chapter 7)*

> *Oral.*
> Divide the class into small groups. Everyone should contribute to the group's answers, and one person should write them down. The same person or another can report to the class. After all groups have finished the exercise, go through the items, eliciting at least two different responses for each. Ask the reporters to give only their most interesting responses that do not duplicate another group's.
>
> In item 8, *illiterate* means "unable to read or write beyond a very basic level."

☐ **EXERCISE 42, p. 314.** *Review.* *(Chapter 7)*

> *Controlled completion; multiple choice.*
> Exercises 42 and 43 could be assigned as homework.
>
> *ANSWERS:*   **1.** B   **2.** C   **3.** C   **4.** D   **5.** D   **6.** A   **7.** B   **8.** A
> **9.** D   **10.** B   **11.** C   **12.** C

☐ **EXERCISE 43, p. 315.** *Review.* *(Chapter 7)*

> *Error analysis.*
> Go over some of the unfamiliar vocabulary first if you think students will have difficulty with some items (e.g., 2: *interrupt*, 5: *the universe*, 9: *vase*).
>
> *ANSWERS:*   **1.** My brother wasn't able <u>to call</u> me last night.   **2.** <u>Don't interrupt</u>.
> **3.** May I <u>please borrow</u> your dictionary?   **4.** We <u>will go/can go</u> to the museum tomorrow afternoon.   **5.** There are <u>too</u> many.   **6.** The diamond ring was <u>too expensive for John to buy</u>.   **7.** Can <u>you stand</u> on your head?   **8.** My son isn't <u>old enough to</u> go to school. He's only <u>two</u> years old.   **9.** I saw a beautiful vase at a store yesterday, but I couldn't <u>buy</u> it.
> **10.** We have too <u>much homework</u>.   **11.** <u>Close</u> the door please.   **12.** Robert was <u>too</u> tired to go <u>to</u> his class at <u>two</u> o'clock.

☐ **EXERCISE 44, p. 316.** *Review.* *(Chapter 7)*

> *Fill-in-the-blanks.*
> You might call attention to the traditional opening words of this folktale: "Once upon a time . . . ." They set the story in the past, which requires the past tense for most verbs. However, when someone is speaking in the story, usually the present tense is required.

ANSWERS: **(1)** was **(2)** hunted . . . took **(3)** listened **(4)** dreamed/dreamt
(5) decided **(6)** are you leaving **(7)** are you going/will you go **(8)** am going
(9) am going **(10)** do you want to go **(11)** want to experience **(12)** need to learn
(13) can learn **(14)** stay . . . stay **(15)** can't stay **(16)** is **(17)** will have★ . . . get
(18) will face **(19)** may never see **(20)** will try **(21)** Are you having/Do you have
(22) can I cross **(23)** don't know **(24)** can't cross **(25)** won't be
(26) will help **(27)** will give **(28)** can jump . . . will also give **(29)** don't lose . . .
will reach **(30)** are you lying . . . Are you **(31)** can't see **(32)** drank . . . am
(33) will die **(34)** can't find **(35)** gave **(36)** can I give **(37)** will give
(38) can see **(39)** can't see **(40)** will you find **(41)** Jump . . . will carry
(42) can't go **(43)** will I do **(44)** have **(45)** Keep . . . will find **(46)** can't see
(47) can hear **(48)** can't help **(49)** am dying **(50)** are you dying
(51) lost **(52)** can't find **(53)** am starving/will starve **(54)** can help
(55) will give **(56)** can smell **(57)** can I help **(58)** am trying **(59)** need to go
(60) Come . . . will put **(61)** (will) take **(62)** couldn't see **(63)** couldn't smell
(64) lost . . . heard **(65)** help **(66)** Don't cry **(67)** aren't **(68)** never lost
(69) Jump . . . Use **(70)** am flying/can fly

☐ **EXERCISE 45, p. 321.** *Review.* *(Chapter 7)*

Oral and written.
In addition to presenting the play to classmates, your students might enjoy performing for other groups of students, teachers, and school administrators.

CHART 7-18: MORE IRREGULAR VERBS

- Lead students through the list, pointing out spelling patterns.
- Some learners mix up the past forms of *fall* and *feel*. Give extra attention to those words.

☐ **EXERCISE 46, p. 321.** *More irregular verbs.* *(Chart 7-18)*

Oral (books closed).
Don't write these verbs on the chalkboard; have students listen to them. For each item, you should read the two verb forms and have the class repeat them after you. Then read the sentences that follow, keeping an informative yet conversational tone in your voice. One or more students can respond to the question.

★*Will*, not *be going to*, is used in the answers to Exercise 44 in this key, but *be going to* is also often a possible correct completion in the sentences with a future meaning.

☐ **EXERCISE 47, p. 322.** *More irregular verbs.* *(Chart 7-18)*

Controlled completion.
Exercises 47 and 48 could be assigned as homework and reviewed in class.

ANSWERS: **1.** won   **2.** fell   **3.** hurt   **4.** kept   **5.** drew   **6.** grew
7. knew   **8.** swam   **9.** blew   **10.** felt [*have a frog in one's throat* = speak for a moment with an unclear, rough voice, perhaps because of an infection or obstruction in the throat]   **11.** threw

☐ **EXERCISE 48, p. 323.** *More irregular verbs.* *(Chart 7-18)*

Controlled completion.
Many of these verbs were introduced in earlier chapters. There is a complete list in APPENDIX 5.

ANSWERS: **1.** took   **2.** wore   **3.** cost   **4.** caught   **5.** knew   **6.** met
7. grew   **8.** fell   **9.** lost   **10.** spent   **11.** threw   **12.** made   **13.** stole
14. told   **15.** broke   **16.** began   **17.** sang   **18.** flew   **19.** left   **20.** won

Chapter 8: NOUNS, PRONOUNS, AND ADJECTIVES

ORDER OF CHAPTER	CHARTS	EXERCISES
Pretest		Ex. 1
Modifying nouns	8-1	Ex. 2 → 6
Word order of adjectives	8-2	Ex. 7 → 11
Expressions of quantity	8-3 → 8-5	Ex. 12 → 18
Using *every*	8-6	Ex. 19 → 20
Possessive nouns	8-7 → 8-8	Ex. 21 → 26
Possessive pronouns	8-9	Ex. 27 → 29
Questions with *whose*	8-10	Ex. 30 → 31
Summary: uses of the apostrophe	8-11	Ex. 32 → 33
Summary: uses of nouns	8-12	Ex. 34
Connected nouns: noun + *and/or* + noun	8-13	Ex. 35 → 37
Summary: uses of adjectives	8-14	Ex. 38 → 42
Summary: personal pronouns	8-15	Ex. 43
Indirect objects	8-16 → 8-19	Ex. 44 → 56
Review		Ex. 57 → 60
More irregular verbs	8-20	Ex. 61 → 64

General Notes on Chapter 8

This chapter deals with many ways to modify a noun. Learners become aware of the order of nouns and their modifiers, some of which come before and some of which follow the noun. The chapter begins with the terminology of adjective and noun, then shows that a noun can modify another noun. Next, multiple modifiers are practiced, and some new vocabulary is introduced.

The next section gives practice with phrases of quantity that modify nouns, and the problem of subject–verb agreement becomes a focus.

Attention is given to ways that the notion of possession changes the form of nouns and pronouns. Following this is a section on the possessive question word *whose*.

After summaries of the uses of apostrophes, nouns, adjectives, and pronouns, the text presents indirect objects.

□ **EXERCISE 1, p. 325.** *Nouns and adjectives.*

Structure identification.
This exercise allows you to review what the students already know about nouns and adjectives.
The purpose of the exercise is for you to check on the students' understanding of the grammar
terms "noun" and "adjective" before proceeding with the chapter.

SAMPLE SENTENCES: **3.** ADJ—My brother is *tall.* **4.** NOUN—I live in an *apartment.*
5. NOUN— *Tom* is in class today. **6.** ADJ—My dog is an *intelligent* animal.
7. NOUN—Rita hurt her *hand* yesterday. **8.** ADJ—Jane's dinner was *good.*
9. NOUN—I saw a *monkey* at the zoo. **10.** ADJ—The *young* child played in the yard.
11. NOUN—*Music* is very relaxing. **12.** ADJ—The ring I wanted was too *expensive.*
13. NOUN—I'm studying English *grammar.*

CHART 8-1:	**MODIFYING NOUNS WITH ADJECTIVES AND NOUNS**

- The word "modify" is explained in Chart 4-2 in the textbook.

- One unusual feature of English is that a noun can modify another noun. These nouns are called
"noun adjuncts" and do not add any letters or sounds. Call attention to example (d), where the modifier
has incorrectly been given a plural form. Making a noun adjunct plural is a common error. (The
explanation in the text says that a modifying noun is "always" singular. The author should and indeed
does know better by now than to ever use "always" or "never" when explaining English grammar! There
are of course exceptions, one of which is *sports* in *a sports car/a sports jacket.*)

- The order of modifiers is shown in example (e), and more examples are in Chart 8-2.

□ **EXERCISE 2, p. 326.** *Adjectives modifying nouns.* *(Chart 8-1)*

Structure identification.
Some of the vocabulary might be new, so check students' comprehension as you lead them
through this exercise.

ANSWERS: **2.** *wise* modifies *woman* **3.** *native* modifies *language* **4.** *busy* modifies
waitress . . . empty modifies *cup* **5.** *young* modifies *man . . . heavy* modifies *suitcase*
6. *uncomfortable* modifies *chair* **7.** *international* modifies *news . . . front* modifies *page*
8. *wonderful* modifies *man*

□ **EXERCISE 3, p. 326.** *Nouns modifying nouns.* *(Chart 8-1)*

Structure identification.
Noun adjuncts are a common feature in English. Exercises 3, 4, and 5 give only a very few
examples for the students to play with.

In a related structure, a noun adjunct is attached to the noun it modifies, resulting in a
compound noun (e.g., *bookstore, textbook, moonlight, mailman*). The textbook does not deal with
compound nouns, but you may choose to mention this phenomenon. If students want to know
if a word such as *bookstore* is one word or two words, they simply need to consult their
dictionaries.

The following examples are fun—but they can be confusing.
Chocolate milk is a delicious drink. (*Chocolate* modifies *milk.*)
Milk chocolate is a delicious kind of candy. (*Milk* modifies *chocolate.*)

ANSWERS: 2. *music* modifies *store*   3. *train* modifies *station*   4. *Vegetable* modifies *soup*   5. *movie* modifies *theater* . . . *furniture* modifies *store*   6. *lunch* modifies *menu*   7. *traffic* modifies *light* [*traffic light* = stop-and-go signal. Note: *light traffic* = not many cars on the street.]   8. *business* modifies *card*

☐ **EXERCISE 4, p. 326.   Nouns modifying nouns.   (Chart 8-1)**

Transformation.
Students must learn here that the modifier is not in plural form.
In item 1, *vases* = AmE /vesəz/; BrE /vazəz/.
Also, the modifier is usually spoken with more stress (higher pitch) than the noun.

ANSWERS: 3. a newspaper story   4. hotel rooms   5. bean soup   6. an office worker   7. a computer room   8. airplane seats   9. a park bench   10. a price tag

☐ **EXERCISE 5, p. 327.   Nouns modifying nouns.   (Chart 8-1)**

Controlled completion.
In item 5, the noun *official* is spoken with more stress. In all other items, the modifier is spoken with more stress.

ANSWERS: 2. store   3. class   4. race   5. official   6. soup   7. program   8. trip   9. keys   10. number   11. tickets   12. room

☐ **EXERCISE 6, p. 328.   Nouns modifying nouns.   (Chart 8-1)**

Controlled completion.

ANSWERS: 2. good television program   3. dangerous mountain road   4. bad automobile accident   5. interesting magazine article   6. delicious vegetable soup   7. funny birthday card   8. narrow airplane seats

---

CHART 8-2:   WORD ORDER OF ADJECTIVES

• When more than one adjective modifies a noun, English prefers a sequence. This chart and the following exercises introduce that sequence.

• In the author's experience, the word order of adjectives is not a major problem for students in their spontaneous usage, but the teaching of this word order can sometimes force errors. The author is not sure how to avoid this, other than treating this unit as "information you might find interesting" as opposed to "information you must memorize."

• The term "opinion adjective" is used in this textbook. Other grammar books may use other terms for this, such as "descriptive" or "evaluative" adjective. The point to learn is that such adjectives express the speaker/writer's opinion. *Beautiful* is an opinion; *red* is not.

• Adjectives can be divided into eighteen or more categories, but the six in this chart are the most useful to learn.

• Note that commas are not used between adjectives in different categories. However, more than one adjective in a category can modify a noun; in that case, commas are necessary between the adjectives within that same category. For example: *She bought a beautiful, expensive old glass vase.*

□ **EXERCISE 7, p. 329.** *Word order of adjectives.* *(Chart 8-2)*

Controlled completion.
Give the class time to work out their answers, then have them check with a partner and discuss any questions. Finally, remind them to write nationalities with a capital letter at the beginning. It's a good idea for everyone to say these phrases out loud, so you could lead the class in choral repetition of the answers.

ANSWERS: **2.** delicious Thai   **3.** small red   **4.** big old brown   **5.** narrow dirt
6. serious young   **7.** beautiful long black   **8.** famous old Chinese   **9.** thin brown
leather   **10.** wonderful old Native American

□ **EXERCISE 8, p. 330.** *Word order of adjectives.* *(Chart 8-2)*

Controlled completion.
Give students time to work out their answers, then lead the class through the items.
    The choice of *a* or *an* in items 4, 5, 7, and 8 depends on the first sound of the following word.

ANSWERS: **2.** Asian   **3.** leather   **4.** an unhappy   **5.** a soft   **6.** brick
7. an important   **8.** a polite   **9.** coffee   **10.** Canadian

□ **EXERCISE 9, p. 331.** *Word order of adjectives.* *(Chart 8-2)*

Open completion.
Students can use their imaginations to add interesting words to these items.
    The sample completions here are only some possibilities. Your students may think of other answers that are just as good.
    The choice of *a* or *an* in items 2, 6, and 9 depends on the first sound of the following word.

SAMPLE COMPLETIONS: **1.** Chinese [*hot* = spicy, peppery, or at a high temperature]
2. a large   **3.** woolen   **4.** small   **5.** brown   **6.** an attractive   **7.** red
8. leather   **9.** a beautiful   **10.** cotton

□ **EXERCISE 10, p. 332.** *Word order of adjectives.* *(Chart 8-2)*

Error analysis.
Remind students that some sentences have no mistakes.
    In item 1, *wood* could also be the adjective form *wooden*.

ANSWERS: **3.** a famous Chinese landmark   **4.** an interesting newspaper article
5. *(no change)*   **6.** the cold mountain stream   **7.** my favorite Italian food
8. *(no change)*   **9.** comfortable old brown leather   **10.** tiny black insects [*gnats* /næts/]
11. a brown cardboard box   **12.** *(no change)*   **13.** a handsome middle-aged man . . . short
brown hair   **14.** an expensive hotel room

□ **EXERCISE 11, p. 333.** *Word order of adjectives.* *(Chart 8-2)*

Oral.
Students work with a partner, following the instructions. Go through the examples first. Remind them to change A and B roles after item 20 and to work quickly.
    It is hoped that the students will be pleasantly surprised by how easily they can think of typical completions, e.g., *a kitchen table, a kitchen knife, a kitchen door.*

CHART 8-3:   EXPRESSIONS OF QUANTITY: *ALL OF,*
                      MOST OF, SOME OF

- Example (e) illustrates a common mistake made by learners: confusing *most of* with *almost all of.* The phrase *⋆almost of* is not possible.

- In this chapter, the phrase *all of* is learned and practiced. Speakers often omit *of* after the word *all: She ate all (of) her food.* It is not possible to omit *of* after the words *most* or *some,* so it is a good idea to teach the preposition *of* with all three of these words of quantity.

☐ **EXERCISE 12, p. 334.   *ALL OF, SOME OF, MOST OF.*   (Chart 8-3)**

Controlled completion.
Items 1–5 use the words *odd* and *even* to describe numbers. Students should find this a useful concept. Items 6–9 use present progressive *(are flying)* to describe the action in a picture. Items 10–13 should reflect the situation in your class.

ANSWERS: **2.** All of   **3.** Most of   **4.** Some of   **5.** Almost all of   **6.** Almost all of   **7.** Most of   **8.** All of   **9.** Some of   **10.–13.** *(free response)*

CHART 8-4:   EXPRESSIONS OF QUANTITY:
                      SUBJECT–VERB AGREEMENT

- Not all expressions of quantity follow this rule, as the next charts explain.

☐ **EXERCISE 13, p. 336.   *Subject–verb agreement.*   (Chart 8-4)**

Controlled completion.
In this exercise, students learn to focus on the noun and choose the verb that agrees with it. Give them time to think before they respond.
   In items 7 and 8, point out that *word* is a count noun, but *vocabulary* is a noncount noun.
   The drawing at the bottom of page 336 illustrates a common saying: "An optimist sees the glass and says it is half full, but a pessimist sees the same glass and says it is half empty." This shows opposite ways of interpreting the same information.

ANSWERS: **2.** are   **3.** was   **4.** were   **5.** are . . . are   **6.** is   **7.** are   **8.** is   **9.** is   **10.** are   **11.** arrive   **12.** arrives

CHART 8-5:   EXPRESSIONS OF QUANTITY: *ONE OF,*
                      NONE OF

- The use of *one of* causes students a lot of singular-plural problems. Common errors: *⋆One of my friend is coming. ⋆One of my friends are coming.*

- You could make a circle on the chalkboard and draw several small circles inside it. The small circles represent your friends in example (a). Label one of the circles to represent Sam. Point to the filled-in circle as you explain examples (a) and (c).

- The footnote below Chart 8-5 explains the usage of examples (e) and (f).

☐ **EXERCISE 14, p. 337.** *ONE OF, NONE OF.*   *(Chart 8-5)*

Combination.
Students may work in pairs, but you should lead everyone through the answers. Check to see or hear that the *-s* is added where required.

ANSWERS: **2.** (. . .) is one of my classmates.   **3.** One of my books is red.
4. One of my books has a green cover.   **5.** (. . .) is one of my favorite places in the world.
6. One of the students in my class always comes late.   **7.** (. . .) is one of my best friends.
8. One of my friends lives in (. . .).   **9.** (. . .) is one of the best programs on TV.
10. (. . .) is one of the most famous people in the world.   **11.** One of my biggest problems is my inability to understand spoken English.   **12.** (. . .) is one of the leading newspapers in (. . .).   **13.** None of the students in my class speaks (. . .).   **14.** None of the furniture in this room is soft and comfortable.

☐ **EXERCISE 15, p. 339.** *ONE OF, NONE OF.*   *(Chart 8-5)*

Open completion.
Students can write their answers, then compare them with classmates. The freedom to use their own ideas can produce interesting responses.

☐ **EXERCISE 16, p. 339.** *Expressions of quantity.*   *(Charts 8-3 → 8-5)*

Controlled completion.
This exercise focuses on singular-plural agreement. The map is for item 7.

ANSWERS: **2.** are   **3.** is   **4.** are   **5.** is   **6.** is   **7.** live   **8.** lives
9. have [*lap-top computer* = a small, portable computer (which can be set on one's lap instead of on a desk or table)]   **10.** has   **11.** is/are   **12.** is

☐ **EXERCISE 17, p. 340.** *Expressions of quantity.*   *(Charts 8-3 → 8-5)*

Controlled completion.
This is another review of singular-plural agreement. You might use some of these items on a test.

ANSWERS: **2.** are   **3.** is   **4.** are   **5.** is   **6.** are   **7.** is   **8.** is   **9.** are
10. is

☐ **EXERCISE 18, p. 340.** *Expressions of quantity.*   *(Charts 8-3 → 8-5)*

Oral (books closed).
Tell students that you don't want an exact number in their answers unless the number is very small. They'll spend too much time counting! In items 1, 4, and 5, you can substitute some familiar or similar words in the parentheses.

CHART 8-6:   USING *EVERY*

• Learners sometimes ask why *everyone, everybody,* and *everything* are written as one word, but *every day, every person,* etc., are written as two words. This is just a tradition in English. (Note: *everyday* is spelled as one word when it is used as an adjective: *everyday life, everyday experiences, everyday food,* etc.)

☐ **EXERCISE 19, p. 341.** *Using EVERY and ALL OF.* **(Charts 8-3 and 8-6)**

Controlled completion.
Items 11–14 are questions.

ANSWERS: **2.** book . . . is **3.** students . . . are **4.** student . . . is **5.** teacher . . .
gives **6.** teachers . . . give **7.** child . . . likes **8.** children . . . know **9.** people . . .
are **10.** wants **11.** Do . . . students **12.** Does . . . person **13.** Do . . . people
14. Does **15.** city . . . has

☐ **EXERCISE 20, p. 342.** *Review. (Charts 8-1 → 8-6)*

Error analysis.
This exercise contains some of the most frequent mistakes that learners make. It is important to
review it carefully.

ANSWERS: **1.** I work hard every <u>day</u>. **2.** I live in an apartment with one of my <u>friends</u>.
3. We saw a pretty <u>flower</u> garden in the park. OR We saw <u>some</u> pretty flowers in the park.
4. Almost <u>all</u> of the students are in the class today. **5.** Every <u>person</u> in my class <u>is</u> studying
English. OR <u>All (of) the</u> people in my class are studying English. **6.** All of the cities in
North America <u>have</u> traffic problems. **7.** One of my books <u>is</u> green. **8.** Nadia drives a
<u>small blue</u> car. **9.** Istanbul is one of my favorite <u>cities</u> in the world. **10.** Every <u>one</u> of <u>the</u>
students in the class <u>has</u> a grammar book. OR <u>Every</u> student in the class <u>has</u> a grammar book.
11. We can't finish <u>everything</u> today. **12.** Everybody in the world <u>wants</u> peace.

CHART 8-7: POSSESSIVE NOUNS

- *Apostrophe* /əpˈastrəfi/ or /əpˈɔstrəfi/.

- The pronunciation of this possessive *-s* follows the same rules as the *-s* ending on nouns and verbs.
(See Charts 2-4 and 2-5.)

☐ **EXERCISE 21, p. 343.** *Possessive nouns.* **(Chart 8-7)**

Structure identification and punctuation.
Students can check their answers with a partner, then you should lead the class through the
items to be sure they are correct.

ANSWERS: **2.** Bob's **3.** teachers' **4.** mother's **5.** parents' [The telephone number
is spoken as a series of individual numbers: five-five-five-nine-eight-seven-six.] **6.** father's
7. girl's **8.** girls' **9.** Tom's **10.** Anita's **11.** students' **12.** Alex's /ˈæleksəz/
13. elephant's **14.** monkey's **15.** Monkeys'

☐ **EXERCISE 22, p. 344.** *Possessive nouns.* **(Chart 8-7)**

Open completion.
Pronunciation of these names in their English possessive forms may be difficult, but students
should follow the usual rules for pronouncing *-s* endings.
   If a person's name ends in *-s*, there are two possible ways of writing the possessive form:
(1) by adding an apostrophe + *-s*, as in *Charles's last name is Smith*, and (2) by adding only an
apostrophe, as in *Charles' last name is Smith*.

□ **EXERCISE 23, p. 345.** *Possessive nouns.* *(Chart 8-7)*

    Written.
    You might set a time limit and a target number of sentences for the students to produce in this exercise.

□ **EXERCISE 24, p. 345.** *Possessive nouns.* *(Chart 8-7)*

    Controlled completion.
    It might be helpful to draw a diagram of family relationships to review some of the vocabulary needed in this exercise.
        Pronunciation: *niece* /nis/; *nephew* /nɛfyu/

    ANSWERS: **2.** brother   **3.** mother   **4.** children   **5.** sister   **6.** mother
    7. wife   **8.** mother . . . father   **9.** daughter   **10.** son

---

CHART 8-8:   **POSSESSIVE: IRREGULAR PLURAL NOUNS**

- Punctuation of possessive nouns is unnecessarily complicated in English, but that's the way it is. Some of your students may not be especially interested in these finer points of punctuation.

- Pronunciation of the final *-s* follows the usual rules. (See Charts 2-4 and 2-5.)

□ **EXERCISE 25, p. 345.** *Possessive: irregular plural nouns (Chart 8-8)*

    Fill-in-the-blanks.

    ANSWERS: **2.** girl's   **3.** girls'   **4.** women's   **5.** uncle's   **6.** person's
    7. people's   **8.** Students'   **9.** brother's   **10.** brothers'   **11.** wife's   **12.** dog's
    [*Fido* /faydo/]   **13.** dogs'   **14.** men's   **15.** man's . . . woman's [*nickname* = a short form or a special familiar form of a name (e.g., *Chris* is a short form of Christopher or Christine)]   **16.** children's

□ **EXERCISE 26, p. 346.** *Possessive: irregular plural nouns.* *(Chart 8-8)*

    Structure identification and punctuation.
    You might have students examine the drawing for a variety of possessive forms, then review the rules for those forms.

    ANSWERS: **2.** Yuko's   **3.** women's   **4.** roommate's   **5.** parents' (two people)/ parent's (one person)   **6.** father's   **7.** Rosa's   **8.** classmates'   **9.** people's
    10. husband's   **11.** men's   **12.** children's

CHART 8-9:   **POSSESSIVE PRONOUNS:** *MINE, YOURS, HIS, HERS, OURS, THEIRS*

- Languages vary in their ways of indicating possession with pronouns. Learners continue to make mistakes with these English forms for a long time.

- You may want to point out that the *-s* on *yours, hers, ours,* and *theirs* does not depend on a singular or plural reference:

    That book is hers.   *When does your class begin?*
    Those books are hers.   *When does yours begin?*

□ EXERCISE 27, p. 347. *Possessive adjectives and pronouns.* *(Chart 8-9)*

Semi-controlled and open completion.
This exercise can be confusing, so give students time to think before they respond. They should write the correct form in each blank so they can review their answers later.

ANSWERS: **2.** them . . . their . . . theirs **3.** you . . . your . . . yours **4.** her . . . her . . . hers **5.** him . . . his . . . his **6.** us . . . our . . . ours

□ EXERCISE 28, p. 348. *Possessive adjectives and pronouns.* *(Chart 8-9)*

Fill-in-the-blanks.
Remind students that every answer must be a possessive noun or pronoun. You might have students work with a partner, taking turns with the items.

ANSWERS: **2.** a. ours b. theirs c. Our d. Theirs **3.** a. Tom's b. Mary's c. His d. Hers [*raincoat* = a coat or jacket that gives protection from the rain] **4.** a. mine b. yours c. Mine . . . my d. Yours . . . your **5.** a. Jim's b. Ours c. His d. Ours **6.** a. my b. yours c. Mine . . . my d. Yours . . . your **7.** a. Our b. Theirs c. Ours d. Their [*Chevrolet* /ˇʃɛvrəley/ and *Volkswagen* = names of automobiles; *gets 17 miles to the gallon* = travels 17 miles using one gallon of gasoline or petrol] **8.** a. Ann's b. Paul's c. Hers . . . her d. His . . . his

□ EXERCISE 29, p. 349. *Possessive adjectives and pronouns.* *(Chart 8-9)*

Controlled completion.
Students can work with partners.

ANSWERS: **2.** hers **3.** A: your B: my . . . Mine **4.** yours [*wood carving* = a picture or form cut into wood with a knife] **5.** theirs . . . Their [*the Smiths'* = the Smith family's (a married couple or a family may be called the Smiths, the Joneses, the Browns, etc.)] **6.** A: our . . . yours B: Ours **7.** A: your B: his **8.** A: your B: yours . . . yours A: Mine **9.** A: your B: yours A: Yours B: hers A: My . . . His [*spaghetti sauce* = a tomato or cream mixture that is poured over spaghetti /spəgɛti/ (a kind of Italian noodle or pasta); *In truth* = speaking truthfully, to tell the truth, really, actually]

CHART 8-10:   QUESTIONS WITH *WHOSE*

- In examples (a) and (b), *whose* is like a possessive adjective followed by a noun. In examples (c) and (d), *whose* is like a possessive pronoun.

- Learners often confuse *whose* with *who's* (*who is* or *who has* when *has* is used as the auxiliary in the present perfect). The drawing on page 351 shows the difference in these two words.

- The word *whose* is the same for singular and plural references, as in examples (c) and (d).

□ EXERCISE 30, p. 351. *Questions with WHOSE.* *(Chart 8-10)*

Controlled completion.
Lead the class through this exercise slowly so that everyone hears the correct answers. Discuss any questions that arise about singular/plural forms.

ANSWERS: **2.** are those **3.** are these **4.** is that **5.** are those **6.** is this

☐ **EXERCISE 31, p. 352.** *Questions with WHOSE.* *(Chart 8-10)*

> *Oral.*
> After the class hears two or three examples, you might divide them into groups and continue.
> Announce a time limit, and encourage each student to participate.

CHART 8-11:   SUMMARY: USES OF THE APOSTROPHE

- This chart summarizes that pesky little punctuation mark, the apostrophe. You might tell your students that even native speakers have a lot of trouble using apostrophes and that apostrophe-usage mistakes are common.

- Note examples (m) through (o). The use of the possessive adjective *its* has not been presented before in the text. That is an oversight by the author. Please correct this oversight by presenting its use now. Some examples you could use:

> *We saw a tiger at the zoo. **Its** eyes were green.*
> *The horse lifted its head.*
> *The fish moved its tail and swam away.*
> *Virtue is its own reward.*
> *Jack lifted the knife. Its handle was carved wood. Its blade was sharp.*

- If you use the footnote, use care when you say "in formal English" and "in informal English." It is difficult to hear the difference, and learners easily become confused.

☐ **EXERCISE 32, p. 353.** *Summary: uses of the apostrophe.* *(Chart 8-11)*

> *Structure identification and punctuation.*
> ANSWERS: **3.** Jim's   **4.** Jim's   **5.** He's   **6.** I'm [*a little hungry* = somewhat hungry, not a lot]   **7.** Tony's   **8.** Tony's   **9.** Who's   **10.** She's Bob's   **11.** *(no change)*   **12.** *(no change)*   **13.** It's Gina's   **14.** Where's   **15.** won't . . . doesn't   **16.** It's also famous . . . [*a destination* = a place that people go to; *an attraction* = something that catches your attention; *night life* = social activities after dark, such as dancing or going to the theater]

☐ **EXERCISE 33, p. 353.** *Summary: uses of the apostrophe.* *(Chart 8-11)*

> *Structure identification and punctuation.*
> ANSWERS: **2.** Yoko's   **3.** He's   **4.** Pablo's [*someone's full name* = the complete name]   **5.** You're   **6.** I'm . . . Lee's   **7.** Mary's . . . Anita's   **8.** Mary's . . . Anita's   **9.** That's   **10.** What's . . . What's . . . Who's . . . Where's   **11.** I'm . . . It's a grammar book. It's on my desk. It's open.   **12.** There's . . . It's black and red . . . It's sitting on a branch.   **13.** It's a magnificent animal . . . It's an endangered species. There're . . . [*admire* = respect, regard with approval and wonder; *magnificent* = outstanding, wonderful, grand, noble in appearance; *a species* /spiš iz/ = a category or type; *in doubt* = uncertain, not guaranteed; *endangered* = in danger]

CHART 8-12:   SUMMARY: USES OF NOUNS

- A noun can have many functions in a sentence. Those functions are listed in this chart.
- The term "complement" is new here. In (d), the noun *student* complements the subject *Yoko*. That is, *student* completes the information about the subject. We could say *Yoko = student*.

Structure identification.
Use each group of sentences to complete a group of diagrams. Use items a and b to complete diagrams 1 and 2, etc. The drawing on page 356 illustrates the meaning of item j.

ANSWERS:

2.

A kangaroo	is	an animal.
subject	*be*	noun complement

3.

Restaurants	serve	food.
subject	verb	object

4.

Jason	works	in	an office.
subject	verb	prep.	object of prep.

5.

Karen	held	the baby	in	her arms.
subject	verb	object	prep.	object of prep.

6.

Korea	is	in	Asia.
subject	*be*	prep.	object of prep.

7.

Korea	is	a peninsula.
subject	*be*	noun complement

8.

Monkeys	eat	fruit.
subject	verb	object

9.

Children	play	with	toys.
subject	verb	prep.	object of prep.

10.

Jack	tied	a string	around	the package.
subject	verb	object	prep.	object of prep.

CHART 8-13:   CONNECTED NOUNS: NOUN +
***AND/OR* + NOUN**

- The words *and* and *or* are called "coordinating conjunctions." They connect grammatically similar words or phrases. In this chart, they connect nouns. In this chart, the students are beginning to learn about parallel structures.

- In (d), the meaning of *or* is a choice; the speaker wants something to drink but does not have a preference, so the listener can make the choice.

- Point out the locations of commas. They will be practiced in some exercises in this section.

- In Example (c), the comma immediately preceding *and* is optional. (CORRECT: *I have a book, a pen, and a pencil.*) See the footnote on page 358.

☐ **EXERCISE 35, p. 357.** *Noun + AND/OR + noun.* **(Chart 8-13)**

Structure identification.
Discuss each item with the class.

ANSWERS: **2.** apples, bananas, and oranges = used as the object of the verb *bought* **3.** Jack and Olga = used as the subject **4.** apples or bananas = used as the object of the verb *wants* **5.** Jack and Olga = used as the object of the preposition *with* **6.** Tennis and golf = used as the subject **7.** museums and libraries = used as the object of the verb *has* **8.** trunk, branches, leaves, and roots = used as the object of the verb *has* **9.** Automobiles, trains, and trucks = used as the subject [*a vehicle* /v̲i̲hɪkəl/ (many people do not pronounce the *h*) = a device for carrying passengers, goods, or equipment] **10.** soup or a sandwich = used as the object of the verb *will have*

☐ **EXERCISE 36, p. 358.** *Noun + AND/OR + noun.* **(Chart 8-13)**

Punctuation.
The text presents the use of a comma immediately preceding *and* as being standard, with the omission of that comma presented as an option. Both are equally correct. The text chooses to present the pattern that includes the comma because the author feels it helps the students recognize the individual parallel elements in a connected series.

ANSWERS: **3.** Bears, tigers, and elephants **4.** *(no change)* **5.** rice, fruit, and vegetables **6.** *(no change)* **7.** Canada, the United States, and Mexico **8.** *(no change)* **9.** *(no change)* **10.** soup, a salad, and a sandwich **11.** days, music, good friends, and books **12.** birds, butterflies, and airplanes [*have in common* = share, have similarly]

☐ **EXERCISE 37, p. 358.** *Noun + AND/OR + noun.* **(Chart 8-13)**

Structure identification.
The drawing on page 350 illustrates turtles, the topic of these sentences.

ANSWERS: **2.** turtle = subject; shell = object of the verb *has* **3.** turtle = subject; head, legs, and tail = object of the verb *pulls;* shell = object of the preposition *into* **4.** turtles = subject; lives = object of the preposition *of;* water = object of the preposition *in* **5.** turtles = subject; land = object of the preposition *on;* lives = object of the preposition *for* **6.** Turtles = subject; teeth = object of the verb *don't have;* jaws = object of the verb *have* **7.** Turtles = subject; eggs = object of the verb *bury* [*bury* = put something under the ground*]; sand or mud = object of the preposition *in* **8.** Baby = noun used as an adjective to modify the noun *turtles;* turtles = subject; dangers = object of the verb *face* [*face . . . dangers* = meet, confront, encounter] **9.** Birds and fish = subject; baby = noun used as an adjective to modify the noun *turtles;* turtles = object of the verb *eat* **10.** sea = noun used as an adjective to modify the noun *turtles;* turtles = subject; years = object of the preposition *for* **11.** Turtles = subject; dangers = object of the verb *face;* people = object of the preposition *from* **12.** People = subject; turtles' = possessive noun used as an adjective to modify the noun *homes;* homes = object of the verb *destroy* **13.** People = subject; beaches, forests, . . . areas = object of the verb *replace* [*replace . . . with* = substitute]; towns and farms = object of the preposition *with* **14.** People = subject; areas = object of the verb *poison;* pollution = object of the preposition *with* **15.** species = subject; turtles = object of the preposition *of;* extinction = object of the verb *face* [*extinction* = death of every one]

┌───┐
│ **CHART 8-14: SUMMARY: USES OF ADJECTIVES** │
└───┘

• This chart introduces a few common linking verbs. Other common linking verbs not presented are *appear, become, grow, seem,* and *stay.*

☐ **EXERCISE 38, p. 360.** *Summary: uses of adjectives.* *(Chart 8-14)*

Structure identification.

ANSWERS: **2.** cold = modifies the noun *water* **3.** cold = follows *be* and describes the subject of the sentence, *nose* **4.** cold = follows the linking verb *feels* and describes the subject of the sentence, *Ice* **5.** easy = follows the linking verb *looks* and describes the subject of the sentence, *exercise* **6.** easy = modifies the noun *tests* **7.** English = modifies the noun *grammar;* easy = follows *be* and describes the subject of the sentence, *grammar* **8.** sour = follows the linking verb *taste* and describes the subject of the sentence, *Lemons* **9.** unhappy = follows the linking verb *look* and describes the subject of the sentence, *You* **10.** sad = follows *be* and describes the subject of the sentence, *I* **11.** favorite = modifies the noun *author* **12.** angry = follows the linking verb *sound* and describes the subject of the sentence, *You* **13.** wonderful = follows the linking verb *smell* and describes the subject of the sentence, *flowers* **14.** soft and comfortable = follow the linking verb *looks* and describe the subject of the sentence, *chair* [Note that the conjunction *and* can connect two adjectives.] **15.** good = modifies the noun *teacher;* history = a noun used as an adjective to modify the noun *teacher*

☐ **EXERCISE 39, p. 361.** *Summary: uses of adjectives.* *(Chart 8-14)*

Oral.

With a partner, students can take turns responding. In PART I, they might say, "I feel good." or "I don't feel good today." In PART II, they make truthful sentences about their opinions, such as "Pineapples taste good." In PART III, they express opinions, such as "The floor looks very clean."

☐ **EXERCISE 40, p. 361.** *Summary: uses of adjectives.* *(Chart 8-14)*

Oral.

Students can work in pairs or small groups, or you could ask for volunteers to show an emotion to the whole class. Lead them through the example first. This exercise can lead to a lot of laughter.

☐ **EXERCISE 41, p. 361.** *Summary: uses of adjectives.* *(Chart 8-14)*

Controlled and/or open completion.
Vocabulary: *terrific* = very wonderful (informal); *it sounds* + adjective = it seems *(adjective)* to me.
    In item 3, *the community theater* = the theater that a small town or neighborhood owns; amateur theatrics.
    In item 4, *overpopulation* = too many people living in one area, causing a strain on resources and facilities.
    In item 11, *darling* and *honey* = names that lovers or spouses call each other.
    In item 12, *I sure do* = Yes, I most certainly smell it (informal).

☐ **EXERCISE 42, p. 362.** *Summary: uses of adjectives.* *(Chart 8-14)*

Oral and written.
The team with the longest (and most correct) list for each item is the winner.

CHART 8-15:	SUMMARY: PERSONAL PRONOUNS

- You might have students cover the lower right sections of the chart and explain the function of each pronoun or adjective to you in their own words.

☐ **EXERCISE 43, p. 363.** *Summary: personal pronouns.* *(Chart 8-15)*

Error analysis.
After students correct all the errors, you might ask them to write the whole letter correctly on a piece of paper. This gives them another opportunity to use these forms accurately and to remember them.

ANSWERS: **(1)** It's **(2)** my . . . His . . . him **(3)** you . . . me . . . He's . . . He's . . . We're **(4)** *(no change)* **(5)** we **(6)** his . . . I . . . mine . . . His **(7)** her . . . she . . . him . . . They **(8)** *(no change)* **(9)** Our . . . They're . . . them **(10)** Our . . . theirs . . . They . . . She's **(11)** Her . . . They . . . It's black and white. **(12)** It's a friendly cat . . . their **(13)** our **(14)** I'm . . . your

---

CHART 8-16:	INDIRECT OBJECTS

- English has two ways to express indirect objects. Examples (a) and (b) illustrate these. You might have students look at those examples and tell you all the differences they see before you give the explanation.

- For a review of *who/whom*, see Chart 5-15.

- Many learners make mistakes with word order and the use of the preposition *to*. The following exercises give them practice with the correct forms.

☐ **EXERCISE 44, p. 364.** *Indirect objects.* *(Chart 8-16)*

Combination.
Lead the class through the example, making sure they understand that both answers have the same meaning.

ANSWERS:

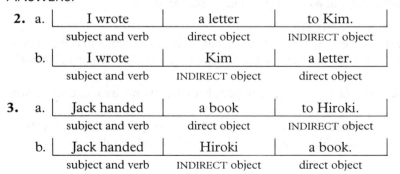

4. a. | I passed | the salt | to Stacy. |
       subject and verb   *direct object*   INDIRECT *object*

    b. | I passed | Stacy | the salt. |
       subject and verb   INDIRECT *object*   *direct object*

5. a. | I lent | my car | to Tom. |
       subject and verb   *direct object*   INDIRECT *object*

    b. | I lent | Tom | my car. |
       subject and verb   INDIRECT *object*   *direct object*

6. a. | I sent | a postcard | to Alice. |
       subject and verb   *direct object*   INDIRECT *object*

    b. | I sent | Alice | a postcard. |
       subject and verb   INDIRECT *object*   *direct object*

7. a. | Ann told | a story | to us. |
       subject and verb   *direct object*   INDIRECT *object*

    b. | Ann told | us | a story. |
       subject and verb   INDIRECT *object*   *direct object*

8. a. | Jack showed | a picture | to us. |
       subject and verb   *direct object*   INDIRECT *object*

    b. | Jack showed | us | a picture. |
       subject and verb   INDIRECT *object*   *direct object*

☐ **EXERCISE 45, p. 366.** *Indirect objects.* *(Chart 8-16)*

Oral/transformation.
Many learners have difficulty with the placement of the preposition *to*. This exercise focuses on that problem.

ANSWERS: **2.** Please hand me that book.   **3.** Rose wrote her brother a letter.
4. I gave Ahmed a birthday present.   **5.** Please tell us a story.   **6.** Did you send your parents a package?   **7.** Mr. Hong showed me a photograph of his wife.   **8.** Would you lend me your camera?

☐ **EXERCISE 46, p. 366.** *Indirect objects.* *(Chart 8-16)*

Oral (books closed).
This exercise may be confusing to some learners. Lead them carefully through the example so they know how to respond.

ANSWERS: **1.** I gave (. . .) my pen.   **2.** I wrote (. . .) a letter.   **3.** I sent (. . .) a package.   **4.** I told (. . .) a funny story.   **5.** I showed (. . .) a photograph.   **6.** I sent the telephone company a check.   **7.** I passed (. . .) my dictionary.   **8.** I handed (. . .) my notebook.   **9.** I lent (. . .) $20.

☐ **EXERCISE 47, p. 366.** *Indirect objects.* *(Chart 8-16)*

Oral.
You can decide if you want both forms of each answer from the students.

ANSWERS: **2.** I sent my parents a telegram two days ago. OR I sent a telegram to my parents two days ago.   **3.** Mrs. Kelly gave her children some candy after dinner. OR Mrs. Kelly gave some candy to her children after dinner.   **4.** Sue is going to lend me her car tomorrow. OR Sue is going to lend her car to me tomorrow.   **5.** Sam told the class a joke yesterday. OR Sam told a joke to the class yesterday.   **6.** I'm going to write the newspaper a letter. OR I'm going to write a letter to the newspaper.   **7.** Did you hand John the scissors? OR Did you hand the scissors to John?   **8.** Could you please pass me the soy sauce? OR Could you please pass the soy sauce to me?   **9.** Mr. Schwartz showed Liz a picture of his baby daughter. OR Mr. Schwartz showed a picture of his baby daughter to Liz.
10. Yesterday the teacher gave the students some good advice. OR Yesterday the teacher gave some good advice to the students.

☐ **EXERCISE 48, p. 367.**   *Indirect objects.*   *(Chart 8-16)*

> *Oral (books closed).*
> Lead the class through the example. Continue the exercise in a conversational way. Accept either form of the indirect object answer, but note that "What did you do?" requires a past tense verb in the response. In item 3, the past of *lend* is *lent*. In item 8, there are two verbs that must be changed to the past tense in the student's response.

CHART 8-17: INDIRECT OBJECTS: USING *FOR*	

* The meaning of *for* + indirect object is usually "as a favor" or "in order to help."

* You might have students cover the right side of the chart and discover the rules together. Discuss any questions that arise.

* Pronunciation: The final prepositional phrase is spoken with almost no stress. The stressed syllable is in the noun (direct object) that comes before *for* + indirect object.

☐ **EXERCISE 49, p. 368.**   *Indirect objects: using FOR.*   *(Chart 8-17)*

> *Controlled completion.*
> Learners must understand the general meaning of *for* + indirect object phrases. This exercise should help them develop that understanding. Items 3 and 8 may be especially difficult because the students may think that someone is talking <u>to</u> someone else. However, the meaning in both cases is "to help" or "to do someone a favor." The drawing illustrates item 11.
>
> *ANSWERS:*   **1.** for   **2.** for   **3.** for   **4.** to   **5.** for   **6.** for   **7.** to   **8.** for
> **9.** for   **10.** for   **11.** for

☐ **EXERCISE 50, p. 368**   *Indirect objects: using FOR.*   *(Chart 8-17)*

> *Oral (books closed).*
> You might begin with a review of polite questions with "Could you (please)" and various responses in Charts 7-13 and 7-14.

☐ **EXERCISE 51, p. 369.**   *Indirect objects: using FOR.*   *(Chart 8-17)*

> *Oral (books closed).*
> Lead the class through the example, making sure they understand the choices in A's and B's responses. You read each cue to Student A, whose book is closed.

CHART 8-18: INDIRECT OBJECTS WITH *BUY, GET, MAKE*

- In Chart 8-17, students learned that there is only one position for *for* + indirect object—after the direct object. Now they must learn that three common verbs have a different pattern. This tradition in English usage is the result of historical changes.

☐ **EXERCISE 52, p. 369.** *Indirect objects with BUY, GET, MAKE.* *(Chart 8-18)*

Oral.
You might have two students respond to each item, each student giving a different form.

ANSWERS: **2.** Jack got a stuffed animal for his daughter. OR Jack got his daughter a stuffed animal. [*a stuffed animal* (illustrated in the drawing) = a toy animal filled with soft cotton or similar material] **3.** I bought some gloves for Robert. OR I bought Robert some gloves.   **4.** I made Mike a cake. OR I made a cake for Mike.   **5.** Carmen got a new television set for her parents. OR Carmen got her parents a new television set.   **6.** Eric bought a necklace for his mother. OR Eric bought his mother a necklace. [*necklace* /nɛkləs/ = a piece of jewelry worn around the neck] **7.** Oscar made his guests dinner. OR Oscar made dinner for his guests.   **8.** Heidi bought a nice birthday gift for her brother. OR Heidi bought her brother a nice birthday gift. **9.** Could you please get me a glass of water? OR Could you please get a glass of water for me?

CHART 8-19: INDIRECT OBJECTS WITH *EXPLAIN* AND *INTRODUCE*

- You might have the students cover the right side of the chart and discover the rule for themselves. They should note the difference between these verbs and the ones in Chart 8-18. They must remember that some verbs require one sentence form but not another.

- Note this situation:

    (b) *Anna introduced her sister to me.* (Anna said, "Bob, I'd like to introduce my sister Mary." OR "Bob, this is my sister Mary.")

    (b.1) *Anna introduced me to her sister.* (Anna said, "Mary, I'd like to introduce Bob." OR "Mary, this is Bob.")

Both are correct. The difference depends on whose name Anna said first in the introduction. You might have two students act out both sequences of introducing two people to each other.

☐ **EXERCISE 53, p. 370.** *Indirect objects with EXPLAIN and INTRODUCE.* *(Chart 8-19)*

Oral.
Give students time to think before they respond. They must put the words in the correct order. Discuss any questions that arise.

ANSWERS: **2.** The professor explained the chemistry formula to the students. **3.** Tina introduced her son to me.   **4.** Mr. Schwartz explained his problem to the doctor. **5.** Could you please translate this sentence for me?   **6.** Could you please explain this sentence to me?   **7.** Fred told me his ideas. OR Fred told his ideas to me.   **8.** I explained Fred's ideas to my husband.

□ **EXERCISE 54, p. 370.   Review of indirect objects.   (Charts 8-16 → 8-19)**

Transformation.

Give students time to think before they respond. They must decide whether *to* or *for* is better, then put the words in the correct order. Some sentences have two correct alternatives. Discuss any questions that arise.

ANSWERS: **2.** I sent my cousin a postcard. OR I sent a postcard to my cousin.
3. The teacher answered a question for me.   **4.** Jim opened the car door for his girlfriend.
5. Ann Miller gave the bride and groom a nice wedding present. OR Ann Miller gave a nice wedding present to the bride and groom.   **6.** The teacher pronounced the new vocabulary words for the class.   **7.** The teacher explained the meaning of the word to us.
8. I translated the title of a book for my roommate.   **9.** My friend answered the phone for me because my hands were full.   **10.** I sent an application to the University of Texas. OR I sent the University of Texas an application.   **11.** Ron fixed the sewing machine for his wife.
12. Don told us a funny joke at the party. OR Don told a funny joke to us at the party.
13. Jane explained her problems to me.   **14.** My father wrote me a letter. OR My father wrote a letter to me.   **15.** Samir showed a picture of his family to the teacher. OR Samir showed the teacher a picture of his family.   **16.** I bought a gift for my friend. OR I bought my friend a gift.

□ **EXERCISE 55, p. 371.   Review of indirect objects.   (Charts 8-16 → 8-19)**

Oral (books closed).

You might want to make a copy of this exercise so you can walk around without the book and carry on conversations with students. Lead them through the example, and discuss the various responses. When a student responds, only one form should be used in order to keep the conversation more natural. (In other words, the student should not respond with all the possible variations of the answer.)

In item 5, *desperately* = urgently, immediately; *get kicked out* = be forced to move out (informal).

In item 6, *hide* = put something where no one can see it.

In item 10, *a paper airplane* = a piece of paper that is folded so that it flies through the air easily.

□ **EXERCISE 56, p. 372.   Review of indirect objects.   (Charts 8-16 → 8-19)**

Open completion.

You could use some of these items for a test.

SAMPLE COMPLETIONS: **1.** I wrote my sister a letter yesterday. OR I wrote a letter to my sister yesterday.   **2.** I sent a package to my friend last week. OR I sent my friend a package last week.   **3.** Please pass me the salt. OR Please pass the salt to me.   **4.** The taxi driver opened the door for me.   **5.** (. . .) gave me a birthday card. OR (. . .) gave a birthday card to me.   **6.** Could you please pronounce "Jakarta" for me?   **7.** Could you please lend me a dictionary? OR Could you please lend a dictionary to me?   **8.** (. . .) translated a letter for me.   **9.** Could you please answer a question for me?   **10.** My friend explained the bus schedule to me.   **11.** I bought my mother a bouquet of flowers. OR I bought a bouquet of flowers for my mother.   **12.** Could you please get me a glass of water? OR Could you please get a glass of water for me?

□ **EXERCISE 57, p. 372.** *Review.* *(Chapter 8)*

Controlled completion; multiple choice.
After students complete the exercise, they can compare their answers with one another and discuss any misunderstandings.

ANSWERS: **1.** B **2.** A **3.** B **4.** D **5.** B **6.** D **7.** C **8.** D **9.** D **10.** B

□ **EXERCISE 58, p. 373.** *Review.* *(Chapter 8)*

Error analysis.
Students can either compete with each other to find and correct the mistakes, or they can cooperate with partners. Discuss any questions that arise.

ANSWERS: **1.** I bought an <u>airplane</u> ticket. <u>It was</u> expensive. **2.** Some of those <u>books are</u> mine. **3.** Hiroki is a <u>Japanese</u> businessman. **4.** There's <u>a big old</u> tree in our backyard. **5.** Did you give <u>Jim</u> my message? OR Did you give my message <u>to Jim</u>? **6.** The cat licked <u>its</u> paw. **7.** Everybody <u>wants</u> to be happy. **8.** One of the <u>buildings</u> on Main Street is the post office. **9.** <u>Who's/Who is</u> that woman? **10.** What are those <u>people's</u> names? **11.** Is the <u>bedroom</u> window open? **12.** Mr. and Mrs. Swan like <u>their</u> apartment. <u>It's</u> large and comfortable. **13.** I walk in the park every <u>day</u>. **14.** <u>Whose</u> book is this? **15.** <u>I'm/I am</u> studying English. **16.** <u>Tina's</u> last name <u>is</u> Miller. **17.** Please explain this sentence <u>to me</u>. **18.** My <u>roommates'</u> desks are always messy. **19.** Could you pronounce this word <u>for me</u>? **20.** I know the names of almost <u>all</u> of the <u>students</u> in my class.

□ **EXERCISE 59, p. 374.** *Review.* *(Chapter 8)*

Oral.
This is a test of vocabulary for both the student who describes the item and the classmates who have to guess the noun. Lead everyone through the examples, then divide the class into small groups. Announce a time limit; 5 minutes is usually enough.

□ **EXERCISE 60, p. 374.** *Review.* *(Chapter 8)*

Oral.
If all of your students are from the same place, you could bring items to the class. Choose old or unusual items that most young people would not necessarily be familiar with.

CHART 8-20: MORE IRREGULAR VERBS	

• Pronounce each word and have the class repeat it. Then ask one student to spell the word aloud.

• Clarify the meanings.

□ **EXERCISE 61, p. 375.** *More irregular verbs.* *(Chart 8-20)*

Oral (books closed).
The class must listen carefully to what you say, then respond to the question. Try to keep your speech as natural and interesting as a normal conversation.
In item 5, *have* /hæv/, but *have to* /hæftə/. (See Chart 10-3.)

□ EXERCISE 62, p. 375.   More irregular verbs.   (Chart 8-20)

Fill-in-the-blanks.
Lead the class through this exercise so that everyone hears the answers and discusses the vocabulary.

ANSWERS: **1.** hid   **2.** bit   **3.** shook [*shook his head no* = moved his head from side to side with a negative meaning]   **4.** became . . . became [*lost touch with* = did not continue to communicate after some time (Note: *I've lost* is the present perfect *I have lost*.)]   **5.** chose [*a lollipop* = a piece of candy on a stick]   **6.** held   **7.** built   **8.** bent   **9.** fought   **10.** fed [*fed information into the computer* = typed information into the computer's memory]

□ EXERCISE 63, p. 376.   More irregular verbs.   (Chart 8-20)

Controlled completion.
After students write their answers, ask for only the verbs. When the students respond, ask them to pronounce and spell each answer aloud.

ANSWERS: **2.** fought   **3.** bite . . . bit [*poisonous* /pɔyzənəs/ = full of poison, deadly]   **4.** built [*woodworking class* = a school course in making things out of wood]   **5.** bent   **6.** fed   **7.** hid [*stole* (past tense of *steal*) = took without permission (a crime)]   **8.** became

□ EXERCISE 64, p. 377.   More irregular verbs.   (Chart 8-20)

Oral (books closed).
Every answer must begin with "Yes." Keep the pace fairly fast. If a student can't answer, he/she can say "Pass" so you continue to the next student quickly. Later come back to the student who passed and ask another item.

You may want to use this exercise as pair work, or you may want to make a team contest of this exercise. Divide the class into two or three equal teams. Ask one question to the first person on one team. That person must answer immediately and correctly to get two points for the team. If the answer is not correct, the second person on that team has a chance to answer correctly for one point. Continue with the next question to a different team. At the end of the game, the team with the most points is the winner. You can decide whether they get some kind of prize or just the honor of winning.

ANSWERS: **1.** I flew   **2.** I drank   **3.** I came   **4.** I went   **5.** I ate   **6.** I lent   **7.** I lost . . . I found   **8.** I gave   **9.** I threw . . . (. . .) caught   **10.** someone stole . . . I got   **11.** I woke   **12.** I got up   **13.** the wind blew   **14.** I shut   **15.** class began   **16.** I said   **17.** I told . . . (. . .) sat down   **18.** I heard   **19.** I taught   **20.** I brought   **21.** I forgot   **22.** I saw   **23.** I met   **24.** I left   **25.** I read   **26.** I went   **27.** I drove   **28.** I rode   **29.** a barber cut   **30.** I ran   **31.** my pen cost   **32.** I understood   **33.** I came   **34.** I made   **35.** I took   **36.** I wrote . . . I sent   **37.** telephone rang   **38.** I broke   **39.** I shook   **40.** I drew   **41.** I bent   **42.** I won   **43.** I felt   **44.** I fed   **45.** I bit   **46.** I hurt   **47.** I held   **48.** I built   **49.** I stood   **50.** I sang   **51.** I grew up   **52.** I became   **53.** (. . .) won   **54.** I fell   **55.** I thought   **56.** I fought   **57.** I want . . . I chose   **58.** I hid   **59.** my car hit   **60.** I put

Chapter 9: MAKING COMPARISONS

ORDER OF CHAPTER	CHARTS	EXERCISES
Comparisons: using *the same (as)*, *similar (to)*, and *different (from)*	9-1	Ex. 1 → 5
Comparisons: using *like* and *alike*	9-2	Ex. 6 → 7
The comparative: using *-er* and *more*	9-3	Ex. 8 → 16
Using *as . . . as*; using *less*	9-4	Ex. 17 → 22
Using *but*	9-5 → 9-6	Ex. 23 → 28
The superlative: using *-est* and *most*	9-7	Ex. 29 → 32
Using *one of* + superlative + plural noun	9-8	Ex. 33 → 36
Adjectives and adverbs	9-9	Ex. 37 → 39
Making comparisons with adverbs	9-10	Ex. 40 → 41
Using *as . . . as* with adverbs	9-11	Ex. 42 → 45
Review		Ex. 46 → 48

General Notes on Chapter 9

Learners need to learn how to combine ideas within sentences. This chapter gives them several ways to do this when making comparisons. The purpose of most comparisons is to form or express a judgment that favors one thing more than another. Thus, both comparison and contrast are introduced in this chapter.

    The first section introduces some adjectives with prepositions: *the same as, similar to,* and *different from.* Then the adjectives *like* and *alike* are explained and practiced. Next is a section on the *-er* ending and the modifier *more (than),* followed by a section on the phrases *as . . . as* and *less (than).* A different kind of contrast is expressed with the conjunction *but* between two clauses.

    The next section of the chapter deals with the superlative, introducing the ending *-est* and the modifier *most* to express comparisons of more than two items. The chapter concludes with an examination of some adverbs and adjectives that are often confused by learners. These are practiced with various kinds of comparisons. By the end of the review exercises, learners should have a good understanding of comparisons and contrasts and how to express them in English.

**CHART 9-1: COMPARISONS: USING *THE SAME (AS)*,
SIMILAR (TO), AND *DIFFERENT (FROM)***

- It is recommended that you teach *the same* as a phrase so that learners always use the article *the* in this expression. The omission of *the* before *same* is a common error.

- It is also recommended that you teach the prepositions as part of each phrase so that learners think of them as a whole.

- Note that the preposition is not used when only the adjective follows the verb, as in the first sentence below each picture in the chart.

☐ **EXERCISE 1, p. 379.** *Comparisons.* *(Chart 9-1)*

Oral.
Students should answer with complete sentences. (In a conversation, the answers would probably be "Yes, they are." or "No, they're not." This is an exercise, not a conversation, and the questions are intended as prompts for using the target structures and vocabulary.)

ANSWERS: **1.** Yes. **2.** No. **3.** Yes. **4.** Yes. **5.** No. **6.** Yes.

☐ **EXERCISE 2, p. 380.** *Comparisons.* *(Chart 9-1)*

Controlled completion.
Tell the class to listen carefully to each response and to be sure that the sentence is complete with the necessary preposition, *the*, and singular or plural verb.

A, F, and G are *triangles* /traɪˈæŋgəlz/ (A and F are equilateral triangles; G is a right triangle). B and D are *rectangles* /ˈrɛktæŋgəlz/. E is a *square*. (NOTE: a square can be considered a kind of rectangle.) C is a *circle* /ˈsɹkəl/.

ANSWERS: **3.** C is different from D. **4.** B is the same as D. **5.** B and D are the same. **6.** C and D are different. **7.** A and F are the same. **8.** F and G are similar. **9.** F is similar to G. **10.** G is similar to A and F, but (it is) different from C.

☐ **EXERCISE 3, p. 380.** *Comparisons.* *(Chart 9-1)*

Error analysis.
Lead the class through each item after giving them time to find the mistakes.

ANSWERS: **1.** A rectangle is similar <u>to</u> a square. **2.** Pablo and Rita come from <u>the</u> same country. **3.** Girls and boys are <u>different</u>. [Adjectives do not add -*s*.] Girls are different <u>from</u> boys. **4.** My cousin is the same age <u>as</u> my brother. **5.** Dogs are similar <u>to</u> wolves. **6.** Jim and I started to speak at <u>the</u> same time.

☐ **EXERCISE 4, p. 381.** *Comparisons.* *(Chart 9-11)*

Written.
Most students enjoy simple puzzles like these. Give them time to figure out the answers, perhaps assigning this as homework.

ANSWERS: **1.** Figures 1, 4, 8, and 10 are the same. Figures 3 and 5 are the same. Figures 4 and 8 are the same. Figures 2, 7, and 9 are the same. **2.** Figure 6 is different from all the rest. **3.** Seven. **4.** Nine. **5.** Eleven.

☐ **EXERCISE 5, p. 381.** *Comparisons.* *(Chart 9-11)*

    Oral (books closed).
    Lead the class through the example so they know what to do. Then in a conversational manner,
    continue with the other items. Help with vocabulary as necessary, and adapt the items to the
    situation in your classroom.

CHART 9-2: COMPARISONS: USING *LIKE* AND *ALIKE*

• Some learners want to say ★"Your pen likes my pen," which is nonsensical. Call their attention to the
meaning of the verb *like* in Chart 3-9 on page 101. The verb in Chart 9-2 is *be*.

• The word *alike* is always the last word in the sentence in these exercises. Its pattern is similar to words
like *asleep*, *awake*, and *aloud*.

• The word *like* is something like a preposition; it follows a verb and is followed by an object.

☐ **EXERCISE 6, p. 382.** *Using LIKE and ALIKE.* *(Chart 9-2)*

    Controlled completion.
    Of course, other words can complete these sentences correctly, but for the purpose of this
    exercise, students should choose either *like* or *alike*.

    ANSWERS: **2.** like . . . alike   **3.** alike   **4.** like   **5.** like   **6.** alike   **7.** alike
    8. like

☐ **EXERCISE 7, p. 382.** *Using LIKE and ALIKE.* *(Chart 9-2)*

    Oral.
    Some imaginative students might produce unusual responses, but the expected comparisons are
    listed here. The interesting ideas can be in the explanations the students give for their answers in
    the second sentence of each response.

    EXPECTED RESPONSES:

An alley is like a street.	A monkey's hand is like a human hand.
A bus is like a taxi.	An orange is like a lemon.
A bush is like a tree.	A pencil is like a pen.
A cup is like a glass.	A sea is like an ocean.
A hill is like a mountain.	A sofa is like a chair.
Honey is like sugar.	A sports jacket is like a suit coat.

CHART 9-3: THE COMPARATIVE: USING *-ER* AND *MORE*

• You might have students look at the examples and the lists of adjectives to discover the rules. Ask
them to explain the rules in their own words, if possible.

• NOTE about *farther* and *further*: Both are used to compare physical distance: *My house is farther/further
away from school than Bob's house. Further* (but not *farther*) can also mean "additional": *I need further
information.*

□ **EXERCISE 8, p. 383.** *Using -ER and MORE.* *(Chart 9-3)*

Spelling.

There are two purposes to this exercise: using the word *than* with a comparison and spelling the comparisons correctly. It is recommended that students learn to add the word *than* to each comparison. You could tell them to think of *more/-er . . . than* as a complete unit. In addition, students must decide which words use *-er* and which use *more*. Give them time to think before they respond, and ask them to spell the *-er* words aloud or write them on the chalkboard.

ANSWERS: **2.** smaller than **3.** bigger than **4.** more important than **5.** easier than **6.** more difficult than **7.** longer than **8.** heavier than **9.** sweeter than **10.** more expensive than **11.** hotter than **12.** cheaper than **13.** better than **14.** worse than **15.** farther than **16.** lazier than

□ **EXERCISE 9, p. 384.** *Comparatives.* *(Chart 9-3)*

Fill-in-the-blanks.

You may want to assign exercises 9 and 10 as homework. When students respond, check their spelling.

ANSWERS: **2.** larger than **3.** warmer . . . than **4.** darker than **5.** more important than **6.** lazier than **7.** taller than **8.** heavier than **9.** more difficult than **10.** better than **11.** longer than **12.** more intelligent than **13.** better than **14.** worse than **15.** shorter than [*the little finger* = the outside finger on a hand; *the middle finger* = the longest one] **16.** prettier than **17.** farther . . . than **18.** stronger than **19.** curlier than **20.** more beautiful than [*a weed* = a wild plant that grows where no one wants it to be]

□ **EXERCISE 10, p. 385.** *Comparatives.* *(Chart 9-3)*

Fill-in-the-blanks.

ANSWERS: **1.** better than **2.** worse than [*worse* /wrs/] **3.** funnier than **4.** more interesting than **5.** smarter than **6.** more famous than **7.** wider than **8.** deeper than **9.** more confusing than **10.** hotter than **11.** thinner than [*giraffe* / jəræf/] **12.** farther . . . than **13.** better than **14.** easier than **15.** more nervous . . . than

□ **EXERCISE 11, p. 386.** *Comparatives.* *(Chart 9-3)*

Oral.

Lead the class through item 1 as the example. The students can work in pairs, taking turns with alternate items. In items 7 and 8, they must look at other people in the room.

□ **EXERCISE 12, p. 386.** *Comparatives.* *(Chart 9-3)*

Oral (books closed).

You need to bring several books to the classroom, making sure they are different.
    In Part B, you might ask a student to draw the pictures.

□ **EXERCISE 13, p. 387.** *Comparatives.* *(Chart 9-3)*

Controlled and/or open completion.

ANSWERS: **2.** sweeter than **3.** colder/hotter than **4.** more expensive than **5.** cheaper than **6.** faster than **7.** smaller than **8.** more intelligent than **9.** higher than **10.** brighter than **11.** larger than **12.** more comfortable than **13.** easier than **14.** more important than

□ EXERCISE 14, p. 388. *Comparatives.* *(Chart 9-3)*

Oral (books closed).
You should say each cue as a sentence: "*(Student's name),* compare an elephant to a mouse."
Help with new vocabulary. Be prepared for some interesting (perhaps controversial) responses that might need further discussion.

□ EXERCISE 15, p. 388. *Comparatives.* *(Chart 9-3)*

Oral (books closed).
This is similar to Exercise 14, but now the students must supply the items for comparison. You should encourage them to use their vocabularies and imaginations, but they should also be prepared to explain their opinions.

□ EXERCISE 16, p. 388. *Comparatives.* *(Chart 9-3)*

Written and structure identification.
If your students don't want to tear up paper, they can make jumbled sentences for their classmates like this: heavier \ yours \ bookbag \ than \ is \ my

---

CHART 9-4:   USING *AS . . . AS;* USING *LESS*

- The use of *less . . . than* vs. *not as . . . as* is difficult for some students to grasp.
- Students should learn *less . . . than* as a complete unit, just as they learned *more/-er . . . than.*

□ EXERCISE 17, p. 389 *Using AS . . . AS.* *(Chart 9-4)*

Controlled completion.
This exercise on form should go quickly, but ask about the meaning of sentences with negative verbs. Students should understand that they mean "less than."

ANSWERS: **2.** as sweet as   **3.** as big as   **4.** as friendly as   **5.** as dark as   **6.** as cold today as   **7.** as pretty as   **8.** as expensive as

□ EXERCISE 18, p. 390. *Using LESS.* *(Chart 9-4)*

Transformation.
Remind students that *less* is usually used with adjectives of two or more syllables.

ANSWERS: **3.** Arithmetic is less difficult than algebra.   **4.** *(no change)*   **5.** This chair is less comfortable than that chair.   **6.** *(no change)*   **7.** *(no change)*   **8.** Swimming is less dangerous than boxing.   **9.** *(no change)*   **10.** This letter is less important than that letter.

□ EXERCISE 19, p. 390. *Using AS . . . AS.* *(Chart 9-4)*

Transformation.
Give students time to think before answering. They need to use a negative verb, change the adjective, and change the comparative to *as . . . as.*

ANSWERS: **3.** I'm not as tall as my sister. **4.** This exercise isn't as easy as the last one. **5.** My new shoes aren't as comfortable as my old shoes. **6.** My little finger isn't as long as my index finger. **7.** A radio isn't as expensive as a TV set. **8.** This book isn't as good as that book. **9.** My apartment isn't as big as yours. **10.** In my opinion, chemistry isn't as interesting as psychology.

☐ **EXERCISE 20, p. 391.** *Using AS . . . AS.* *(Chart 9-4)*

Transformation.

ANSWERS: **2.** An animal isn't as intelligent as a human being. **3.** Soda pop isn't as expensive as fruit juice. **4.** The Mississippi River isn't as long as the Nile River. **5.** Tom's pronunciation isn't as good as Sue's. **6.** Algebra isn't as easy as arithmetic. **7.** Money isn't as important as good health. **8.** American coffee isn't as strong as Turkish coffee. **9.** A wooden chair isn't as comfortable as a sofa. **10.** A van isn't as large as a bus.

☐ **EXERCISE 21, p. 392.** *Using AS . . . AS.* *(Chart 9-4)*

Oral (books closed).
Set up the students in pairs, one with the book open. Lead the class through the example, and remind them to switch roles after item 9. Tell them to substitute their own words in parentheses.

☐ **EXERCISE 22, p. 392.** *Using AS . . . AS.* *(Chart 9-4)*

Open completion.
This can be assigned as homework or used as a test. The responses should be spelled correctly and be truthful.

CHART 9-5: USING *BUT*

- *But* is a coordinating conjunction like *and;* that is, it connects two clauses or phrases that are grammatically parallel in structure.

☐ **EXERCISE 23, p. 393.** *Using BUT.* *(Chart 9-5)*

Open completion.
In this exercise, learners must use antonyms—words with opposite meanings. They will note two meanings of the adjective *light* in items 4 and 5. They will have to help each other or perhaps consult a dictionary for difficult items. Give them time to work out the best answers.

EXPECTED COMPLETIONS: **2.** cold **3.** dirty **4.** light **5.** dark **6.** comfortable **7.** short **8.** wide **9.** hard/difficult **10.** small **11.** bad/terrible **12.** intelligent/smart **13.** invisible **14.** wrong **15.** wet **16.** empty **17.** quiet **18.** beautiful **19.** clear **20.** dangerous **21.** strong **22.** cheap **23.** lazy **24.** neat/clean **25.** hard

CHART 9-6: USING VERBS AFTER *BUT*

- The students are being asked to understand the grammar in this chart simply from the examples. There is no explanation given of verb usage in the clause following *but*. You might point out that a form of main verb *be* or an auxiliary verb is used after *but*.

- The preferred style in English is to avoid repeating words in a sentence. This is done either by shortening the sentence, as in these examples, or by using synonyms.

- The verb in the second clause is heavily stressed. This makes the contrast clear.

☐ **EXERCISE 24, p. 395.** *Using verbs after BUT.* *(Chart 9-6)*

Open completion.
The students need time to think about negative/affirmative, singular/plural, and the necessary verb. After you lead the whole class through about eight of the items, they can work with partners on the rest.

ANSWERS: **2.** is **3.** aren't **4.** was **5.** weren't **6.** doesn't **7.** do **8.** didn't **9.** can't **10.** won't **11.** wasn't **12.** isn't **13.** are **14.** doesn't **15.** does **16.** didn't **17.** doesn't **18.** does **19.** wasn't **20.** didn't **21.** can't **22.** can **23.** will **24.** won't **25.** will

☐ **EXERCISE 25, p. 396.** *Using verbs after BUT.* *(Chart 9-6)*

Oral (books closed).
Lead the class through the example. Pause after each question for one student to answer.

☐ **EXERCISE 26, p. 397.** *Comparisons.* *(Charts 9-1 → 9-6)*

Oral.

☐ **EXERCISE 27, p. 397.** *Comparisons.* *(Charts 9-1 → 9-6)*

Error analysis.
After everyone has had time to make changes in these sentences, have partners check each other's corrections for accuracy.

ANSWERS: **1.** My cousin is <u>as</u> tall as my brother. **2.** A blue whale is <u>larger than</u> an elephant. **3.** A dog is <u>smaller than</u> a wolf. **4.** Your handwriting is <u>better than</u> mine. **5.** Robert and Maria aren't <u>the</u> same age. Robert is <u>younger</u> than Maria. **6.** A lake isn't as deep <u>as</u> an ocean.

☐ **EXERCISE 28, p. 398.** *Comparisons.* *(Charts 9-1 → 9-6)*

Written.
You could tell students how many sentences they should include in each response. If this is written in class, set a time limit.

CHART 9-7: THE SUPERLATIVE: USING -*EST* AND *MOST*

- It is recommended that students learn the definite article with the superlative as a single unit. Also, when you say a superlative form, always include *the* with it.

- In everyday usage, many people use the superlative when comparing only two items, but the formal rule requires at least three items for the superlative.

☐ **EXERCISE 29, p. 399.** *Comparative and superlative forms.* *(Charts 9-3 and 9-7)*

Spelling.
Require that students use *than* and *the* in every answer. That is the best way to help them avoid mistakes later when they use these forms in conversation or writing. Discuss irregular forms and spelling changes.

ANSWERS:　　**2.** smaller, the smallest　　**3.** heavier, the heaviest　　**4.** more comfortable, the most comfortable　　**5.** harder, the hardest　　**6.** more difficult, the most difficult **7.** easier, the easiest　　**8.** hotter, the hottest　　**9.** cheaper, the cheapest　　**10.** more interesting, the most interesting　　**11.** prettier, the prettiest　　**12.** stronger, the strongest **13.** better, the best　　**14.** worse, the worst　　**15.** farther/further, the farthest/the furthest

☐ **EXERCISE 30, p. 399.** *Using -EST and MOST.* *(Chart 9-7)*

Fill-in-the-blanks.
Students can work in pairs, helping each other with the answers and some vocabulary.

ANSWERS:　　**2.** the longest　　**3.** the most interesting　　**4.** the highest　　**5.** the tallest **6.** the biggest　　**7.** the shortest　　**8.** the farthest　　**9.** the most beautiful **10.** the worst　　**11.** the best　　**12.** the most comfortable　　**13.** The fastest **14.** the best　　**15.** the largest　　**16.** the smallest　　**17.** the most expensive **18.** the easiest　　**19.** the most important　　**20.** the most famous

☐ **EXERCISE 31, p. 401.** *Comparisons.* *(Charts 9-3 → 9-7)*

Semi-controlled completion.
Remind students to use the comparative with two items and the superlative when more than two items are mentioned. This exercise gives learners good practice in using these structures in natural situations.

ANSWERS:
PART A:
2. larger than　　**3.** the largest　　**4.** as large

PART B:
5. older than　　**6.** younger than　　**7.** the oldest　　**8.** as old

PART C:
9. Alice　　**10.** Linda　　**11.** Karen . . . Linda . . . Alice　　**12.** Linda . . . Karen OR Karen . . . Alice OR Linda . . . Alice

SAMPLE COMPLETIONS:
PART D:
13. Mike isn't as strong as Joe.　　**14.** Joe isn't as strong as Don.　　**15.** Don is the strongest. **16.** Joe is stronger than Mike but not as strong as Don.

PART E:
17. A bicycle isn't as expensive as a motorcycle.   18. A motorcycle is less expensive than a car.   19. A car is the most expensive of all.   20. A motorcycle is more expensive than a bicycle but not as expensive as a car.

PART F:
21. Mary's paper isn't as good as Steve's or Carol's.   22. Carol's paper is the best. Mary's paper is the worst.   23. Steve's paper is better than Mary's but not as good as Carol's.
24. Carol's paper is better than Steve's. Mary's paper is worse than Steve's.

PART G:
25. *Introduction to Psychology* isn't as interesting as *Love in the Spring*.   26. *Murder at Night* is more interesting than *Love in the Spring*.   27. *Murder at Night* is the most interesting of all.
28. *Love in the Spring* is more interesting than *Introduction to Psychology*.

☐ **EXERCISE 32, p. 404.**   *Comparative and superlative.*   *(Charts 9-3 → 9-7)*

Fill-in-the-blanks.
In items 9, 10, and 11, note the difference in meaning of the prepositional phrases beginning with *in*. *In the world* is similar to *of all*, so it requires the superlative. But *in area* and *in population* indicate "some specific feature" and require the comparative.

ANSWERS: 1. longer than   2. the longest   3. larger than   4. the largest
5. the highest   6. higher than   7. bigger than   8. smaller than   9. the largest
10. bigger than   11. larger than   12. better . . . than   13. the best   14. more comfortable . . . the most comfortable   15. easier than . . . the easiest   16. worse

```
CHART 9-8:   USING ONE OF + SUPERLATIVE +
             PLURAL NOUN
```

- Remind students of Chart 8-5, which shows that *one of* must be followed by a plural noun or pronoun.

- In example (c), remind students that the word *people* is a plural noun in English even though it does not add *-s*.

☐ **EXERCISE 33, p. 405.**   *Using ONE OF + superlative + plural noun.*   *(Chart 9-8)*

Sentence construction.
Students can use their own knowledge of the world in Exercises 33 and 34. Encourage them to make interesting answers.

SAMPLE RESPONSES: 4. New York is one of the biggest cities in the world.
5. The Grand Canyon is one of the most beautiful places in the world.   6. . . . is one of the nicest people in our class.   7. The Yangtze River is one of the longest rivers in the world.
8. . . . is one of the best restaurants in this city.   9. The Taj Mahal is one of the most famous landmarks in the world.   10. The fall of the Roman Empire was one of the most important events in the history of the world.

□ **EXERCISE 34, p. 406.** *Using ONE OF + superlative + plural noun.* *(Chart 9-8)*

Sentence construction.

SAMPLE RESPONSES: **1.** Seoul is one of the largest cities in Asia. **2.** Texas is one of the largest states in the U.S. **3.** Paris is one of the most beautiful cities in the world. **4.** (. . .) is one of the friendliest persons/people in our class. **5.** San Francisco is one of the best places to visit in the world. **6.** . . . is one of the most famous people in the world. **7.** Good health is one of the most important things in life. **8.** . . . is one of the worst restaurants in *(this city)*. **9.** . . . is one of the most famous landmarks in *(name of a country)*. **10.** . . . is one of the tallest buildings in *(this city)*. **11.** Boxing is one of the most dangerous sports in the world. **12.** Famine is one of the most serious problems in the world.

□ **EXERCISE 35, p. 406.** *Comparisons.* *(Charts 9-1 → 9-8)*

Oral.
After you lead the class through two items, divide the students into groups of three and encourage them to have short conversations about the items. Everyone should give an answer to at least two items. Set a time limit for completing the exercise.

□ **EXERCISE 36, p. 407.** *Comparisons.* *(Charts 9-1 → 9-8)*

Multiple choice.
This exercise allows learners to apply their usage ability of comparatives and superlatives to real-life information. The students should make their best guesses to the questions; it matters not at all if they choose the right answers. The goal of the exercise is to get the students talking in small groups as they use the Table of Statistics to figure out the correct answers. In their discussion, they will have to spontaneously use comparatives and superlatives.

ANSWERS:

PART I: **1.** C **2.** A **3.** A **4.** B **5.** B

PART II: **6.** C **7.** A

PART III: **8.** C **9.** B

PART IV: **10.** (1) Asia (2) Africa (3) North America (4) South America (5) Antarctica (6) Europe (7) Australia

PART V: **11.** D **12.** A **13.** A **14.** A

PART VI: **15.** A **16.** A **17.** B **18.** A **19.** A **20.** A

CHART 9-9:   ADJECTIVES AND ADVERBS

• This chart is an introduction to adverbs of manner. Emphasize that adverbs modify verbs (i.e., give information about verbs), whereas adjectives modify nouns. The students need to understand what an adverb is before they study the comparative and superlative forms of adverbs in the following charts.

• A few adjectives end in *-ly,* for example *friendly, lovely, kindly* (e.g., *a friendly person, a lovely day, a kindly gentleman*). These adjectives should not be confused with adverbs that add *-ly.*

☐ **EXERCISE 37, p. 411.** *Adjectives and adverbs.* *(Chart 9-9)*

Controlled completion.
Discuss the functions of the adjectives and adverbs. Ask the students to identify the noun or verb being modified by the completion.

ANSWERS: **3.** clearly **4.** clear **5.** careless **6.** carelessly **7.** easy
8. easily **9.** well **10.** good

☐ **EXERCISE 38, p. 412.** *Adjectives and adverbs.* *(Chart 9-9)*

Controlled completion.

ANSWERS: **1.** carefully **2.** correct **3.** correctly **4.** fast **5.** quickly
6. fast **7.** neat **8.** neatly **9.** hard **10.** hard **11.** honestly **12.** slowly
13. careless **14.** quickly **15.** early **16.** early **17.** well **18.** good
19. loudly **20.** slowly . . . clearly

☐ **EXERCISE 39, p. 413.** *Adjectives and adverbs.* *(Chart 9-9)*

Controlled completion.

ANSWERS: **1.** well **2.** fast **3.** quickly **4.** fast **5.** softly **6.** easy
7. hard **8.** clearly **9.** late **10.** safely **11.** hard **12.** hard **13.** late
14. easily **15.** quietly **16.** fast **17.** honest **18.** honestly **19.** well
20. good **21.** well . . . well **22.** fluently

CHART 9-10: MAKING COMPARISONS WITH ADVERBS

• Adverbs follow the same patterns as adjectives in the comparative and superlative. (See Chart 9-7.)

• Remind students to use *than* with comparatives and *the* with superlatives.

☐ **EXERCISE 40, p. 414.** *Comparisons with adverbs.* *(Chart 9-10)*

Controlled completion.
The verbs in parentheses are optional; the sentences are complete with or without them.
(See the footnote on page 384 of the textbook.)
After you lead the class through four or five items, they can continue working with partners.

ANSWERS: **2.** more quickly than **3.** more beautifully than **4.** the most beautifully
5. harder than **6.** the hardest **7.** more carefully than **8.** earlier than
9. the earliest **10.** better than **11.** the best **12.** more clearly than **13.** faster
than **14.** the fastest **15.** more loudly than **16.** more fluently than **17.** the most
fluently **18.** more slowly than [The drawing illustrates a snail on the left and a crab on the right.]

☐ **EXERCISE 41, p. 415.** *Comparisons with adverbs and adjectives.* *(Charts 9-3 and 9-10)*

Controlled completion.
Lead the class through four or five items, discussing any problems and reminding students to use *than* with comparatives and *the* with superlatives. Then have them continue with partners.

ANSWERS: **2.** more beautiful than **3.** neater than **4.** the neatest **5.** more neatly
than **6.** the most neatly **7.** heavier than **8.** more clearly than **9.** better than
10. better than **11.** the best **12.** harder than **13.** the hardest **14.** longer
15. later than **16.** the most clearly **17.** sharper than **18.** more artistic than
19. more slowly than **20.** more dangerous than

CHART 9-11: USING *AS . . . AS* WITH ADVERBS

- Adverbs and adjectives can both be used with *as . . . as*. (See Chart 9-4.) Both can also be used with *less . . . than*: *I finished my work less quickly than Sue (did.)*

- Examples (d) and (e) have the same meaning. Examples (f) and (g) also mean the same.

☐ **EXERCISE 42, p. 416.** *Using AS . . . AS with adverbs.* *(Chart 9-11)*

Open completion.

SAMPLE COMPLETIONS: **2.** as I do [*reckless* = careless, with little attention to safety]
3. as (. . .) does **4.** as I do **5.** as the rest of the class **6.** as (. . .) does
7. as I do **8.** as his wife does [*an insomniac* /ɪnsɔmniyæk/ = a person who cannot sleep, who has insomnia] **9.** as I do

☐ **EXERCISE 43, p. 417.** *Using AS . . . AS with adverbs.* *(Chart 9-11)*

Oral.

The purpose of this exercise is to accustom the students to extremely common patterns used with *as + adverb + as*.

After you lead the class through the examples, continue with two or three more items. Then the students can complete the exercise working with a partner. They should switch roles halfway through the exercise.

ANSWERS: **1.** Please come as quickly as possible/as quickly as you can. **2.** (. . .) came as quickly as possible/ as quickly as she/he could. **3.** Please write as neatly as possible/as neatly as you can. **4.** I opened the door as quietly as possible/as quietly as I could. **5.** Please come as soon as possible/as soon as you can. **6.** (. . .) came as soon as possible/as soon as he/she could. **7.** Pronounce each word as clearly as possible/as clearly as you can. **8.** Do you study as hard as possible/as hard as you can? **9.** When (. . .) saw a mean dog, she/he ran home as fast as possible/as fast as she/he could. **10.** I write to my parents as often as possible/as often as I can. **11.** (. . .) is working as fast as possible/as fast as she/he can. **12.** Please give me your homework as soon as possible/as soon as you can. **13.** I'll get home as early as possible/as early as I can. **14.** (. . .) answered the question as well as possible/as well as she/he could. **15.** I'll call you as soon as possible/as soon as I can. **16.** (. . .) goes swimming as often as possible/ as often as she/he can. **17.** Please finish the test as soon as possible/as soon as you can. **18.** I'll pay my telephone bill as soon as possible/as soon as I can.

☐ **EXERCISE 44, p. 417.** *Review.* *(Chapter 9)*

Controlled completion; multiple choice.
After students complete the exercise, discuss important points with them, such as prepositions and spelling.

ANSWERS: **1.** D **2.** B **3.** C **4.** B **5.** A **6.** D **7.** B **8.** A
9. B **10.** D

☐ **EXERCISE 45, p. 418.** *Review. (Chapter 9)*

Error analysis.

ANSWERS: **1.** Your pen is <u>like</u> mine. **2.** Kim's coat is similar <u>to</u> mine. **3.** Jack's coat is <u>the</u> same <u>as</u> mine. **4.** Soccer balls are different <u>from</u> basketballs. **5.** Soccer is one of <u>the</u> most popular sports in the world. **6.** Green sea turtles live <u>longer than</u> elephants. **7.** My grade on the test was <u>worse than</u> yours. You got a <u>better</u> grade. **8.** A monkey is <u>more intelligent</u> than a turtle. **9.** Africa isn't <u>as</u> large <u>as</u> Asia. **10.** Pedro speaks English more <u>fluently</u> than Ernesto. **11.** The exploding human population is the <u>greatest</u> threat to all forms of life on earth. [*exploding* = suddenly getting larger, rapidly expanding like a balloon; *a threat* = a strong possibility of danger or injury] **12.** The Mongol Empire was the <u>biggest</u> land empire in the entire history of the world.

☐ **EXERCISE 46, p. 419.** *Review. (Chapter 9)*

Oral (books closed).
Exercises 46, 47, and 48 have no predictable answers. Students should use their knowledge and imaginations in responding to the items. When you evaluate their answers, pay special attention to spelling and the forms studied in Chapter 9. Praise the learners for their successes.

☐ **EXERCISE 47, p. 419.** *Review. (Chapter 9)*

Written/oral.

☐ **EXERCISE 48, p. 419.** *Review. (Chapter 9)*

Written.

Chapter 10: EXPRESSING IDEAS WITH VERBS

ORDER OF CHAPTER	CHARTS	EXERCISES
Should	10-1	Ex. 1 → 4
Let's	10-2	Ex. 5 → 6
Have to and *must*	10-3 → 10-4	Ex. 7 → 12
Modal auxiliaries	10-5 → 10-6	Ex. 13 → 16
Present progressive and past progressive	10-7	Ex. 17 → 19
While and *when* in past time clauses	10-8 → 10-9	Ex. 20 → 22
Simple past vs. past progressive	10-10	Ex. 23 → 25
Have been (the present perfect)	10-11	Ex. 26 → 27
Since-clauses	10-12	Ex. 28
Form of the present perfect	10-13	Ex. 29 → 30
Using *never* with the present perfect	10-14	Ex. 31
Present perfect: questions and negatives	10-15	Ex. 32
Using *ever* with the present perfect	10-16	Ex. 33 → 34
The present perfect: questions with *how long*	10-17	Ex. 35 → 36
Past participles of common irregular verbs	10-18	Ex. 37 → 41

General Notes on Chapter 10

This final chapter introduces some basic ways of using verbs to express opinions and the relationships between ideas. It focuses on modal auxiliaries, the past progressive, and the present perfect.

English uses the verb system in complex ways. Some verbs have special meanings that give force to a sentence, such as making a suggestion, giving advice, or requiring necessary action. This chapter introduces a few new modal auxiliaries and revisits the ones presented earlier in the text. Some verb forms, like the progressive, add special meanings about relationships in time, temporary vs. permanent situations, and background vs. foreground information. These are introduced and practiced in this chapter.

Another important structure is the present perfect form of verbs. This also carries special meanings such as looking back into the past from the present moment. The present perfect is associated with some words like *for, since, never,* and *ever* as well as with the past participle verb form. The present perfect, which is complicated and often difficult for students, is presented in more depth in the other two texts in this grammar series. The goal in this chapter is a basic introduction to common uses of the present perfect.

CHART 10-1: USING *SHOULD*

- This chapter adds *should, let's, have to,* and *must* to the modals and periphrastic modals already presented in the text: *will, be going to, can, could, be able to, may,* and *might.*

- The text presents only present/future *should.* The past form is *should have* + past participle: *I should have finished my homework.* You may wish to mention the past form to your class.

- Ask the class to discover things about the examples before looking at the right side of this chart. You might use this approach throughout the chapter.

☐ **EXERCISE 1, p. 420.** *Using SHOULD.* *(Chart 10-1)*

Controlled or open completion.
Exercises 1 and 2 essentially give additional examples of typical situations in which *should* is used. Discuss the meanings of the sentences.

Go over the vocabulary in the red box: *the landlady* = the owner of a building that someone rents (male form: *the landlord); the immigration office* = the government office that issues visas and passports; *take a nap* = sleep for a short time during the day.

Encourage the students to use their own words to complete the sentences as well as finding the proper completion from the box.

ANSWERS: **2.** You should go to bed and take a nap.   **3.** You should go to the bank.
4. You should see a dentist.   **5.** You should study harder. [*flunk* (informal verb) = get a failing grade, fail to make progress]   **6.** You should call the landlady. [*the plumbing* /pləmɪŋ/ = the pipes that bring water into a building]   **7.** You should go to the immigration office. [*renew* = get an extension for additional time]   **8.** You should buy a new pair of shoes.

☐ **EXERCISE 2, p. 421.** *Using SHOULD.* *(Chart 10-1)*

Controlled completion.
This exercise checks out the students' understanding of the meaning of *should* and gives typical uses. Students can work in pairs and discuss their opinions.

ANSWERS: **3.** shouldn't [*waste* = use for no good purpose]   **4.** should   **5.** shouldn't
6. shouldn't [*cruel* = angry and hurtful]   **7.** should   **8.** shouldn't   **9.** shouldn't [*bothers* = makes uncomfortable and a bit angry]   **10.** should . . . shouldn't   **11.** should [*see a play* = attend a live theater performance]   **12.** shouldn't   **13.** should   **14.** shouldn't

☐ **EXERCISE 3, p. 422.** *Using SHOULD.* *(Chart 10-1)*

Oral.
Divide the class into groups of four. Each student reads one item, and the others give advice. Encourage them to be serious and helpful.

In item 3, *a newcomer* = someone who has come to live in a place for the first time.

☐ **EXERCISE 4, p. 422.** *Using SHOULD.* *(Chart 10-1)*

> *Written.*
> The questions are only suggestions; they do not have to be answered in the exact order given here. The writers should respond to the topic with natural sentences that make an interesting paragraph. You might ask them to underline the word *should/shouldn't,* but don't require them to use it in every sentence.

CHART 10-2: USING *LET'S*

- Often a suggestion with *let's* is followed by a tag question.
  Very formal: *Let's go, shall we?*
  More usual: *Let's go, okay?*

- Another verb *let/lets* means to permit or allow something. This verb is never the first word in a sentence, and it never has an apostrophe.
  Example: *Mrs. Smith lets her children stay up late on Saturday night.*

☐ **EXERCISE 5, p. 423.** *Using LET'S.* *(Chart 10-2)*

> *Controlled or open completion.*
> Preview the vocabulary in the red box: *go dancing* (note that no preposition is used); *a seafood restaurant* = one that specializes in fish and other seafood; *the zoo* /zu/ = the animal park (zoological garden).
>
> For each item, talk to one student as if you were having a conversation. Encourage the students to respond with some expression of interest or feeling, as they would in a conversation with a friend.
>
> *SAMPLE COMPLETIONS:*   **2.** Let's go to Florida.   **3.** Let's go to a seafood restaurant.
> **4.** Let's go to the zoo.   **5.** Let's go to a movie.   **6.** Let's walk.   **7.** Let's eat.
> **8.** Let's go dancing.   **9.** Let's get a cup of coffee.

☐ **EXERCISE 6, p. 424.** *Using LET'S.* *(Chart 10-2)*

> *Oral.*
> Lead the class through the instructions and the example. Tell them to substitute their own words in parentheses.

CHART 10-3:   USING *HAVE* + INFINITIVE
(*HAS TO/HAVE TO*)

- *Have to* is common and useful. Most of your students are probably already familiar with it.
- This modal verb has a special pronunciation:
  have to = /hæftə/
  has to = /hæstə/

□ EXERCISE 7, p. 425. Using HAS/HAVE + infinitive. (Chart 10-3)

Oral.

Tell students to use in their responses the same verb that is in the question. Thus, not every answer will use *has/have to*, which is at times contrasted with *want to*.

The purpose of this exercise is to give the students the opportunity to practice communicating their meaning using *have to*. Keep the pace natural, and show interest in the students' answers. Add a comment if you wish. If time is short, you may want to omit some items.

□ EXERCISE 8, p. 425. Using HAS/HAVE + infinitive. (Chart 10-3)

Oral (books closed).

Lead the class through the example before they close their books. Then give them time to think before they respond. Practicing *because*-clauses is equally important as practicing *have to* in this exercise.

□ EXERCISE 9, p. 426. Using HAS/HAVE + infinitive. (Chart 10-3)

Controlled completion.

This exercise reviews the various forms of *have to*: singular, plural, past, negative, question.

ANSWERS: **2.** A: do you have to go B: I have to find **3.** A: does Sue have to leave for B: She has to be **4.** B: I had to buy A: did you have to buy **5.** I have to go . . . I have to get **6.** she had to study **7.** do you have to be **8.** Does Tom have to find **9.** A: Yoko doesn't have to take B: Do you have to take **10.** B: He had to stay A: He had to finish

---

CHART 10-4: USING *MUST*	

- *Have to* occurs with much greater frequency than *must* in everyday usage.

- *Must* is much stronger than *have to*, but the meaning is essentially the same in the affirmative. Indeed, the past form of *must* (meaning "necessity" as it does in this chart) is *had to*. You may want to mention this to your students.

- In the negative, the meanings of *must* and *have to* are different, as pointed out in examples (d) and (e).

- The differences between *must* and *should* are sometimes difficult to explain. Expand upon the contrastive examples in the chart to help give the learners a clear understanding of the differences in meaning.

□ EXERCISE 10, p. 428. Using MUST. (Chart 10-4)

Controlled completion.

This exercise essentially gives further examples of typical uses of *must*. Discuss the meanings of the sentences. Point out that using *should* instead of *must* would make grammatically correct completions throughout this exercise, but its meaning isn't strong enough; thus, *must* is used.

Preview the vocabulary in the red box: *close the door behind you* = as you go out of the room you should close the door; *a library card* = a card that permits you to borrow books from a library; *an income tax* = payment to the government of a percentage of the money that your employer pays to you; *a pill* = medicine in the form of a tablet or capsule.

ANSWERS: **2.** must stop   **3.** must have a library card   **4.** must pay an income tax
5. must study harder   **6.** must have a passport   **7.** must go to medical school
8. must take one pill every six hours   **9.** must close the door behind you   **10.** must listen
to English on the radio and TV/make new friends who speak English/read English newspapers
and magazines/speak English outside of class every day/talk to myself in English.

☐ **EXERCISE 11, p. 429.** *Using MUST.* *(Chart 10-4)*

Oral.
These questions might produce some interesting responses and discussion. Encourage the
students to use *must* or *have to*.

☐ **EXERCISE 12, p. 429.** *Using MUST.* *(Chart 10-4)*

Controlled completion; multiple choice.
This quiz requires students to think about the difference between *must* and *have to* in the
negative as well as about singular and plural forms.

ANSWERS: **1.** A   **2.** B   **3.** B   **4.** A   **5.** C   **6.** A   **7.** B   **8.** A

CHART 10-5:   MODAL AUXILIARIES

• The text has been presenting modals throughout. Now this chart provides a grammar label and
explains the term "modal auxiliary" /modəl ɔkzɪlyəri/.

• One common mistake for learners is adding the word *to* after every modal auxiliary (e.g., ★*He can to
play the piano.* ★*You must to be careful.*). This chart shows clearly that only a few expressions require *to*.
(The expressions in example (b) are called "modal auxiliaries" by some; others calls them "periphrastic
modals." This text calls them "similar expressions.")

☐ **EXERCISE 13, p. 430.** *Modal auxiliaries.* *(Chart 10-5)*

Structure identification.
This exercise helps learners focus on the use of *to*. You might lead them through it, asking them
to read an item and raise their right hands if they think *to* is required. This helps them to use
some caution and judgment before automatically including *to* in a sentence. Exercises like this
are intended to encourage students' self-monitoring of grammar that is the source of common
and frequent errors.

ANSWERS: **3.** X   **4.** to   **5.** X   **6.** X   **7.** to   **8.** X   **9.** X   **10.** X
11. X   **12.** X   **13.** to   **14.** X

**CHART 10-6:   SUMMARY CHART: MODAL AUXILIARIES
AND SIMILAR EXPRESSIONS**

• By now, the students should know the meaning of each auxiliary in this chart. The students should
be impressed by how much they already know about modal auxiliaries in English!

• This is by no means an exhaustive presentation of these auxiliaries. There are other meanings and
uses of many of these expressions; students will expand their understanding of modals in subsequent
texts in this grammar series.

☐ **EXERCISE 14, p. 432.** *Summary: modal auxiliaries.* *(Chart 10-6)*

Oral.
Lead the class through the example, then divide students into small groups to continue. Give them a time limit for completing the exercise. Groups who finish sooner can work on the next two exercises.

☐ **EXERCISE 15, p. 432.** *Summary: modal auxiliaries.* *(Chart 10-6)*

Error analysis.

ANSWERS: **1.** Would you <u>please help</u> me? **2.** I <u>will</u> go/<u>can</u> go to the meeting tomorrow. **3.** Ken should <u>write</u> us a letter. **4.** I <u>had to go</u> to the store yesterday. **5.** Susie! You must <u>not play</u> with matches! **6.** <u>Would/Could/Can</u> you please hand me that book? **7.** Ann couldn't <u>answer</u> my question. **8.** Shelley can't <u>go</u> to the concert tomorrow. **9.** <u>Let's go</u> to a movie tonight.

☐ **EXERCISE 16, p. 433.** *Verb review.* *(Chart 10-6)*

Controlled completion; multiple choice.
This is a review of singular/plural, verb tenses, and some modal auxiliaries.
    After this exercise, the chapter leaves modal auxiliaries and goes to a unit on the past progressive.

ANSWERS: **1.** A **2.** C **3.** C **4.** C **5.** A **6.** C **7.** C **8.** A **9.** B **10.** B

CHART 10-7: THE PRESENT PROGRESSIVE AND THE PAST PROGRESSIVE

• You might have the class cover the right side of this chart and talk about the differences they see between examples (a) and (b). Then look at the drawings and ask the class about the clocks and their relationship to the meaning of the sentences.

• The progressive has other meanings and functions, but "activity in progress" is the most basic one and easy to understand.

• Grammarians call the progressive an "aspect" instead of a verb tense. However, learners do not need this specialized vocabulary. Here we just call it "the progressive" or "the progressive form." Calling the present progressive or the past progressive a tense works well in the classroom. "Tense" is a term students are familiar and comfortable with.

• Some grammars use the term "continuous" instead of "progressive."

☐ **EXERCISE 17, p. 435.** *Present progressive and past progressive.* *(Chart 10-7)*

Controlled completion.
The purpose of this exercise is a comparison of the form and meaning of the present and past progressive. Students should be able to see how closely related the two are. Both of them use *be + -ing*, and both of them express an activity in progress.

ANSWERS: **3.** are sitting **4.** were sitting **5.** is sitting **6.** was sitting **7.** are sitting **8.** were sitting **9.** is sitting **10.** was sitting **11.** are sitting **12.** were sitting

□ EXERCISE 18, p. 435. *Past progressive.* *(Chart 10-7)*

Fill-in-the-blanks.

The progressive tense is useful in referring to two activities at the same time. The continuing or background activity uses the progressive, and the interrupting activity uses the simple tense. Discuss this with the class after they look at the drawings and complete the answers.

ANSWERS: **1.** was eating . . . came   **2.** called . . . was watching   **3.** was playing

□ EXERCISE 19, p. 437. *Past progressive.* *(Chart 10-7)*

Oral.

The activities in the illustration were in progress at midnight. They began before midnight and were happening at the time the thief stole the jewelry. Hence, the past progressive is used for all the responses.

The purpose of this exercise is for the students to understand the meaning of the past progressive, i.e., that it expresses an activity in progress at a particular time in the past when another event occurred.

EXPECTED RESPONSES: (from bottom to top)   Mr. Brown and Miss Gray were playing pool in the basement. Mr. White was playing the piano for Mrs. Blue, who was singing. Mr. Black and Mr. Green were playing cards and smoking cigars. Ms. Orange was reading in bed at midnight. Mr. Blue was watching TV in his bedroom.   Mr. and Mrs. Gold were sleeping in their bedroom. A bat was hanging in the attic. A mouse was running toward a piece of cheese.

CHART 10-8:   USING *WHILE* WITH THE PAST PROGRESSIVE

- The word *while* is a subordinating conjunction. It subordinates (makes less important, puts in the background) the ongoing, progressive activity.

- *While* introduces a time clause. (See Chart 5-18.)

- Ask students to explain the comma in example (b). (See the footnote on page 216 after Chart 5-18.)

□ EXERCISE 20, p. 438. *Using WHILE with the past progressive.* *(Chart 10-8)*

Oral.

Ask two students to respond to each item differently, as in the example. The drawing illustrates item 4; note the times on the clock.

ANSWERS: **2.** Someone knocked on my apartment door while I was eating breakfast. OR While I was eating breakfast, someone knocked on my apartment door.   **3.** While I was cooking dinner yesterday evening, I burned my hand. OR I burned my hand while I was cooking dinner yesterday evening.   **4.** While I was studying last night, a mouse suddenly appeared on my desk. OR A mouse suddenly appeared on my desk while I was studying last night.   **5.** Yoko raised her hand while the teacher was talking. OR While the teacher was talking, Yoko raised her hand.   **6.** A tree fell on my car while I was driving home yesterday. OR While I was driving home yesterday, a tree fell on my car.

CHART 10-9: *WHILE* vs. *WHEN* IN PAST TIME CLAUSES

- Tell the class to look closely at examples (a) and (c). Ask them to tell you the differences. Then do the same with (b) and (d). Ask the class to explain in their own words how the word *when* is different from *while*.

- Note that the explanation says that these forms are "often" used, not always (100%). Your students should learn these patterns well, but they might see other verb forms with *when* and *while*. For example:

    Jack and I got home at 5:00 p.m. Then, while I took a bath, he cooked dinner. We ate at 6:00.

    The bath and dinner were in the same time period but unrelated. Neither was a background for the other. Therefore, neither was in progress before the other. (Don't teach this now.)
    Another example: Sometimes the verbs in the main clause and the *while*-clause are both past progressive: *While I was washing the dishes, Jane was sweeping the floor.* Students can learn these patterns later in their study of English grammar.

- In the next exercises, it is easy to become confused. Ask the class to think about which activity was in progress; *while* means "in progress."

☐ **EXERCISE 21, p. 439.** *WHILE* vs. *WHEN in past time clauses.* *(Chart 10-9)*

> *Fill-in-the-blanks.*
> The drawing illustrates item 8.
>
> ANSWERS: 2. called . . . was washing   3. came . . . was eating   4. was eating . . . came   5. was wearing . . . saw   6. was sleeping . . . got   7. called . . . was taking 8. was watching . . . relaxing . . . took [Note: it is not necessary to repeat "I was" before *relaxing* because the conjunction *and* makes it clear that I was both watching and relaxing.]

☐ **EXERCISE 22, p. 440.** *WHILE* vs. *WHEN in past time clauses.* *(Chart 10-9)*

> *Oral.*
> You should explain and demonstrate the instructions and the example so that the class understands what to do. Then for item 1, tell Student A what to do. After Student A begins, tell Student B what to do. After they stop, ask Student C to describe the two actions. This is a fun exercise that gives the grammar an immediate and real context.

CHART 10-10: SIMPLE PAST vs. PAST PROGRESSIVE

- This chart seeks to clarify the differences between the simple past and the past progressive.

- Example (g) can be difficult for students to understand. Point out that there was a <u>sequence</u> of actions; one followed the other. Nothing was in progress.

- Compare examples (h) and (i). The students should see that nothing was in progress in (h).

☐ **EXERCISE 23, p. 441.** *Simple past vs. past progressive.* *(Chart 10-10)*

> *Fill-in-the-blanks.*
> Students have to think about the relationship of events in time. Some are sequences. Others are in progress, then interrupted. The verb forms must show these relationships.

ANSWERS: 1. had . . . went . . . ate . . . drove . . . took . . . went . . . watched [Note: Do not repeat "we" after *and*.] . . . talked . . . went   2. was walking . . . saw . . . said . . . walked [Note: Do not repeat "we" after *and*.]   3. was eating . . . remembered   4. was driving . . . saw   5. were having . . . saw . . . introduced   6. heard . . . walked . . . opened [Note: Do not repeat "I" after *and*.]   7. opened . . . saw . . . greeted . . . asked   8. were watching . . . came . . . watched

☐ **EXERCISE 24, p. 442.**   *Simple past vs. past progressive.*   *(Chart 10-10)*

Fill-in-the-blanks.
This is similar to Exercise 23, with longer contexts.

ANSWERS: 1. turned . . . was driving . . . was listening . . . heard . . . looked . . . saw . . . pulled . . . waited [*a siren* /sayrən/ = a device that makes a loud warning sound that rises and falls; *a rearview mirror* = a device that helps a driver see what is in back of the car; *an ambulance* /æmbyələns/ = a transport vehicle that is equipped for medical emergencies]   2. had . . . was reading . . . sat . . . handed . . . didn't want . . . was . . . stood . . . walked . . . was waiting . . . offered . . . opened . . . got   3. A: was . . . were eating . . . jumped . . . didn't seem   B: did you say . . . didn't you ask   A: didn't want [*I lost my appetite* = I suddenly didn't want to eat anything]

☐ **EXERCISE 25, p. 443.**   *Review.*   *(Charts 10-7 → 10-10)*

Controlled completion; multiple choice.
This exercise ends the past progressive unit in this chapter.

ANSWERS: 1. C   2. C   3. C   4. A   5. C   6. B   7. C   8. A   9. C   10. D

CHART 10-11:   USING *HAVE BEEN*
(THE PRESENT PERFECT)

• The present perfect is a complicated and difficult verb tense (or aspect—like the progressive, the perfect is generally considered a grammatical aspect. But this terminology is not necessary for your students, who are generally more familiar with the term "tense."). The text simply takes a few common present perfect uses that the students may find useful in everyday life. The text does not attempt an overview of all the meanings and uses of the present perfect.

• The text uses only the verb *be* in the present perfect *(have/has been)* until Chart 10-13, where the past participle is introduced.

• Useful phrases with the present perfect are "up to now" or "until this moment." These phrases will need to be explained carefully if you decide to introduce them to your class. The speaker is looking back to the past to summarize developments up to the present moment.

• The simple past talks about events that are complete, finished already, that happened "then," at a particular time. The perfect talks about a period of time that leads up to the present moment. (This is a very difficult concept to explain to learners of English. They need a lot of practice to understand it. The text purposely does not compare the simple past and the present perfect. Students can do that in later classes with other texts in this grammar series.)

☐ **EXERCISE 26, p. 445.** *Using HAVE BEEN.* *(Chart 10-11)*

Controlled completion.
Lead the class through the examples, reminding them of the difference between *for* and *since*. The other items should help everyone become clear about this.

ANSWERS: **3.** since **4.** for **5.** since **6.** for **7.** for **8.** since **9.** since **10.** since **11.** for **12.** for

☐ **EXERCISE 27, p. 445.** *Using HAVE BEEN.* *(Chart 10-11)*

Open completion.
After doing the examples together, give students time to complete the other items. They will have to ask you about item 4.

CHART 10-12: USING *SINCE*-CLAUSES

• The *since*-clause names a specific time or event, and the main clause summarizes the situation from that time to the present moment. The present perfect is often used to summarize the history or development of a present situation.

• Spend some time making clear the meaning of *since*. Understanding the meaning of *since* helps the learners understand the meaning of the present perfect.
NOTE: In Chart 10-11, *since* is used as a preposition. In this chart, *since* is a subordinating conjunction that introduces a time clause, which is a type of adverbial clause.

• Perhaps ask the class to discover things about the verbs in the examples before looking at the right side of this chart. Make up additional examples of your own and write them on the chalkboard for discussion.

☐ **EXERCISE 28, p. 447.** *Using SINCE-clauses.* *(Chart 10-12)*

Fill-in-the-blanks.
Lead the class through all the items, discussing questions that arise. Keep the focus on using the simple past in the *since*-clause and the present perfect in the main clause.

ANSWERS: **2.** have been . . . was **3.** has been . . . came **4.** has been . . . graduated **5.** has been . . . rained **6.** has been . . . broke

---

CHART 10-13: FORM OF THE PRESENT PERFECT

• This chart is the learners' introduction to the past participle. Now there are three principal parts of irregular verbs for the students to learn. Only a few irregular past participles are introduced and practiced in this text, which presents a bare minimum introduction to the present perfect.

• Make sure the students understand the structure underlying *have had* in (b): *have* is being used as an auxiliary verb, with *had* being the main verb. This can be confusing for students.

☐ **EXERCISE 29, p. 448.** *Form of the present perfect.* *(Chart 10-13)*

> *Fill-in-the-blanks.*
> Perhaps give the class time to write their answers in the blank spaces. Then ask individuals to read their sentences. Discuss any problems that arise.
>
> *ANSWERS:*   **2.** have known   **3.** has been   **4.** have lived   **5.** have had
> **6.** has worked   **7.** have been   **8.** has owned   **9.** has had   **10.** have seen

☐ **EXERCISE 30, p. 449.** *Form of the present perfect.* *(Chart 10-13)*

> *Oral.*
> Students could work in pairs. Each one could make a different sentence for each item. They need to help each other with the correct forms.

CHART 10-14:   USING *NEVER* WITH THE PRESENT PERFECT

- *Never* is commonly used with the present perfect.

- Using *never* with the present perfect may help learners understand the sweeping view of time that the present perfect can express.

☐ **EXERCISE 31, p. 449.** *Using NEVER with the present perfect.* *(Chart 10-14)*

> *Oral.*
> Students can use their knowledge and vocabulary in this exercise. You should try to react in interesting ways to their responses.

CHART 10-15:   PRESENT PERFECT: QUESTIONS AND NEGATIVES

- Ask your class to look at each example carefully. Discuss word order, singular/plural forms, and the *for/since* phrases.

☐ **EXERCISE 32, p. 450.** *Present perfect: questions and negatives.* *(Chart 10-15)*

> *Fill-in-the-blanks.*
> Give the class plenty of time to work on these items. They have to think about singular/plural, word order, and the spelling of participles.
>
> *ANSWERS:*   **3.** Have you known   **4.** haven't known [*only* = merely, just]   **5.** Has she
> been   **6.** hasn't been   **7.** Have your parents lived   **8.** haven't lived   **9.** Have Janet
> and Sam had   **10.** hasn't had   **11.** Has your uncle worked   **12.** hasn't worked

CHART 10-16:	USING *EVER* WITH THE PRESENT PERFECT

- Ask students to examine (a) and (b) and explain what they mean. They can read the definition on the right side of the chart. Point out how the present perfect looks back over a long period of time up to the present moment. The word *ever* communicates this idea of one's whole lifetime.

- Next, focus attention on the section with short answers. In a conversation, it is natural to follow a general short answer with a more specific explanation in the simple past tense. For example:

    A: *Have you ever been in London?*
    B: *Yes, I have. I went there three years ago for a summer vacation.*

You may want to get into a brief comparison of the simple past and the present perfect with examples such as these, but beware of getting bogged down by lengthy explanations at this point. The students can do an in-depth comparison when studying the other two texts in this grammar series.

- In examples (g) through (j), the sentences with *never* are more frequently used. The phrase *not ever* is more strongly emphatic. The focus in the text is simply on the relationship between the meanings of *ever* and *never: never* means *not ever.*

☐ **EXERCISE 33, p. 451.** *Using EVER with the present perfect.* *(Chart 10-16)*

Fill-in-the-blanks.
Lead the class through the examples, then continue with the whole exercise.

ANSWERS: **2.** A: Have you ever been   B: have . . . have been [*been in* a place = *been to* a place = *visited* a place (See the footnote on page 452.)]   **3.** A: Have you ever visited   B: haven't . . . have never visited   **4.** A: Has Sam ever been   B: hasn't . . . has never been   **5.** A: Has Carmen ever been   B: has . . . has been   **6.** A: Have you ever had   B: haven't . . . have never had   **7.** A: Has your brother ever lived   B: hasn't   **8.** A: Have you ever talked   B: haven't   **9.** Have you ever seen . . . have [The drawing illustrates a hummingbird drinking nectar from a flower.]

☐ **EXERCISE 34, p. 452.** *Using EVER with the present perfect.* *(Chart 10-16)*

Oral (books closed).
Lead the class through the example and a couple of more items. Then if you wish, divide them into groups of three or four, and tell them all to answer every question. Each student in the group should ask some questions and answer others.

CHART 10-17:	THE PRESENT PERFECT: QUESTIONS WITH *HOW LONG*

- Questions with *how long* and the present perfect are useful in everyday conversation.

- Lead the class through the examples, noting the word order in the questions and the forms of the short answers. Review the two kinds of structures after *since.* (See Charts 10-11 and 10-12.)

- In example (a), people frequently omit the preposition *for* in the short answer.

☐ **EXERCISE 35, p. 453.** *Questions with HOW LONG.* *(Chart 10-17)*

Fill-in-the-blanks.
This exercise is simply preparation for Exercise 36.

ANSWERS: **2.** have you known **3.** has Mr. Lake been **4.** have you had
5. has your roommate been

☐ **EXERCISE 36, p. 453.** *Questions with HOW LONG.* *(Chart 10-17)*

Oral.
Lead the class through the examples for both PART I and PART II. Then divide the students into pairs. Remind them to switch roles for PART II. The purpose of this exercise is to help them learn how to have conversations in English on simple topics.

CHART 10-18:	PAST PARTICIPLES OF COMMON IRREGULAR VERBS

- Lead the students through the examples, and ask them to give the three forms of each verb. They should pay attention to the correct spelling of each form. (Spelling of *-ed* endings is covered in Chart 5-7.)

- Lead them through the list, having them repeat after you the three forms of each verb. Discuss patterns of spelling.

- Call the class's attention to the footnote about the pronunciation of *read*. The historical development of English pronunciation and spelling patterns has caused these irregularities, but this is too complex to explain here.

☐ **EXERCISE 37, p. 455.** *Irregular past participles.* *(Chart 10-18)*

Oral (books closed).
This is a quick practice of the verb forms in Chart 10-18. You should read the cue, then pause while the class calls out the participle. Then you might ask one student to spell the participle aloud.

ANSWERS: **1.** eaten **2.** gone **3.** had **4.** known **5.** lost **6.** met
7. read /rɛd/ **8.** seen **9.** spoken **10.** taken **11.** told **12.** worn
13. written /rɪtən/

☐ **EXERCISE 38, p. 456.** *Irregular past participles.* *(Chart 10-18)*

Controlled completion.
This is an exercise in participles and vocabulary. Discuss spelling and meaning if questions arise.

ANSWERS:

PART I:
2. met **3.** lost **4.** gone **5.** told **6.** written

PART II:
7. known **8.** seen **9.** read **10.** eaten [*raw meat* = uncooked meat] **11.** worn
12. spoken

□ **EXERCISE 39, p. 457.** *Irregular past participles.* *(Chart 10-18)*

Oral.
Lead the class through the examples, then divide them into pairs. Remind them to switch roles. Give them a time limit, and those who finish early can begin the next exercise.

□ **EXERCISE 40, p. 457.** *Review.* *(Chapter 10)*

Error analysis.
Give the class time to find the mistakes, then lead them through a careful discussion of each item. Review verb tenses, irregular forms, spelling, and word order.

ANSWERS: **1.** Let's <u>go</u> to a restaurant for dinner tonight. **2.** I've never <u>seen</u> a whale. **3.** The phone rang while I was <u>eating</u> dinner last night. **4.** How long <u>have you</u> been a student at this school? **5.** Ken doesn't <u>have</u> to go to work today. **6.** I <u>must study</u> tonight. I can't <u>go</u> to the movie with you. **7.** I have been in this city <u>for</u> two months. **8.** Why <u>do</u> you have to leave now? **9.** You <u>shouldn't speak</u> loudly in a library. **10.** I've known Olga since I <u>was</u> a child. **11.** You <u>must not</u> be late for work. **12.** Have you ever <u>gone</u> to a baseball game? **13.** I <u>have been</u> in this class since the beginning of January.

□ **EXERCISE 41, p. 458.** *Irregular verbs.* *(Chart 10-18)*

Written.

Map of the World

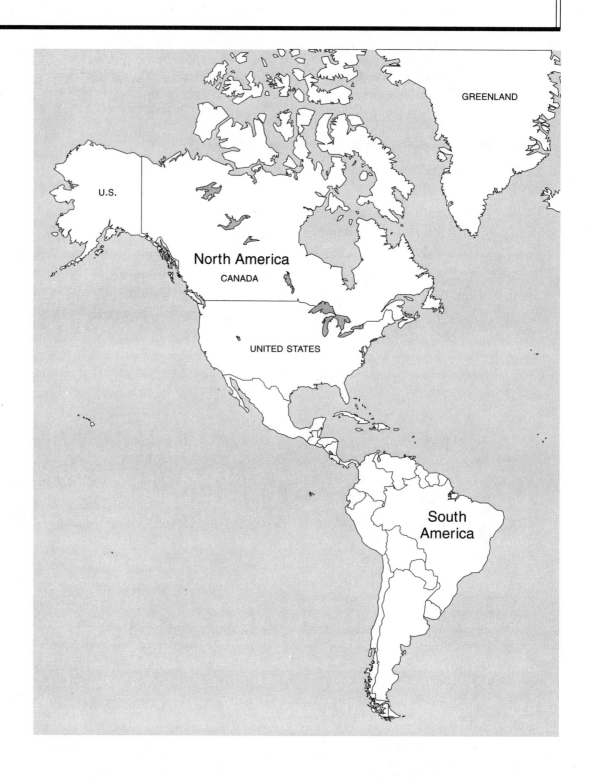

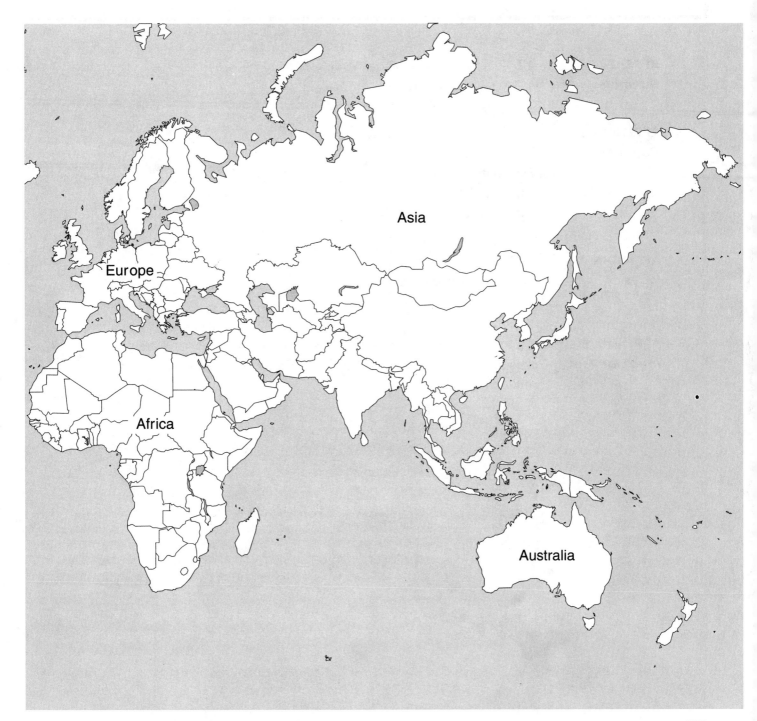

Europe

Asia

Africa

Australia

MAP *177*

Appendix Notes

APPENDIX 2:
Numbers

1,000,000,000 = one billion (AmE)
1,000,000,000 = one thousand million (BrE)

APPENDIX 3:
Days of the Week

Another common spoken form:
January the first
March the second
May the third
Etc.

APPENDIX 4:
Ways of Saying Time

9:45 = It's a quarter till ten. (AmE)
9:30 = It's half ten. (BrE)

APPENDIX 5:
Irregular Verbs

There are many more irregular verbs. The ones in this list are the most useful for beginners. They occur frequently in both spoken and written English.

Index